IN THE SPIRIT WE'RE EQUAL

IN THE SPIRIT WE'RE EQUAL

The Spirit, The Bible, and Women
A Revival Perspective

Susan C. Hyatt

REVIVAL & RENEWAL RESOURCES

by

HYATT PRESS

Publishing Arm of Hyatt Int'l Ministries

Published by Hyatt International Ministries, Inc.
Mailing Address (1998):
P. O. Box 764463
Dallas, Texas 75376

Phone: (214) 374-2454
Fax: (214) 374-0252
E-Mail: SHyatt3641@aol.com

Cover and book design by Susan Hyatt

91 92 93 94 95 96   10 9 8 7 6 5 4 3 2 1

ISBN 1-888435-08-9
Printed in the United States of America

**Library of Congress
Catalog Card Number: 98-92698**

Dedicated to my friends

About the Author

Susan C. Hyatt is a Church research historian and Bible scholar. She graduated *with honors* from the University of New Brunswick Teachers College and Christ for the Nations Institute, and *magna cum laude* from Southwestern Assemblies of God University. She earned two M.A.s *with honors* from Oral Roberts University, one in Historical/Theological Studies with emphasis in Pentecostal/Charismatic Studies; the other, in Biblical Studies. She has studied at the Center for Advanced Theological Studies at Fuller Theological School and will be completing D.Min. requirements in 1999 at Regent University.

She is the recipient of numerous academic awards such as WHO'S WHO Among Students, the National Religion and Philosophy Award, National Dean's Honor's List, Academic All American, *Delta Epsilon Chi* (Honor Society of the American Association of Bible Colleges), and the Canadian Governor-General's Medal.

Susan is also a seasoned minister and professional educator. Her passion is to see genuine Christianity prevail over fallen culture and human-centered religion. Within genuine biblical Christianity, she believes, is everything that will enable believers to flourish in life.

For a decade, Susan has ghost-written for several ministers and ministries that have a global impact. Now she is producing her own renewal/revival oriented material. Her first book was *Where Are My Susannas?* a challenging little book about Susanna Wesley, Phoebe Palmer, and Aimee Semple McPherson. Her new book, *In the Spirit We're Equal*, will be available in course format for personal study and Bible college and seminar use.

Susan and her husband, Eddie L. Hyatt, are partners in life and ministry, in research and writing. Together they have planted and pastored churches, founded and directed Bible schools, and ministered internationally. They are co-founders of Hyatt Int'l Ministries. The mission of H.I.M. is teaching, training, and equipping the people of God for End-Time renewal/revival. Dr. Vinson Synan, Dean of the School of Divinity, Regent University, writes, "Eddie and Susan were two of the best students I have ever taught. They are one of the finest teams of husband and wife researchers that I have ever known."

Susan is a member of the Society for Pentecostal Studies, the Evangelical Theological Society, Christians for Biblical Equality, Victory Fellowship Ministries, and Friends in Harvest.

Contents

IN THE SPIRIT WE'RE EQUAL

Preface

This book is especially for men and women who embrace a Pentecostal, Charismatic, Revival, or Renewal Christian experience, but I trust that those of other persuasions will also find it helpful. It is not designed as an argument for biblical equality. It is, instead, an affirmation for men and women for whom this biblical truth is already a living reality. Traditionally, this truth has been denied by the institutional Church, but it is the position that the 540 million-and-growing Spirit-oriented believers should joyfully embrace because it is taught in Scripture and ratified by the activity of the Holy Spirit. In addition to that, heartfelt endorsement of this will widen and deepen the mighty River of God flowing in our midst today.

Like many other books, this book has arisen out of a passionate search for truth. This search began in earnest when I recognized a marked difference between the manner in which the Lord Jesus related to me personally and the manner in which His Body, the Church, has related to me simply because I am a woman. Because this is an important, personal, and passionate issue, I do not apologize for the book's direct and, perhaps, passionate tone.

My search did not begin in earnest until I had earned my first Master of Arts degree, a graduate degree in Pentecostal/Charismatic Studies. Classroom studies had emphasized the exploits of men, seldom mentioning the contributions of women. This left me oblivious to the egalitarian activity of the Spirit. But in my research, I kept stumbling upon the profound work of the Spirit in and through women despite prevailing religious and social restrictions. My first exercise related to this issue grew into a 100 page paper about the fact that women tended to take the lead in early Pentecostal Bible and leadership training, especially between 1901-10. My husband, Eddie L. Hyatt, also a Pentecostal/Charismatic scholar, aptly named it *Women Who Led the Way*.

Much of the material in this book is, in fact, the product of further research and additional academic papers that I wrote for graduate, post-graduate, and doctoral courses in the areas of biblical, theological, and historical studies. As a result of this research, I was becoming increasingly aware of the gap between the real work of the Spirit and the oppressive measures taken by the Church. Always in times of revival, there was that mysterious uplift of women by the Spirit toward equality with men.

As truth unfolded before my eyes, I became increasingly aware of the active presence of the Holy Spirit directing my research and thinking. Clearly, I was to document my findings for revival people, and the main point of the presentation was to be that the Holy Spirit consistently elevates women and that that elevation is always toward equality with men, a position that agrees with Scripture, accurately interpreted. Since the Holy Spirit is the source of truth (Jn.15:26), it has been invigorating to discover this egalitarian activity of the Spirit on behalf of women and the agreement between Spirit and Scripture on this issue.

The Spirit-oriented reading of Scripture adds a dimension that is both challenging and exciting. It highlights the egalitarian attitude of Jesus in the Gospels. It coincides with the egalitarian position demonstrated by the Holy Spirit in the Book of Acts. And it helps to clarify the so-called difficult passages in Paul's letters, harmonizing them with the egalitarian practices expressed by Jesus and the Spirit.

This stands in stark contrast to the hierarchical and patriarchal theologies that prevail among us today. What is the root of this difference? When did the change occur? I found the answer by exploring the history of the institutional Church and by uncovering the attitudes of the men who formed the traditionally accepted interpretation of biblical manhood and womanhood. For the most part, they display a strongly patriarchal and hierarchical worldview borrowed from pagan philosophy, a worldview that is permeated by unmistakably misogynous attitudes. The summary of this is painful reading, indeed!

By contrast, how refreshing it was to study revival people and movements. These were often persecuted by the institution as heretical, but, clearly, they were divine efforts to reinstate biblical Christianity. In these movements, the activity of the Spirit consistently elevated women, reflecting the egalitarian perspectives of Jesus. Some movements, such as early Quakerism, advocated an overt egalitarianism, while others, such as early Methodism which were less inclined to break with the institution, adopted a stance of inclusivism of women. But it has always been the activity of the Spirit that has always instigated biblical equality. In addition to the purely historical research, I have explored how revival people have interpreted the Bible, especially Paul's passages on headship, in order to facilitate the equality promoted by the Spirit.

Moving from the historical studies, I reflect on Scripture, bringing together the Spirit and the research of contemporary scholarship. What did Genesis really say about women? What did Paul really say? If the Spirit and the Bible agree, it should be possible to harmonize the two without tampering with the text or without manipulating the meaning intended by the author? Indeed, it is! In fact, it takes manipulation to promote patriarchy!

In our century, at various times, we have seen both Spirit-oriented biblical equality and traditional patriarchy at work among Pentecostals, Charismatics, and Revival people. In this, what has been most disturbing has been the forsaking by revival movements of the equality delivered by the Spirit and the replacing of this equality with the traditional patriarchy of the institutional Church. Why has this happened?

Also in recent years, an inordinate fear of feminism has kept many from exploring the biblical truth of equality. Pulling back the veil and shining the light of truth on this bogey-man should alleviate this ignorance-based fear. Awareness of truth should ignite evangelical fervor in the hearts of revival people to see a great harvest among one of the largest, most strategic, and neglected mission fields in the world today: educated, gifted women and highly educated feminists.

Finally, it has been obvious to me that, even when truth is presented, some still vehemently oppose it. They war against the Spirit. Clearly, this resistance is not a theological issue. For deep-seated reasons, some men and women hide behind theological arguments. What, then, are the controlling elements that would keep people from accepting truth?

Having precluded patriarchy's right to rule, I provide principles from Jesus' teaching to guide an egalitarian lifestyle. In addition, I incorporate gleanings from the writings of egalitarian scholars to faciliatate application of these principles.

In writing this book, my heart's desire has been to respond to the Holy Spirit. As I have uncovered skeletons in the closets of the institutional Church, I have had to come to grips personally with the horrors of prejudice and injustice against, not only myself, but women in general. But as passionate as I am about this, I have made a conscious effort not to allow bitterness to motivate me. As passionate as I am about truth, I have yet made a serious effort to present documented facts, not mere emotion. I have attempted to share clearly but emphatically what I have found because my desire is to see those captive to falsehood set free, those blinded by bigotry begin to see, and those pained by the knife of prejudice be made whole. I desire that we all might come to a greater realization of truth that will empower all of us—men and women—to be better partners with the Holy Spirit and with one nother.

Acknowledgements

Thank you, Eddie!
   Your blessed wife,
         Sue

Where the Spirit Wind Is Blowing

by

Lamar Wadsworth

Where the Spirit-wind is blowing, see the manmade barriers fall!
Saints grow bolder in their witness, sinners on the Lord do call.
God regards not race or gender, and the poor He'll not deny;
Freely God pours out the Spirit, sons and daughters prophesy!

Equal partner in Christ's service, sister, will you work with me?
As the Spirit gives us power, we'll do works of ministry.
Sister, claim the gifts God gives you, use them for the common good,
As you keep the bedside vigil, as you stand to preach the Word.

Brother, serve Christ with your sister, in the Gospel you agree!
Tell of Jesus and His mercy, how from sin He set you free!
Celebrate your sister's grace-gifts as you exercise your own,
Colleagues in the Master's service, make His saving power known!

Not beneath you, nor above you, but beside you I will stand;
As your brother, as your sister, I will take your outstretched hand.
When you falter, I will help you, be Christ's presence in that hour;
When I falter, will you help me, lift me up by Jesus' power?

Men and women, join together, serving others, serve the Lord!
We received the same baptism, the same Spirit, the same Word.
Equal in our lost condition, equally endowed with grace,
Equal in our Master's service, equal our eternal place.

*This hymn was composed for the ordination of deacons Marie Chaney and Steve
Takacs at Woolford Memorial Baptist Church in Baltimore, MD, on October 6,
1996. We have sung it to the BEECH SPRING tune. Other tunes that work
well are HOLY MANNA, NETTLETON, and ODE TO JOY. It is not copy-
righted, nor will it be. May it always be free to be used by those who believe its
message.*

A brother, Lamar   Date: 97-08-08

Introduction

1

It Is Important that
We Get It Right.

Recently an influential Christian woman caught my attention when she said, "In the spirit we're equal, but in the natural it's different. In the natural, my husband is my head, so I submit to him." This statement clearly summarizes the idea currently popular among Pentecostal, Charismatics, and Revival people. While preserving the traditional Christian teaching that women are to submit to men, it acknowledges that equality exists in the Spirit. But I wonder how this recognizes that all Christians are to live according to the Spirit, where, as this woman correctly suggests, she is man's equal. There is surely something here worth investigating.

It is important that we get this right because we live in a day when the Spirit is being poured out and thousands of women are being awakened in a new way. As people of revival, we diligently uphold the authority of Scripture. If the Bible says it, that is the way we want it.

But as people of revival, we are also eager to experience the manifest activity of the Holy Spirit. We know that the Spirit and the Word, accurately understood, agree. Therefore, when the Holy Spirit behaves in a manner contrary to our understanding of what the Bible says, we have a problem. We are experiencing this dilemma in Spirit-oriented circles today, and the woman's statement is her honest attempt to reconcile the obvious equality of women demonstrated by the Holy Spirit with her interpretation of male headship in the writings of the apostle Paul.

In this book, as we explore church history and examine Scripture, we will see that no such discrepancy exists. In God's economy, we are equal and we are to function interdependently with one another in a Spirit of true humility. In fact, Jesus warns against any domination of one person over another, saying, "Don't rule over one another!" (Mt. 20:25-26), and "Don't call one another by authority laden titles!" (Mt. 23:1-12). All of this is challenging to our flesh, especially to our religious flesh! But it is important that we get it right.

The Response and Reaction of Women

It is important that we get it right because women live according to their belief system, and if their belief system does not line up with truth, problems arise on all fronts. The belief system of Christian women has been shaped by the traditional teaching of the institutional Church. This teaching has been strongly patriarchal, saying that under the headship, covering, or control of men, women have, at best, been "honored" as second class citizens. Men have been elevated and women have been either marginalized or patronized.

- Because of this, some women have rejected the Church as irrelevant, but they have not rejected the Jesus of Scripture.

- Other women have rejected both the Church and Jesus Christ, turning instead to secular feminism, witchcraft and various other forms of paganism, Eastern cults, and New Age practices in their efforts to satisfy their spiritual needs, and in some cases, simply to have control their own lives.

- Many women have accepted marginalization by the Church as their fate as women. They live in the shadow of a husband or other designated man. From him, they derive their identity and purpose in life. The words of Mrs. J. Fowler

Willing, writing in 1898, ring true even today. She charges that the average Christian woman "contents herself with shining, like the moon, with borrowed splendor, as the mother, sister, or wife of the great so-and-so." She continues, [She has] "left her talent in its napkin while she has been obeying the world's dictum by helping to make the most of his."[1]

- Still other women openly subscribe to the idea of male domination/female subjugation. Privately, however, they either become hopelessly depressed through lack of personal control of their lives, or they compensate for the lack of personal control of their lives by becoming skillful manipulators. By this behavior, however, they deny the position they profess! One well-known woman minister recently told me that it is all a game and that she is just playing the game to get ahead.

Is there a biblical answer to this dilemma? If there is, we have a responsibility to find it because Christianity is not a game. Turning from God, relinquishing personal responsibility, and manipulating others are not biblical solutions.

Abuse—The Bad Fruit of Fallen Humanity

Again, it is important that we get this right because in both pagan and Christian cultures, women suffer in ways that men do not. On the basis of male domination/female subjugation, they are used, misused, and abused simply because they are women. A few relevant notes will serve as examples to awaken us.[2]

- The international sex trade sold no less than 30 million

---

[1] Mrs. J. Fowler Willing, "Woman and the Pentecost," *Guide to Holiness* (September 1898): 87.

[2] Unless otherwise stated, all statistics are from UNICEF/WHO cited by Alice Bratton, *A Woman's Voice*, Tyler, TX 75701-9460.

girls between 1991-93.[3]

- In Ghana today, girls as young as 10 years old are sold as sex partners to pagan priests by their parents. Recently 436 of these slaves have been redeemed at a cost of 5 cows and $1000 each. Thousands remain in captivity in this Christian nation.

- In Bosnia, 20,000 women have been raped as part of Serbian ethnic cleansing.

- In Kenya, December is the traditional month for female circumcision (i.e. *genital mutilation*). Two million girls a year risk genital mutilation, or 8,000 daily; in fact, UNICEF/WHO estimates that 85-114 million girls and women in the world are genitally mutilated.

- In Nigeria, an old husband cut the legs off his 9 year old bride for running away.

- In India, bride burning is on the increase, and the killing of infant girls (infanticide) is increasing because Indian families prefer boys to girls. In Usilampatti, for example, female infanticide is almost universal with records showing that out of 600 female births per year, 570 disappear for "social causes."[4]

- In China, young women are sold as sex slaves for $150-$600, and women are forced to have abortions until the 7th month.

- In Bangladesh, women are buried to the chest and stoned to death.

- In Thailand, young kidnapped girls are locked in brothels until they die, usually of AIDS.

- In Afghanistan, where the Taliban Militia have won the

---

[3] Margot Hornblower, "Special Report: The Skin Trade," *Time International* (21 June 1993): 24.
[4] *ChildLink* (October 1997): 7-8.

civil war, a few notes about the status of women are in order:

* Women not wearing the veil are beaten.
* Employment of women is forbidden and violators are beaten.
* Education of girls and women has ceased.
* Women have become prisoners in their homes and have disappeared from public in some regions.
* Women who go out on the streets to seek medical care are beaten. In Kabul, a pregnant woman delivered her baby on the street as guards beat her husband for attempting to take her to the hospital.[5]

- In Algeria, women have been told to abandon their jobs because the Moslem law requires that they stay home and care for children and husband. In the town of Ain Adden, gunmen caught 11 women teachers who were returning home from school, bound them hand and foot, and cut their throats. This is not an isolated event.[6]

Indeed, it is important that we get it right!

Abuse . . . Among Christians?

The basis of female abuse is wrong thinking about women whether we are considering pagan or so-called Christian cultures. Indeed, we have not had it right! In America during the Vietnam War era, for example, more women were murdered in domestic violence in America than men were slain on the battlefield.[7] Statistics show "that battering, incest, and other abuse occur in about the same percentage of Christian homes as is found in the general

---

[5] Alice Bratton, *A Woman's Voice Int'l Newsletter* (September 1997).
[6] *Telegraph Journal*, Saint John, New Brunswick, Canada, 30 September 1997, sec. B, p. 14.
[7] Catherine. Kroeger, "An Agenda for Biblical Feminism at the End of the Century," *Prism Magazine* 2, no. 7 (September-October 1997): 11.

population"[8] And the *Cape Cod Times* (Oct. 13, 1992) reports:

> Murder is the leading cause of death for young women in the United States. Four women a day are murdered in domestic disputes. A third of all women in the United States currently are victims of domestic abuse. Domestic abuse is the No. 1 cause of emergency room visits by women.[9]

Abuse may be physical, emotional, verbal, sexual, or a combination of these. All are destructive, devastating, and demoralizing. Speaking personally, I am thankful never to have been abused as a woman in any of these ways, that is, except emotionally and verbally in ministry and in higher Christian education—the places I would least expect it! I have had and still have some wonderful, supportive teachers and mentors, and I am grateful for these men and women. But again, I would emphasize that in both Christian ministerial activities and Christian educational environments, I have experienced the emotional and verbal abuse from those prejudiced against women.

To my amazement, I have observed other women being used and abused in Christian settings—domestic, ecclesiastical, ministerial, and educational. For example, a friend of mine was in her final semester of seminary when she felt the numbing blow of emotional and verbal abuse. Soon to receive double masters degrees in Bible and Divinity, she was deeply shaken by the reality that the Church does not esteem her on a level equal with that of her male colleagues. Her rude awakening came in a homiletics class when one of her male colleagues, taking his turn practice preaching, skillfully delineated the traditional view about "the place of women." Another colleague, commending the preacher for his presentation, mentioned in passing that she did not agree with the theology of his message. Suddenly the professor in charge

---

[8] Kroeger, 11.
[9] *Cape Cod Times* (13 October 1992) quoted by Kroeger, *Prism*, 11.

lashed out. Approaching the startled woman, he shook his finger in her face and said, "You cannot argue with the Bible! He is right! That's your fate as a woman!" A cold silence fell and class ended.

My friend retreated, silently questioning herself, God, and the Bible. You see, if what the professor had said were, in fact, true, it would shatter her self-esteem, her faith in the goodness of God, and her confidence in The Book she had studied and loved. All through the night, she agonized. The pain just would not go away.

My friend did talk to the dean about the incident, but the man remains in his post as a professor at the seminary and as a pastor of a local congregation. Do you think that this man's female students enjoy the same opportunity to develop and excel that is enjoyed by his male students? Do you think that the women in his congregation can really fulfil their divine destiny?

My friend graduated and has moved on, but something happened to her in that so-called "Spirit-filled" classroom. At best, she is forever sensitized to a very real problem.

This is not an isolated incident, and as was true in this case, most prejudicial treatment of this sort goes unchecked. Fueled by a belief in male dominance and female subjugation, the demoralizing and marginalization of women in Christian circles is very real and ever-present. It signals a need for people of the Spirit to get a picture of men and women that is consistent with the heart of God. We need to get it right!

The prevailing theology that men are to exercise authoritative headship while women are to submit graciously is problematic, unbiblical, and destructive. The fruit is bad; it does not resemble the fruit of the Spirit in any respect. So why has the Church continued to teach this doctrine? How did it get this way? Why does it continue?

Dealing with Our Procrustes

A few months ago at a conference, I met a retired librarian named Alma. From her wealth of knowledge, she shared with me the Greek legend about Procrustes. As the story goes, Procrustes kept an inn by the side of the road, and it was his habit to invite weary travelers to rest in the comfort of his bed. But this apparent kindness had a dark side! Every guest, once in bed, was required to fit it exactly. In that no guest ever met this stipulation, Procrustes took measures to assure the fit. If a guest were too short, he would stretch him, and if he were too long, he would simply cut him down to size.

When Alma shared this tale with me, she remarked, "I used to think this was just a silly story until, one day, the depth of its meaning suddenly dawned on me!" She explained, "When a new idea comes along, we are compelled to make it fit our point of view. We lop off pieces or add on parts—whatever it takes to preserve our point of view!"

Procrustes lurks within each of us and has a habit of appearing from time to time as we journey through life. Although he seems so comforting, he is always busy stretching and cutting to make new and different ideas fit his preconceived notions.

But then, on our journey, we meet Jesus Christ. What happens next is up to us. Do we let Procrustes determine our attitudes, or do we truly let Jesus Christ reign in our hearts and minds? That challenge faces us in this book, specifically in relation to our beliefs about women, and it is important that we get it right.

Jesus, Friend of Women

2

Jesus, Friend of Women

The Bible tells us that Jesus went about doing good. As our Supreme Example, He showed us how to relate to one another. In the Bible, we see Him in action in an historical setting, and in our daily life, by His indwelling Holy Spirit, we experience His prompting and empowerment to emulate Him.

Jesus lived in "a man's world," yet He often went against the norms of patriarchal culture by treating women as persons equal with men. In general, we miss this when we read the Gospels and we fail to grasp the radical nature of Jesus' actions because we lack knowledge of the oppressive conditions suffered by women of that day. We can gain some insight, however, through listening to the hostility expressed in religious writings of the day. Consider the following examples:[1]

- The oral law of Jesus' day said, "Let the words of the Law be burned rather than committed to women. . . . If a man teaches his daughter the Law, it is as though he taught her lewdness" (*Sotah* 3:4).[2]

- "The woman, says the Law, is in all things inferior to man. Let her accordingly be submissive" (*Apion* 2:210).[3]

- Let a curse come upon the man who must needs have his wife or children say grace for him.[4]

- Praised be to God that he has not created me a gentile;

---

[1] Leonard Swidler, "Jesus Was a Feminist," *Catholic World* (January 1971) as reported on the Christians for Biblical Equality website: www.ChrBibEq.org

[2] Cited by A. Schmidt, *Veiled and Silenced: How Culture Shaped Sexist Theology* (Macon: Mercer Univ. Press, 1989), 83.

[3] Schmidt, 82.

[4] Cited by Swidler.

praised be God that created me not a woman; praised be
God that he has not created me an ignorant man (This is a
thanksgiving prayer of Jews in Jesus' day). (*Menahot* 43b)

- It is well for those whose children are male, but ill for those
whose children are female . . . At the birth of a boy all are
joyful, but at the birth of a girl all are sad . . . When a boy
comes into the world, peace comes into the world; when a
girl comes, nothing comes . . . Even the most virtuous of
women is a witch (*Niddah* 31b).

Examples of social practices in Jesus' day also help us understand the deprecation of women.

- In the Jerusalem temple, women were limited to one outer
portion, the women's court, which was five steps below the
court for the men.
- A rabbi regarded it beneath his dignity to speak to a woman
in public.
- Women were kept for childbearing and rearing and were
always under the strict control of a man.

The Gospel writers show us that Jesus countered these attitudes. Never do they portray a negative attitude toward women.
Never do they attribute a prescribed, subservient role to women
that would be in keeping with the cultural role given women in
that day. Instead, they reflect Jesus' attitudes and actions. That
the Christian community did so "underscores the clearly great religious importance Jesus attached to his positive attitude . . . toward women," notes Leonard Swidler. "Personalism extended to
women," he adds, "is a constitutive part of the Gospel, the Good
News, of Jesus."[5]

Perhaps we think nothing of the fact that Jesus taught women
the Scriptures and revealed to them the Gospel, but in that cul-

---

[5] Cited by Swidler

ture, what He did was revolutionary. And do we forget that women, as well as men, were Jesus' disciples and that they traveled with Him? It was a woman whom Jesus raised from the dead in Mt. 9:18-26, and it was largely because of women that He raised two other people from the dead (Lk. 7:11-17; Jn. 11:1-44). Then, too, it was to a woman named Martha that Jesus declared Himself to be *The Resurrection* (Jn. 11:25), thus revealing first to a woman the central event and message of the Gospel. It was a woman of ill repute whom Jesus allowed to anoint Him (Lk. 7:36-50). And it was a woman, Mary, whom Jesus sent first to preach His Resurrection (Jn. 20:10-18). She was, in fact, the first person to be given an apostolic commission from the Resurrected Lord. In a culture where the testimony of women was not considered valid, Jesus sent this woman to testify to men about the most important event in the history of humanity: The Resurrection of the Lord Jesus Christ. Clearly, He was making a radical statement about women.

Jesus Demonstrates the Personhood of a Woman

John 8:3-11. When the religious leaders brought to Jesus a woman who had been caught in the act of adultery, they wanted to know if He would have her stoned as the law required (Deut. 22:23-30). In the minds of the religious leaders, the woman was merely property owned by a husband or a husband-to-be. He was, in fact, the one who had been violated in the sense that his property—his woman—had been misused. As "damaged goods," she had brought disgrace on him and was no longer worthy of life. According to the law, the man involved in the offense, as well as the woman, were to be stoned, but again, the reason for stoning the man was not because he had violated the woman or the law, but because he had misused another man's property.

But Jesus demonstrated an entirely different set of values in the situation. He did not treat the woman as a man's property, but as a person of great value. He showed respect for her by speaking to her, a thing that was prohibited in that culture. And He spoke to her with tenderness and compassion, thereby carefully demonstrating the high regard God places on women.

Matthew 9:20-22. In the story of Jesus healing the woman with the issue of blood, we are told that she touched Him. According to the law, this made Him ritually unclean, but once again, Jesus disregarded religious rules and rulers, to help a woman. He demonstrated that God sees even one woman as being of great value.

Jesus Shows Woman's Equality in Marriage

Matthew 19:1-11. Since women were considered the property of men, a man could divorce his wife at the slightest whim; on the other hand, a woman could not divorce her husband. Jesus rejected this double standard in His discourse on marriage and divorce. He also rejected the notion that women are the property of men. He clearly demonstrated that the man and the woman were to have the same rights and responsibilities in their relationships toward each other (Mk. 10:2-12; Mt. 19:3). This is *mutuality*.

Jesus Shows Woman's Equal Social Status

John 4:1-26,39-42. In Jesus' encounter with the Samaritan woman, He demonstrates that she to is receive honor equal to that afforded men. Despite strong, cultural prohibitions to the contrary, He responded to the woman with the same regard He would have shown a man. Furthermore, as a Jew, He was not permitted to speak to a Samaritan. And as a man, He was not to speak publicly to a woman. Since He was a teacher, He was aware of the prohibition against teaching women theology. But Jesus spoke publicly to this Samaritan woman about theology! He consciously ignored three major, cultural prohibitions in this encounter. In addition, in the process, He revealed to her that He was the

Messiah. What an astounding revelation! She then proclaimed the Good News to both the men and the women of her village. Many Samaritans believed in Him because of the woman's testimony.

Jesus Projects God in the Image of Woman

Luke 15:8-10. We make much of the image of God as father in Jesus' teaching, but his presentation of the image of God as woman or mother is often overlooked. Nevertheless, He did so, and it is helpful to consider such references. For example, He compares His desire to protect and care for Jerusalem with the protective instincts of a mother hen spreading her wings over her brood (Mt. 23:37; Lk. 13:34). In the parable about the woman who found the lost coin (Lk. 15:8-10), He used the image of a woman to portray God. Swidler thinks that Jesus included "this womanly image of God quite deliberately" because "the scribes and Pharisees were among those who most of all denigrated women."

Jesus Rejects the Notion of "Woman's Role"

Luke 8: 19-21. What can we learn from Luke 8:19-21?

[19]Now Jesus' mother and brothers came to see him, but they were not able to get near him because of the crowd. [20]Someone told him, "Your mother and brothers are standing outside, wanting to see you." [21]He replied, "My mother and brothers are those who hear God's word and put it into practice."

It is customary in discussions about male/female relationships, to presume the notion of gender-restricted roles; that is, that women have their place and it is only a rebellious woman who would resist or override this role. In this incident, however, Jesus demolishes this notion, for when the messenger notifies Him that His mother and brother are wanting to see Him, Jesus redefines the meaning of the terms! He says that His mother and brothers do not have favored status because of their gender or familial relationships. He states, instead, that what determines intimate relationship with Him is attentiveness to and regard for God's Word. By his behavior, He also indicates that the honor due mother and brothers is an honor to be extended equally to everyone.

Luke 10:38-42. Jesus teaches this principle again when He visits Martha and Mary and praises Mary for listening attentively instead of Martha for doing "woman's work." Consequently, Swidler says He regarded her "first as a person . . . who was allowed to set her own priorities, and in this instance has 'chosen the better part.'" Schmidt's remarks are also well worth repeating.

> Jesus saw woman as a full-fledged human being, rather than subordinate, submissive property. In the Mary-Martha incident Martha is the sociocultural conformist. Apparently, she had deeply internalized the patriarchal idea that woman's place was in the kitchen. She busied herself preparing a meal for Jesus, her guest. Mary, her sister, did what only men did, namely sit down and learn theology. No woman in her right mind, according to the Hebraic-rabbinic teachings, would think of doing what Mary did. Luke says that Mary "sat at Jesus' feet and listened to His teaching" (Luke 10:39). But what is even more significant in this account is that Jesus was the greater deviant. He, after all, taught Mary. Such behavior was a flagrant violation of the established theology.[6]

Jesus Rejects the Cultural Perception of Womanhood

Luke 11:27-28. One day a woman complimented Jesus by referring to how happy His mother must have been to have had such a wonderful son. "Blessed the womb that bore You, and breasts which nursed You!" she said. She meant well, but Jesus rebuked her sharply. Her reference to woman in purely reproduc-

---

[6] Schmidt, 167. See Deut. 6:7; 11:19; 12:28; 29:22, 29; 32:46.

tive terms, seemed to have bothered Jesus. Swidler remarks, "Jesus clearly felt it necessary to reject the 'baby-machine' image of women."[7] He points out that Jesus insisted "on the personhood, the intellectual and moral faculties, being primary of all." Luke records Jesus' response in verse 28. He says, "Nay rather, blessed are the ones hearing and keeping the word of God." Jesus made no gender distinction in clarifying what the defining priority is to be: "hearing and keeping the word of God." Furthermore, both the word choice and word order in the Greek text indicate that He carried out his corrective action with intense emphasis.[8]

The Risen Christ Commissions the First Apostle—A Woman

John 10:10-18; Matthew 28:1-10. It is a well known fact that the women were the last ones to leave the Cross and the first ones to arrive at the Tomb. When Mary Magdalene visited the tomb early on Resurrection morning and found it empty, without delay, she reported to the disciples that Jesus' body was missing. They all hastened to the scene, but they did not grasp the significance of the empty tomb because "they still did not understand from Scripture that Jesus had to rise from the dead" (Jn. 20:9). So they returned home, but Mary lingered behind. It was then that Jesus appeared to her and said, "Go and tell my brothers. . . ."

This appearance and commission are significant for several reason. During the forty days between His resurrection and ascension, Jesus appeared to His disciples at various times, and on one occasion he appeared to over five hundred of His followers. The Gospel writers, however, are explicit in noting that it was Mary Magdalene to whom He appeared <u>first</u> after His resurrection. The importance which the evangelists attach to this fact indicates that

---

[7] Swidler writes, "But her image of woman was sexually reductionist in the extreme (one that largely persists to the present): female genitals and breasts" (n.p.).

[8] I. Howard Marshall, *The Gospel of Luke: A Commentary on the Greek Text, The New International Greek Commentary* (Grand Rapids: Eerdmans, 1978), 482.

it was not an accidental occurrence, but that Jesus purposely appeared first to this woman. He could just as easily have appeared to a man; instead, He honored a woman.

In appearing first to Mary Magdalene, Jesus was making a very important statement. It was a statement, perhaps, that the disciples could not have grasped by a mere lecture. This statement was further clarified by the words which Jesus spoke to her on this occasion: "Go and tell my brethren. . . ."

- "Go and tell" defines the commission. Interestingly, the New Testament word *apostle* literally means "one who is sent." Mary thus received the first apostolic commission from the Risen Lord to proclaim the greatest fact in history, the resurrection.

- "Go and tell *My bothers*. . . ." defines her audience. Jesus was sending her to men, not women. In other words, her commission was not limited to a "women's ministry," as is so often the restriction placed on women today.

This was revolutionary thinking, indeed, for in both Roman and Jewish courts of law, the testimony of a woman was not permitted as evidence. By appearing first to Mary Magdalene, Jesus was, therefore, cutting through any remnants of disdain and prejudice in His male disciples toward His female disciples. He no doubt was also teaching the women something revolutionary about their responsibility. Thus, Jesus declared His equal acceptance and expectation of women while also confirming their public responsibility as ministers of the New Covenant.

Conclusion

Jesus was a friend of women. He vigorously promoted the dignity and equality of women in terms of both value and function, and He left us this example. Is it not our responsibility now to emulate His attitudes and actions?

3

Evidence of Equality
in Early Christianity

The first generation of believers reflected Jesus' teaching about women. Despite the pressures of a patriarchal world, the believers in the Book of Acts demonstrate a remarkable tendency toward equality. This is obvious in daily life, decision making, salvation, Spirit baptism, ministry, business, and marriage.

In keeping with Jesus' egalitarian social pattern, both men and women participated in prayer and decision-making in the Upper Room (Acts 1:13-26). Some of the women probably present were Mary Magdalene, Mary the mother of James, Mary His mother, Joanna the wife of Herod's household manager, Susanna, those who had followed Him from Galilee, and many others (Lk. 8:1-3;23:49,55;24:10).

The Holy Spirit confirmed the egalitarian pattern demonstrated by Jesus, when, on the Day of Pentecost, women were equal recipients of the Pentecostal outpouring (Acts 2:1-4,17-18). Scholars point to this event as the birthday of the church. Thus, equality was an essential characteristic of the Church at its beginning. From the outset, then, God's purpose for women and His empowerment of women were equal in every respect with His purpose for and empowerment of men.

Early in Acts, the Holy Spirit introduced another important precedent. He held women directly, personally, and equally responsible with men to God. Numbers 30 had given fathers and husbands control over women, but God clearly set a new standard—an egalitarian standard—when He dealt with Ananias and

Saphira (Acts 5:1-11). He holds Ananias, the husband, responsible for his actions, and He holds Saphira individually and personally responsible for her behavior. Ananias was not held responsible for his wife, and Saphira was directly accountable to God. She could not excuse herself with the claim that she was submitted to her husband and so shift responsibility to him.

Another area in which gender equality was highly visible in the church in Acts was in redemption. Women were redeemed to the same degree as men, and all the benefits, requirements, and ramifications belonged to both equally (eg. Acts 5:14). Consequently, women were experiencing salvation and Spirit baptism, and were proclaiming the Gospel. They were also being persecuted and imprisoned (Acts 8:3-4;12; 9:1-2;22:4).

Paul clearly acknowledged gender equality in redemption. This is characteristic of Paul's proclamation and practice wherever he went. In Thessalonica, for example, a number of prominent women were converted to *The Way* (Acts 17:4). In Berea, converts included a number of prominent Greek women (Acts 17:12). In Athens, a woman named Damaris was among the converts (Acts 17:34). In Romans 16:1-15, Paul specifically greets ten women by name, including Phoebe, Prisca, May, Junia, Tryphaena, Tryphosa, Persis, the mother of Rufus, Julia, and the sister of Nereus.

In Jerusalem, Christian women exercised considerable freedom and equality in both domestic and spiritual functions.[1] They were neither slave nor subordinate, and because both men and women shouldered the affairs of daily life, "the burden of the daily provisions, which still falls so heavily on the vast majority of women, was here rendered extremely light." "Equal fellowship also in the great spiritual possessions caused all marks of woman's inferiority to vanish," reports one study, "and the sexes freely mingled in a

---

[1] Karen Jo Torjesen, *When Women Were Priests: Women's Leadership in the Early Church and the Scandal of Their Subordination in the Rise of Christianity* (San Francisco: HarperSanFrancisco, 1993); Elizabeth A. Clark, *Women in the Early Church*, ed. Thomas Halton, *The Message of the Fathers of the Church*, vol. 13 (Collegeville: The Liturgical Press, 1983), 20.

pure and noble companionship."[2]

It might be said that on the Day of Pentecost, God made an egalitarian proclamation when He poured out the Holy Spirit without regard for gender. It might also be said that Paul's central egalitarian proclamation is: *There is neither Jew nor Greek, slave nor free, male nor female, for you are all one in Christ Jesus* (Gal. 3:28). Indeed, in Jesus Christ, God removed the hierarchical distinctives that had arisen in regard to race, social class, and gender. Aware of this principle and empowered by the Spirit, women functioned as equals with men.

Women and Ministry in the Beginning

What Is "Ministry"? This book is about biblical womanhood. It is not about women in ministry, but ministry is one area of consideration in the discussion. Because every reader brings to this discussion a preconceived notion about ministry, in order to understand this book's perspective, a definition of ministry is needed. *Ministry* is the self-disclosure of God to and through His people.

A consistent theme from Genesis to Revelation is the self-revelation of God motivated by divine desire to establish a love relationship with humanity. This self-revelation began in Creation, climaxed in the Incarnation, and continues through the Holy Spirit.

This self-revelation of God as seen in Jesus Christ and replicated by the Holy Spirit in and through believers individually and corporately is God's ministry. As Scripture says, "We love Him because He first loved us" (1 Jn. 4:19). As we respond to His love, He discloses Himself *through* us. Thus, ministry is about knowing Him and making Him known. It is the expression of a relationship

---

[2] Alfred Brittain and Mitchell Carroll, *Women in All Ages and in All Countries: Women of Early Christianity* (Philadelphia: Rittenhouse Press, 1907-08), 38.

based on intimate, two-way communication with God.

The Old Testament is the historical love drama depicting God's efforts to establish and maintain relationship with humanity. This personal, holy, transcendent and immanent God expressed Himself in Creation, was rejected by humanity, but relentlessly reached out to communicate with humanity. He selected the Israelites as the Chosen People through whom He would disclose Himself to the nations and through whom He would come in human form in the Person of Christ. This relationship is God-centered and God-directed, not human-centered and human-directed, and it is based on encounter facilitated only by divine self-disclosure, not on manipulation or metaphysical proposition. God revealed Himself to special people at special times in special places. Thus, in the Old Testament, ministry—God's self-disclosure—was reserved for a select few.

The New Testament is the ongoing drama of God's effort to establish and maintain relationship with humanity. The ultimate self-disclosure of God is the Person of Jesus Christ. He was rejected, but He persisted, sending His Spirit to abide in those who would reciprocate the love relationship He initiated. The believer is the prophet-priest and the dwelling place on earth of the Spirit of God. God continues to reveal Himself to whoever will receive Him at any time and in any place. He does this by His Spirit, in general revelation through His creation and in specific, personal revelation through the Bible and the Church (believers). Ministry in the New Testament is the Spirit-empowered privilege and responsibility of all believers.

Thus Christian life today is ministry. How can there be a distinction between ministry and life? As we participate with God in His ongoing attempts to establish relationship with people, we are ministering. Thus, it is a two dimensional event or process. In a vertical sense, it is our personal response to God's loving initiative. In a horizontal sense, it is our God-directed initiative toward people on His behalf. Because God is Love, ministry is character-ized by compassionate courage and commitment. And because God is faithful, ministry proceeds from the rest of faith. Out of dynamic union with God flows Spirit-empowered action. This is ministry.

With this foundation in place, we can proceed with our dis-cussion of women and ministry. In the pristine state of the young Church, ministry was relatively untainted by human ideas. It was still God's self-disclosure to and through people by the power of the Spirit. In this, God did not seem concerned about gender! Clearly, He did not favor men over women or women over men. *Ministry*, then, was as egalitarian as God's self-disclosure! And the Church flourished and spread.

This continued—although perhaps not with the unsullied char-acter of the earliest days—for two-hundred years. During this time, believers met primarily in homes, a natural venue for women *to minister*. It also provided an egalitarian atmosphere for corporate meetings. Worship was simple, personal, and *charismatic* (i.e. Spirit-empowered and Spirit-led),[3] and whatever *leadership* was, it was informal and *charismatic*. Perhaps more than anything else, it consisted of facilitating the activity of the Spirit among the indi-vidual participants. This activity of the Spirit is the self-disclosure of God. It is *ministry*.

A good example of a charismatic meeting is recorded in 1 Cor-inthians 14:22-31. It is clear that all were encouraged to partici-pate in the gatherings according to their Holy Spirit giftings and to the activity of the Spirit in their midst. It is interesting to note that Paul never appeals to a leader or a leadership group to deal with the problems he is addressing—even the problem that had arisen in the practice of communion (1 Cor. 11:17-34). Instead, Paul appeals to the entire congregation to do what is right in the situation. Professor James D. G. Dunn interprets this to mean

---

[3] See Eddie L. Hyatt, *2000 Years of Charismatic Christianity* (Dallas: Hyatt Int'l Ministries, 1996).

that there was no obvious, visible leadership group to whom he could appeal. For Dunn the implication is plain, "If leadership was required, Paul assumed that the charismatic Spirit would provide it."[4]

In both 1 Corinthians 12 and Romans 12, Paul provides a picture of the church as a body made up of many different members. Each time he shares this concept, it is within the context of spiritual gifts. This is because it is the empowerment of the Holy Spirit in a believer and the expression of particular giftings of the indwelling Spirit that give each member of the body his or her particular function in the body. That function is an expression of God through a person. It is simply a response to God's desire to disclose Himself to people. The essence of Paul's illustration is that our responsibility to serve springs forth simply from a man or woman's spiritual gifting. Hans von Campenhausen sees this as the early church's vision of Christian community which he describes as "one of free fellowship, developing through the living interplay of spiritual gifts and ministries, without the benefit of official authority or responsible elders."[5]

Clearly, among early Christians, *ministry* was seen as the responsibility and privilege of every believer. A select "ordained," "clergy" class, as we know it today, did not exist. This is confirmed by the fact that the word *laos,* from which we get *laity,* is everywhere used in the New Testament to refer to "the whole people of God." For example, in 1 Peter. 2:9, Peter refers to the entire church as a holy *laos,* or "people." In the same way, the Greek word *kleros,* from which we get "clergy," is also used to refer to all the people of God. In Romans 1:6, for example, Paul refers to the believers in Rome as the *kleros* (called) of Jesus Christ. Dunn, in fact, insists that there is no precedent or justification in

---

[4] James D.G. Dunn, *Jesus and the Spirit* (Philadelphia: Westminster, 1975), 291.

[5] Hans von Campenhausen, *Ecclesiastical Authority and Spiritual Power in the Churches of the First Three Centuries* (Stanford: Stanford Univ. Press, 1969), 58.

the New Testament for a theology or practice of ordination as something indispensable before one can preach, baptize, or serve communion.[6]

The basic New Testament pattern of leadership and ministry was set by Jesus Himself. It was one of service not dominance (Mk. 9:33-37; Mt. 18:1-5;23:8-8-11; Lk. 9:46-48; Jn. 13:15-16). It was not to reflect Jewish or pagan patterns of dominance (Mk. 10:41-45; Mt. 20:24-28; Lk. 22:24-27). Jesus' pattern of leadership also included men and women without regard for gender. He instituted no offices, and he taught that discipline within the body was the responsibility of the entire community of believers (Mt. 1:15-20;1 Cor. 5;14:37-38;2 Thess. 3:14-15).[7]

In his paper, "Patterns of Authority in the Early Church," David M. Scholer, Dean of the Center for Advanced Theological Education at Fuller Theological School, traces charismatic, functional leadership through the New Testament. In this thoroughly researched document, he shows clearly the functional nature of ministry and leadership. Ultimately, Scholer is showing that ministry is the self-disclosure of God through his people. This, of course, is contrary to the way that many of us tend to understand ministry today, that is, in terms of office and apostolic succession.[8]

As the New Testament introduces new Greek words to describe the functions that individuals performed in the growing body of believers, we tend to assume that this indicated the development of offices. But this is not the case; these were not offices as we know them. Consider the New Testament meaning of three terms: *presbuteros* (elder), *episkopoi* (bishops), and *diakonoi* (deacons). These terms are interchangeable expressions with no inherent hierarchical meaning. In the pastoral letters, the term *presbuteros* (elder) is used for the first time by Paul, and qualifications are

---

[6] James G.D. Dunn, "Ministry and Ministry: The Charismatic Renewal's Challenge to Traditional Ecclesiology," *Charismatic Experiences in History*, ed. Cecil M. Robeck Jr. (Peabody: Hendrickson, 1985), 94.

[7] See Ch. 2; David M. Scholer, "Patterns of Authority in the Early Church," *Servant Leadership, Volume One: Authority and Governance in the Evangelical Covenant Church*, ed. J. R. Hawkinson and R. K. Johnston (Chicago: Covenant Publications, 1993), 46-48.

[8] Scholer, 45-65.

given for those who would serve as *episkopoi* (bishops) or *diakonoi* (deacons). Adolph Harnack suggests, however, that *presbuteros* or *elder* may simply denote the *old* as opposed to the *young*, and John Knox insists, "We are not dealing with formal offices, but with functions for which persons were as certainly spiritually endowed as for prophecy and healing."[9] Rudolph Bultman, a liberal theologian but astute historian, says, "Neither in the earliest Palestinian congregation nor in earliest Hellenistic Christianity was there originally any thought of instituting church regulations and offices."[10]

In this setting where the life and ministry of the Church are one and the same—an expression of the life of Jesus Christ through individual believers and groups of believers—it is easy to see how men and women would function together as equal partners. Had not the Scriptures promised that the Holy Spirit would be poured out on all flesh and that consequently, men and women alike would be empowered to prophesy, that is, to proclaim God's word. Did not Paul say that in God's redemptive plan, which is made real by the power and presence of the Holy Spirit, there is neither male nor female (Gal 3:28)? It is, then, not surprising to see women functioning in what we call *ministry* alongside men throughout the New Testament, including Paul's epistles?

Women Were Co-laborers with Paul. Paul mentions women as being *co-laborers* or *coworkers* (Greek, *sunergoi*) with him in ministry (1 Cor. 16:16, 19; Rom. 16:1-16; Phil. 4:2-3). In Romans 16, he names 29 people and of these, ten are women. He lists two women in Philippians 4:2-3, and four who were "house church leaders." In describing these women, Paul uses the same Greek words that he used for men who were co-laborers with him. One researcher admits the possibility that women may not have been doing the same things as the men, but he quickly points out that there is no evidence supporting that notion!

---

[9] John Knox, "The Ministry in the Primitive Church," *The Ministry in Historical Perspective*, ed. Richard H. Niebuhr and Daniel D. Williams (New York: Harper and Row, 1956), 10.

[10] Rudolph Bultman, *New Testament Theology*, 2 vols. (New York: Charles Scribner, 1965), 2:100.

In Romans 16:3-16, Paul speaks of Mary (16:6), Tryphaena, Tryphosa, and Persis (16:12). He says that they "work very hard," an expression Paul used to describe both his ministry and the ministry of others.[11] Reference to these women in these terms, notes Scholer, indicates they were "engaged in the authoritative work of ministry."[12]

Two other coworkers of Paul need to be introduced at this point. In Philippians 4:2-3, Paul refers to Euodia and Syntyche, two women who worked *beside* him, not *under* him. And he pleads, "Help these women. . . ."

> *I beg Euodia and I beg Syntyche to agree with each other in the Lord. Yes, and I ask you, my loyal yoke-fellows, to help them because they are women who fought at my side in the spread of the gospel along with Clement and the rest of my coworkers.*[13]

Paul says that these two women "struggled along with" him. He uses a rare Greek verb that describes "athletes working as a team, side by side, playing the game not as several individuals but together as one person with one mind for one goal." A sense of equality is inherent in this passage, and in no way is there any hint that "these two must have been among those [women] who, having believed, labored among their own sex for" the spread of the gospel. "These were rather Paul's coworkers (*sunergoi*), equal in importance to Clement and the rest (*oi loipoi*) of Paul's fellow laborers."[14]

Women Functioned as Pastors. In New Testament days, the believers gathered in homes to worship and to be strengthened in the faith. Today we call these New Testament gatherings *house churches,* as if, perhaps, they were a unique kind of church, but in that era, they were the Church. This remained the case until at

[11] 1 Cor. 4:12;15:10; 16:15-16; Gal. 4:11; Phil. 2:16; Col. 2:29; 1 Tim. 4:10; 5:17; Acts 20:35; Thess. 5:12.

[12] David M. Scholer, "Paul's Women Coworkers in Ministry," *Theology, News and Notes*, 42:1, March 20, 1995: 20.

[13] Translation by Gerald F. Hawthorn, *Philippians, Word Bible Commentary*, vol. 43 (Waco: Word Books, 1983), 175.

[14] Hawthorne, 57. 180.

least the third century, and even then, it continued to be the normal venue for church gatherings until Constantine's conversion in the fourth century.

In the New Testament, several of the homes where believers gathered on a regular basis are described in terms of the woman of the home. Acts 12:12, for example, speaks of Mary, the mother of John Mark, and Acts 16:13-15 and 40 speak of Lydia. 1 Corinthians 1:11 mentions Cloe, and 1 Corinthians 16:19 and Romans 16:3-5 refer to Priscilla and Aquila.

Paul sends greetings to Nympha (Col. 4:15) in whose home a church met. The gender of Nympha has been debated raising the question whether the passage should read, "Nympha and the church in her house" or "Nymphas and the church in his house." The evidence favors the feminine form *Nympha*. It has been suggested that that scribes would have been more inclined to change a woman's name into a man's name rather than the reverse.[15]

2 John is a letter written to a particular woman and to the believers who met in her home. Through the centuries, however, interpreters of Scripture have taught that the address, "chosen lady," is a code name for *church*, and "children," for *church members*. Clearly, this is a biased interpretation forcing a meaning on the passage that is not present in the text.

Perhaps worthy of note here is some discussion that surrounds the reference to Phoebe as a *servant, minister,* or *deacon* (Rom. 16:1-2). The latter part of verse 2 has been translated, "She has been a helper of many and of myself also." The word *helper* is a translation of the Greek word *prostatis* which literally means "one who stands before."[16] This word can also mean "ruler or leader" or "protector, patron or guardian." Some have, therefore, suggested that the clause should read: "She was designated as a ruler over

---

[15] Peter T. O'Brien, vol. 44 of *Colossians, Philemon, Word Biblical Commentary,* (Waco: Word Pub., 1982), 245-46; Craig Keener, *The IVP Bible Background Commentary: New Testament* (Downers Grove: IVP. 1993), 582.

[16] Snodgrass, 6.

many by me."[17] But this translation is not in keeping with the spirit of New Testament Christianity which clearly indicates that we are not to rule over others. In addition, as one scholar points out, the *kai* in the Greek construction indicates that "whatever Phoebe was to the many she was also to Paul."[18] The best translation, therefore, embraces the notion that Phoebe stood before many as a protector, patron, and guardian. This sounds like a wonderful description of a true, New Testament pastor! *Diakonos* is used by Paul to describe his own ministry.

Women Functioned as Teachers. One of the most obvious New Testament teachers was Priscilla. In Corinth, Paul shared ministry with her and her husband Aquila (Acts 18:1-4). The couple instructed the learned Apollos (Acts 18:18-28). As one scholar notes, "One does not get the impression that Priscilla was sitting by quietly while the instruction was taking place."[19]

There is no reason to suppose that teaching in the New Testament was strictly a male function. For example, Colossians 3:16 says, "Let the word of Christ dwell in you richly as you teach. . . ." This is obviously directed to the believers in Colosse without gender restriction (Col. 1:2; 3:12). Also, nothing in 1 Corinthians 14:26,31 exclude women from "having a teaching" or "a word of instruction" to share with the whole body. The overarching New Testament principle is that every believer is responsible to God to teach if and as the Spirit leads. If women are to prophecy, surely they are to teach, for prophecy is the function of delivering the word of the Lord. Prophecy could, then, include teaching. In the sense of speaking forth the word of the Lord, prophecy is not unlike teaching. To suggest that the New Testament excludes women from this activity is simply unacceptable.

Women Functioned as Prophets. Women, such as Deborah,

---

[17] Letha Scanzoni and Nancy Hardesty, *All We're Meant to Be* (Waco: Word Books, 1974), 62.

[18] Snodgrass, 6.

[19] Snodgrass, 6.

Miriam, Huldah, and Anna, had functioned as prophets before the Day of Pentecost, but one result of the coming of the Spirit "upon all flesh" (Acts 2) was that "Your sons and daughters will prophecy" (Acts 2:17). It is not surprising, then, to hear of Philip's four prophesying daughters (Acts 21:8-9). In fact, the historian Eusebius points to these women, four men, and Ammias, a woman of Philadelphia, as examples of prophetic ministry in the Church.[20]

According to 1 Corinthians 11:4-5;14:3-4;26,31, both men and women in Corinth prophesied. In these passages, Paul was not silencing women but was offering Christian protocol in the use of the genuine gift of prophecy. This was necessary because the men and women to whom he was writing were familiar with prophetic phenomena since prophecy was the most universal cult practice in the New Testament world and since the famous pagan Oracle of Delphi was only a few miles from Corinth.[21]

Women Functioned as Apostles. Paul refers to Junia of Rome, a woman, as an apostle (Rom. 16:7). Several ancient commentators, including Chrysostom (A.D. 347-407), patriarch of Constantinople, understood Andronicus and Junia to be husband and wife. Chrysostom also writes, "Oh, how great is the devotion of this woman [Junia], that she should be even counted worthy of the appellation of apostle."[22]

The female gender of Junia went unquestioned until the Middle Ages when translators "attempted to change the gender by changing the name to Junias. But such a name is unknown in antiquity, and there is absolutely no . . . evidence for it."[23] In fact, the first known commentator to understand Junia as the male name Junias was Aegidius of Rome (1245-1346).[24]

---

[20] Eusebius, *The History of the Church*, trans. G.A. Williamson (New York: Dorset Press, 1965), 222.

[21] Susan Hyatt, *Prophecy in the Greco Roman World* (Dallas: Hyatt Int'l Ministries, 1995), 1-2. An extensive bibliography is available in D. E. Aune, *Prophecy in Early Christianity and the Mediterranean World* (Grand Rapids: Eerdmans, 1983).

[22] Chrysostom, "Homily XXXI," *Homilies on Romans*; Snodgrass, 5.

[23] Catherine Kroeger, "The Neglected History of Women in the Early Church," *Christian History*, vol. VII, no. 1, 17: 7.

[24] Bernadette Brooten cited by David M. Scholer, "Paul's Women Coworkers in Ministry," *Theology, New and Notes*, 42:1, March 1995: 22.

Women in Business Outside the Home

Christian women were not confined to domestic roles as is often suggested today as the proper biblical model for women. In fact, the New Testament mentions women who worked outside the home in commerce. In Jerusalem and Alexandria, women were not confined to home. In rural Palestine and in wider Greco-Roman culture, despite male dominance, they generally experienced a degree of public activity. In fact, in Roman culture, a few women "enjoyed great power and influence on politics and culture, . . . and increasingly pursued interests outside the home, including commerce."[25] This enabled women to participate effectively in the expansion of the Gospel.

Lydia (Acts 16:14), a business woman who dealt in purple cloth, was converted along with her entire household. Subsequently, she provided hospitality for Paul and his companions. Lydia was from Thyatira in the Roman province of Lydia. Since a freed slave customarily took the name of her country of origin, it is possible that she was a freed slave. At this point, however, she was obviously "a competent business woman in Philippi, knowledgeable about trade routes westward from Thyatira, with a large house and her own slaves."[26]

Damaris (Acts 17:32) was a convert in Athens where Paul preached in the Areopagus, a council that met in the Stoa Basilicos, in the Agora (public market). It seems likely that Damaris was converted when she heard Paul preach to the Areopagus. Craig Keener says that most educated and publicly visible women in Athens were probably still prostitutes and foreigners.[27] Others note, however, that Greek women were accepted as philosophers, and so it is possible that Damaris was in public as a philosopher.

---

[25] Stanley Grenz, *Women in the Church: A Biblical Theology of Women in Ministry* (Downers Grove: IVPress, 1995), 72-73

[26] *Study Bible for Women: The New Testament*, ed. C. Kroeger, M. Evans, and E. Storkey (Grand Rapids: Baker, 1995), 264.

[27] Craig S. Keener, *The IVP Bible Background Commentary: New Testament* (Downers Grove: IVPress, 1993), 373.

Thus, although Scripture does not tell us who she was, the fact that she is mentioned indicates the likelihood that she was a prominent figure.

Other notable women who functioned in business were Priscilla and Phoebe. Priscilla and her husband Aquila (Acts 18:2-3), tentmakers by trade, may have set up shop in Ephesus and Rome, as well as Corinth where they worked together with Paul who was also a tentmaker.[28] Phoebe (Rom. 16:1-2) was a business person in Rome with considerable influence, and it is thought that she delivered Paul's Epistle to the Romans.[29]

Mutuality in Marriage

It goes without saying that the world of the New Testament operated as a highly patriarchal and androcentric system. It is revolutionary, then, that Christian marriage in the Bible was egalitarian. Some would immediately grasp the Ephesians 5 proof-text to refute this notion, but as David M. Scholer points out, Ephesians 5:21-33 does not promote male headship in marriage. "It is, rather, an early Church witness to an emerging new perspective on mutual submission in marriage."[30] Yet, among Spirit-oriented Christians, the home is the stronghold of female subservience and male dominance. Later chapters will clarify the Scriptural basis of egalitarian marriage.

Inclusive Meaning

The New Testament was not written to men only, but to men and women alike. This truth remains even though the language may be tainted by the patriarchal influences of the day and by translators who oft-times have interpreted the text from a patriar-

---

[28] *Study Bible for Women*, 264.
[29] *Study Bible for Women*, 320.
[30] David Scholer, "Male Headship: God's Intention or Man's Invention?" *WATCHword* 12:1 (Feb.-March 1988): 3, 5,7.

chal bias. The fact that statements, promises, and directives are spoken with both men and women in mind and without regard for gender differences may be one of the strongest arguments for equality. For example, consider Paul's instructions to Timothy.

*And the things you have heard me say in the presence of many witnesses entrust to reliable **people** who will also be qualified to teach others (2 Tim. 2:2, NIV Inclusive).*

Many versions of the New Testament have translated the word *anthropos* as "men." If Paul had intended the passage to refer to males only, he would have chosen the word *andros.* This is an example of a gender inclusive statement in the Greek which is best rendered with the word "people" rather than "men." This is in keeping with the fact that the Holy Spirit was and is given to women and to men in the same way and for the same purposes. Clearly, the person and gifts of the Spirit are not different in women and men. The passages dealing with the *charismata,* therefore, apply to both men and women (Rom. 11:29;12:4-8; 1 Cor. 12:1,7-11,28-31;14:1-5; Eph. 4:7,11-12; 1 Peter 4:10-11). If the Holy Spirit did not suggest a chain-of-command based on gender, why should we?

Conclusion

Jesus was a friend of women, and His Holy Spirit, too, is a friend of women. Like Jesus, the Spirit vigorously promotes the dignity and equality of women in terms of both value and function. How, then, have we as revival people accepted a doctrine of female submission and male rulership? Before we explore the true meaning of proof texts used to uphold this position, we need to understand the traditional, centuries-old notions that influence modern perspectives—even among Pentecostals, Charimatics, and Revival people.

Intrusion of Paganism

4

Good News and Bad News for Women

By the latter half of the second century, the trend away from Spirit-life and biblical equality to institutionalism and patriarchy was gaining momentum. Because it is the Spirit who empowers the principle of biblical equality, as the manifest presence of the Spirit was replaced by outward form and ritual, the status of Christian women was diminished. But when the Church experienced its first renewal through a movement known as *Montanism*, hope momentarily flickered in the hearts of Spirit-filled women.

Institutionalism—Bad News for Women!

As the first generation of believers passed away and as Christianity spread rapidly, two very different movements arose within Christendom: one was a move of God; the other, a move of man. The move of man gained precedence manifesting itself in what is known as *institutionalism*. Institutionalism is an emphasis on organization at the expense of other factors. It is a mode of organization whereby human control displaces the leadership of the Holy Spirit. In the early Church, institutionalism crept in at the expense of Spirit-life.

One symptom of institutionalism was (and is) the division of Christians into two classes: a ruling class called *clergy* (*kleros*) and a subservient class called *laity* (*laos*). This is a misuse of these two New Testament terms since both are consistently used to refer to all the people of God.[1] All believers are both "the called ones" (*kleros*) and "the people of God" (*laos*). Nevertheless, the institutional trend prevailed and this move of man defined the term *clergy* as "called ones" who ruled and *laity* as "the masses" who were ruled.

By the third century, the political, clerical ruling class had virtually replaced the charismatic leadership of the Spirit. The clergy gradually assumed all the ministerial responsibilities of the Church, and a distinct priesthood parallel to that of the Old Testament emerged.[2] The Roman emperor, Constantine, made Christianity the official religion of the state and organized the Church on the basis of the Roman Empire. Subsequently, the Church moved rapidly toward a highly developed patriarchal system of government identical in structure to the political empire.[3] In this scenario, the outward forms of office, ritual, and sacraments displaced personal, Spirit-empowered relationship with God. And with this quenching of the Holy Spirit came the simultaneous stifling and subordination of women.[4]

The rise of the separate ruling class is borne out in the writings of Ignatius (A.D. 67-c.a.107), who, in the early second century, seems to have been preoccupied with defending the authority and prestige of the bishop.[5] In his bid to centralize control over the

---

[1] The word *laity* comes from the Greek word *laos*, and everywhere in the New Testament, it speaks of the whole people of God. The word *clergy* comes from the Greek word *kleros* which is usually translated *called*. Like *laos*, it always refers to all the people of God. See M. Michelet, *The Life of Martin Luther*, trans. G.H. Smith (New York: A.A. Kelley, 1858), 258, who quotes Martin Luther as saying, "The difference between these two classes is fictitious since by baptism we all become priests."

[2] See Cyprian, *Letters*, vol. 51 of *The Fathers of the Church*, who in his attempt to thwart widespread schisms in the Church makes repeated parallels of the authority of the bishop with that of the Old Testament priesthood. See also Peter Hinchliff, *Cyprian of Carthage* (Great Britain: Geoffrey Chapman, 1974), 103, who points out Cyprian's application of Old Testament texts to the bishop's office and his transference of passages referring to the Old Testament Levitical priesthood to the Christian ministry.

[3] See Rudolph Sohm, *Outlines of Church History* (London: MacMillan, 1913), 44 who says that "the constitution of the Church was in the main modeled on the organization of the empire." See also Lars Qualben, *A History of the Christian Church* (New York: Thomas Nelson, 1933), 99, who says that Constantine "organized the Church on the basis of the political organization of the Empire." He diagrams the corresponding offices of the Church and the Empire.

[4] Jan Peters, "Women in the Functions of the Church," *Apostolic Succession: Rethinking a Barrier to Unity*, ed. Hans Kung, *Ecumenical Theology: Conciliation, A Theology in the Age of Renewal* (New York: paulist press, 1968)), 131-32.

[5] See Gerald F. Hawthorne, *Phillipians*, vol. 43 of *Word Biblical Commentary*, ed. David A. Hubbard and Glen W. Barker (Waco: Word Books, 1983), 8, which points out that the word *bishop* literally means *to watch over*. Not unique to the New Testament, it was used in the Greco-Roman world in reference to tutors, army scouts, watchmen and the superintendents of building projects. Acts 20:17,28 and Titus 1:5-7 show that the word was used interchangeably for *pastor* and *elder*, an

numerous house churches of a city or region, he designed a church structure like the civil government. In this structure, he claimed new authority for the bishop, seeing that person in the sense of the *civitas* or mayor with the sole authority to rule over all the congregations in a locality. In *To the Trallians,* Ignatius declares, "Only that Eucharist which is under the bishop is to be considered valid." He asserted that, apart from the bishop, it is not lawful "either to baptize or to hold a love-feast."[6] In his letter *To the Smyrneans,* he admonishes his readers to "do nothing without the bishop."[7] Professor James Ash, Jr., describes Ignatius' attempt to garner such authority for himself and for an office of bishop as "a novelty."[8] Indeed, when compared with the writings of the New Testament, it is obvious that Ignatius has taken a new path in church government. Regarding this, Burnett Streeter, in his classic work, *The Primitive Church,* says that Ignatius' overly enthusiastic defense seems to imply "the existence of strong opposition" to the concept of ruling bishops. He points out, in fact, "The principle which Ignatius is so concerned to uphold is one by no means universally recognized.[9]

History demonstrates that the institutional trend advocated by Ignatius prevailed. In time, the idea of *bishop* became an office with regal status. Indeed, the concept of bishop had deteriorated from the biblical idea of service to and responsibility for people to one of privilege and power over people! However, as late as the fifth century, Augustine pointed out that the etymology of the word (*episcopas*) refers to responsibility and not authority. "Therefore," says Augustine, "he who loves to govern is no bishop."[10]

---

indication that it was a word designating function involving responsibility and service on behalf of people rather than an office with inherent authority and power to rule over people.

[6] Ignatius, "To the Trallians," *The Apostolic Fathers,* ed. Michael W. Holmes (Grand Rapids, Baker, 1992), 161.

[7] Ignatius, "To the Smyrneans," *The Apostolic Fathers,* ed. Michael W. Holmes (Grand Rapids, Baker, 1992), 189.

[8] James L. Ash, Jr., "The Decline of Ecstatic Prophecy in the Early Church," *Theological Studies* 37 (1976): 249.

[9] Burnett Streeter, *The Primitive Church* (New York: MacMillan, 1929), 169-70.

[10] P. Schaff and H. Wace, eds., vol. 2 of 15 vols., *Nicene and Post-Nicene Fathers of the Christian Church,* 1st series (Grand Rapids: Eerdmans, 1979), 413.

For those who embraced this emphasis on organizational structure, spiritual authority was no longer seen as residing in the person with the spiritual gift. That authority now resided, not in the calling or gifting of the Spirit, but in the one occupying the ecclesiastical office. Bultman points out that the gift of the Spirit to teach and lead "which was originally given by the Spirit to the person, is now understood as an office—*charisma* conveyed by ordination."[11] With ministry no longer rooted in God's call and corresponding gifts of the Holy Spirit, women were pushed aside to their socially acceptable, subservient place.

Some have charged that the reason for the shift away from the manifest activity of the Holy Spirit by this time was that the Written Word of the New Testament Canon had replaced any need for the charismatic gifts. It has, however, been correctly noted, "The bishops, not the Canon, expelled prophecy."[12] Virtually all church historians agree that the institutionalization of the early Church was accompanied by the demise of the charismatic gifts.[13] This loss of spiritual power was accompanied by the marginalization and subjugation of its female members.

The First Renewal—Good News for Women!

Within this context, the Church's first renewal occurred in the latter half of the second century.[14] It was both a reaction to institutionalism as well as a response to the Holy Spirit. These revivalists called themselves *The New Prophecy* but were derisively referred to by their opponents as *The Montanists* after the name of the founder, Montanus. This move of God began in Phrygia in Asia Minor primarily through Montanus and two women named Maxmilla and Prisca. It spread quickly and found favor especially

---

[11] Bultman, 2:52.

[12] Ash, 228.

[13] Ash, 227.

[14] Eddie L. Hyatt, "Montanism: Pagan Frenzy or Pentecostal Fervor?" A paper presented to the 26th Annual Meeting of the Society for Pentecostal Studies, March 13-15, 1997, Patten College, Oakland, CA.

in North Africa where the eminent church father, Tertullian (A.D. 160-240), joined the movement around A.D. 200.

The Montanists, prompted by their experiential relationship with God through His indwelling Holy Spirit, seemed to grasp the concept of the priesthood and prophethood of all believers in the New Testament sense. This challenged not only the Old Testament pattern of priesthood practiced by the institutional Church but also the authority claimed by the Church hierarchs. In fact, the renewal so threatened the hierarchs that the Council of Constantinople (A.D. 381) denounced these revival people as pagans.

But Montanism was good news for women! With the return to New Testament Spirit-life came a tendency toward egalitarian values: women were elevated by the Spirit and emerged as leaders. Also, with the sense of urgency that sprang from the belief in Christ's immanent return, both men and women were encouraged to be filled with the Holy Spirit and to spread the Good News.

Among the Montanists, the empowering of the Holy Spirit— the anointing, the obvious presence of the *charismata*—was the criterion for service. (In the institution, "ministry" was carried out by those who had ecclesiastical approval and appointment.) An example of this comes through Tertullian's writings. He tells of a woman in his congregation in Carthage who experienced the gifts of the Spirit including words of knowledge and wisdom, and gifts of healing. She apparently was highly sensitive to the Spirit of God, and this was a great help and encouragement to others.[15]

Tertullian's acceptance of a movement that was eventually declared to be heretical has often mystified those who recognize his greatness as a defender of orthodox Christianity. But Tertullian, was, no doubt, concerned about the loss of the Church's spiritual power to institutionalism. Roman Catholic historian, Paul Johnson, says that Tertullian could not endorse an institution that

---

[15] Tertullian, *A Treatise on the Soul*, vol. 3 of *The Ante-Nicene Christian Library*, ed. A. Roberts and J. Donaldson (Edinburgh: T&T Clark, 1874), 189.

denied the biblically legitimate activity of the Spirit and that insisted that "all communications should be through the regular ecclesiastical channels."[16]

Johnson also thinks that Tertullian's association with the Montanists resulted in a modification of his views of women.[17] In early writings, he had spoken vehemently against women in leadership. But in later years, he spoke respectfully of Prisca, Maxmilla, and the gifted "sister" in his congregation.

Irenaeus (A.D. 125-165), bishop of Lyons, also defended the Montanists. According to the early historian, Eusebius, Irenaeus had been sent to Rome by the Gaelic Christians to intercede on behalf of the Montanists.[18] Irenaeus lamented the opponents of Montanism who "set aside at once both the Gospel and the prophetic Spirit." He charges that these men probably would reject the apostle Paul, as well, because in his writings to the Corinthians, he "expressly speaks of prophetical gifts, and recognizes men and women prophesying."[19]

Denouncing and Defending Women of Faith

Montanist opponents railed against the Montanist women, especially against Maxmilla and Prisca. They accused them of being filled with a "sham spirit" and of chattering "crazily and wildly." They also falsely accused them of leaving their husbands and of prophesying for financial gain.[20]

These and other accusations were confronted in 1713 by John Lacy in his work, *The General Delusion of Christians Touching the*

---

[16] Paul Johnson, *A History of Christianity* (New York: Simon & Schuster, 1976), 50.

[17] Johnson, 51.

[18] Eusebius, *The History of the Church*, trans. G.A. Williamson (New York: Dorset Press, 1965), 206. See also Philip Schaff, vol. 2 *of History of the Christian Church* (Grand Rapids: Eerdmans, 1910), 420.

[19] Irenaeus, *Against Heresies*, vol. 1 of *The Ante-Nicene Christian Library*, ed. A. Roberts and J. Donaldson (1874; reprint, Grand Rapids: Eerdmans, 1972), 429. Irenaeus is referring specifically to the gospel of John. Some denied its validity and the validity of the prophetic gift; probably in reaction to the Montanists who derived much of their teaching concerning the Paraclete from this gospel. This is the view of Walter Bauer, *Orthodoxy and Heresy in Earliest Christianity*, eds. Robert A. Kraft and Gerhard Krodel (Philadelphia: Fortress Press, 1971), 141; W. H. C. Frend, *The Rise of Christianity* (Philadelphia: Fortress Press, 1984), 254; and Robert M. Grant, *Augustus to Constantine* (New York: Harper & Row, 1970), 136.

[20] Eusebius, 219, 223, 225.

Ways of God's Revealing Himself To and By the Prophets. In it, he presents a convincing argument in favor of the Montanists and dispels the accusations against Maxmilla and Prisca. According to Lacy, their lives were outwardly holy and blameless and they were esteemed by some of the most respected leaders in the Church at that time. He claims that both were from wealthy families and would have had no financial motivation for their prophetic activities.

In 1751, John Wesley read Lacy's book and wrote a reflection in his *Journal*. He said,

> I was fully convinced of what I had once suspected: (1) That the Montanists, in the second and third centuries, were real Scriptural Christians; and (2) That the grand reason why the miraculous gifts were so soon withdrawn, was not only that faith and holiness were well nigh lost, but that dry, formal, orthodox men began even then to ridicule whatever gifts they had not themselves, and to decry them all as either madness or imposture.[21]

Philip Schaff, in his *History of the Christian Church*, also shows support for the Montanist movement. He says Montanism was

> a democratic reaction against the clerical aristocracy, which from the time of Ignatius had more and more monopolized all ministerial privileges and functions. The Montanists found the true qualification and appointment for the office of teacher in direct endowment of the Spirit of God, in distinction from outward ordination and episcopal succession. They everywhere proposed the supernatural element and the free motion of the Spirit against the mechanism of a fixed ecclesiastical order.[22]

He points out that the Church's rejection of the Montanists be-

---

[21] Nehemiah Curnack, ed., vol. 3 of *The Journal of the Rev. John Wesley A.M.*, 8 vols. (London: Epworth, 1938), 490.

[22] Schaff, *History of the Christian Church*, 424.

gan a trend in which a line of demarcation was drawn "between the age of the apostles, in which there had been direct supernatural revelations, and the later age, in which such revelations had disappeared."[23]

More recently, David Aune, author of an exhaustive study of ancient prophecy, *Prophecy in the Early Church and the Ancient Mediterranean World,* rejects the charge that Montanism was an intrusion of paganism into the Church. Such a claim, he says "is completely false." He maintains that all major features of early Montanism "are derived from early Christianity."[24]

Conclusion

The rise of institutional Christianity and its rejection of the manifest activity of the Holy Spirit among the Montanists had serious ramifications for women.

1.   The institutional Church's rejection of Spirit renewal through Montanism accelerated its own progress toward institutionalism. This trend reinforced the emerging class distinction between clergy and laity in the Church's governing structure. With organizational structure and religious ritual replacing the dynamic presence of the Spirit, women found themselves pushed down and under. It was clear that the developing clerical class would be for men only.

2.   The rejection of the Montanists, who represented the renewing work of the Spirit, brought a corresponding suppression of women. Because of the prominence of Montanist women, the rejection of the renewal accelerated the marginalization of women from leadership functions in the church. Johnson says, "Montanism, or rather the efforts to

---

[23] Philip Schaff and Henry Wace ed., *Nicene and Post-Nicene Fathers of the Christian Church,* 2nd Series (Grand Rapids: Eerdmans, 1978), 231.

[24] David Aune, *Prophecy in Early Christianity and the Ancient Mediterranean World* (Grand Rapids: Eerdmans, 1983), 313.

combat it, played a conclusive role in persuading the orthodox to ban the ministry to women."[25]

3. These developments would necessitate the formulation
of theologies to justify both the absence of Spiritual power
in the Church and the secondary status of women.

Throughout the centuries, the Holy Spirit has continued to re-
new true believers, and with these renewals have come efforts by
the Spirit to democratize the Church and to reinstate the egalitarian status of women. However, the rejection of Montanism, the
first renewal movement, was pivotal in the life of the Church. In
fact, it has been said that the Church has never fully recovered
from this early rejection of the Holy Spirit.[26] It could also be said
that women have never fully recovered.

---

[25] Johnson, A History of Christianity, 49.
[26] Killian McDonnell, The Baptism in the Holy Spirit (Notre Dame: Charismatic Renewal Services, 1972), 44.

5

Faulty Foundations

When confronted with new ideas, we tend either to reject them or to assimilate only those parts that we find comfortable. We tend to be captives of our way of thinking and doing. No where is this more true than in our cultural and religious perspectives about women. What we are not so aware of, it seems, is how cultural and religious factors shaped the Church's acceptable way of thinking about women. The Church Fathers, the shapers of how the Church interpreted the Scriptures and the authorities on what the Church should believe, were influenced by their own human flaws and cultural, philosophical presuppositions about women.

The Traditions of Men

The development of the Church's "orthodox theology"—or acceptable way of thinking about things—disregarded Jesus' teaching about women. Perhaps this is because this sanctioned way of thinking evolved in the minds of men who were converts from paganism. In most cases, it seems that these men were not filled with the Holy Spirit as we know it (Acts 2:4). Their theologies, therefore, were not adequately energized by the Spirit, a necessary element in understanding things of the Spirit. In addition, their minds had been molded by the pagan, Greco-Roman philosophies in which they had previously excelled. Sociologist Alvin John Schmidt, in his book *Veiled and Silent, How Culture Shaped Sexist Theology*, charges that they "were more influenced by pagan culture than by Christ, whose name they ritualistically confessed."[1]

Greco-Roman philosophies were no friend of women. Regarding this, John Temple Bristow says something that all Spirit-oriented believers should note,

> In the capital of ancient Greece [Athens], in the brilliant minds of her philosophers and teachers, is the source of the Western world's formalized conviction that women are inferior to men. Here was codified an attitude about females, a prejudice regarding women that Dr. Arthur Verral, a noted classical scholar, identified as "the radical disease, of which, more than anything else, ancient civilization perished."[2]

Two Greek philosophers in particular, Socrates (*ca.* 470-399 B.C.) and Aristotle (384-322 B.C.), influenced the development of thought among early church leaders. Socrates' influence extended through his student Plato (427-347 B.C.), and then through Plato's most distinguished pupil Aristotle. Socrates often referred to women as "the weaker sex" and declared that "being born a woman is divine punishment since a woman is half-way between a man and an animal."[3] He formalized Aristotle's idea that women are inferior to men and are to be treated as such. His classic statement reads:

> Of household management we have seen that there are three parts—one is the rule of the master over slaves, which has been discussed already, another of a father, and the third of a husband. A husband and father, we saw, rules over wife and children, both free, but the rule differs, the rule over his children being a royal, over his wife a constitutional rule. For although there may be exceptions to the order of nature, the male is by nature fitter for command than the female,

---

[1] Alvin John Schmidt, *Veiled and Silenced: How Culture Shaped Sexist Theology* (Macon: Mercer University Press, 1989), 163.

[2] John Temple Bristow, *What Paul Really Said About Women* (New York: Harper and Row, 1988), 3-5.

[3] *Ibid.*, 3.

just as the elder and full-grown is superior to the younger and more immature.[4]

Aristotle taught that a man should be more than twice his wife's age so that he could dominate her.[5]

The attitudes of the church fathers, molded by these pagan ideas toward women, influenced how they interpreted Scriptures about women and about male/female relationships. Statements such as the following illustrate the intensity of their negative perception of womanhood.

"Every Woman Should Blush!"

Clement of Alexandria (*ca.* A.D. 150-220) believed that every woman should blush because she is a woman and that a man's beard was a sign of his superiority over woman.[6] He also said, "Nothing for men is shameful, for man is endowed with reason; but for woman it brings shame even to reflect on what her nature is."[7] He firmly taught that women should be fully veiled so as not to cause men to fall into sin. He argued that it was "the wish of the Word," but he supported his position with pagan evidence.[8]

"Woman Is the Devil's Gateway."

Tertullian (A.D. 160-240), Father of Latin Theology has been called the first real misogynist in the church.[9] He called women "the Devil's gateway."[10] Among many other derogatory state-

---

[4] Aristotle, *Politics* 1.12.1259a-b, trans. Richard McKeon, *The Basic Works of Aristotle* (New York: Random House, 1941), 1143.

[5] Barbara G. Walker, "Marriage," *The Woman's Encyclopedia of Myths and Secrets* (San Francisco: Harper and Row, 1983), 588.

[6] Schmidt, 46, 87; Clement of Alexandria, *The Instructor* 3.3.

[7] Quoted by Elaine Storkey, *Contributions to Christian Feminism*, (London: Christian Impact, 1995), 48.

[8] Clement, *The Instructor*, quoted by Schmidt, 134. Schmidt says, The pagan evidence used by Clement to support his claim "refers to the wife of Aeneas, who, 'did not, even in her terror at the capture of Troy, uncover herself; but through fleeing from the conflagration, remained veiled' (*The Instuctor*, 3.11)."

[9] Schmidt, 134.

[10] Tertullian, "On the Dress of Women," vol. 4 of the *Ante-Nicene Fathers*, 10 vols., eds. James Donaldson and Alexander Roberts (1885; reprint, Peabody, MA: Hendrickson, 1995), 14.

ments about women, he says, "On account of your desert [i.e., punishment], that is, death—even the Son of God had to die." Furthermore, it was Tertullian who first used 1 Corinthians 14 to silence women saying they could neither baptize, sing, pray, nor teach.[11] It is clear that Tertullian modified his views after he became a Montanist! But, unfortunately, the institutional church retained his pre-revival stance.

"God Does Not Stoop to Look Upon What Is Feminine."

Origen (A.D. 185-254), the church's first systematic theologian, castrated himself. He further expressed his disdain for women, saying, "Men should not listen to a woman . . . even if she says admirable things, or even saintly things, that is of little consequence, since they come from the mouth of a woman."[12] He also said, "What is seen with the eyes of the creator is masculine, and not feminine, for God does not stoop to look upon what is feminine and of the flesh" (*Selecta in Exodus* 17.7).[13]

"Woman Is the Origin of All Evil and Deception."

Ambrose of Milan (A.D. 340-397) believed that Eve was seductive and that this was the origin of all evil and lies (*De Paradiso* 10.46, 47).[14] He said, "Even though man was created outside Paradise (i.e., in an inferior place), he is found to be superior, while woman, though created in a better place (i.e., inside Paradise) is found inferior.[15] He also said, "She who does not have faith is a woman and should be called by the name of her sex, but she who believes progresses to perfect manhood. . . . She then

---

[11] Tertullian, "On Baptism" vol. 3 of *Ante:Nicene Fathers*, 667.

[12] Origen, "Fragments on 1 Corinthians, 74," quoted by Roger Gryson, *Ministry of Women in the Early Church*, trans. J. LaPorte and Mary Louise Hall (Collegeville, MN: Liturgical Press, 1976), 28-29. See also George H. Tavard, *Woman in Christian Tradition* (Notre Dame: Notre Dame Univ. Press, 1973), 68.

[13] Quoted by Schmidt, 43.

[14] Schmidt, 65.

[15] Ambrose, "On Paradise," *Corpus Scriptorum Ecclesiasticorum Latinorum*, quoted by Clark, 30.

does away with the name of her sex" (*Evangelius Secundum Lucum* 10.161).[16] He also wrote, "A man may marry again if he has divorced his sinful wife, because he is not restricted in his rights as is the woman, because he is her head."[17]

"The Woman Herself Alone Is Not the Image of God."

Augustine (A.D. 354-430) has been hailed as the greatest of the Fathers of the Western Church because, more than any other, his thoughts laid the foundation of orthodox Western theology. A womanizer prior to becoming a Christian, Augustine, in fact, "bequeathed his sexual fears and hangups to Christian theology,"[18] and his idea that only the man is made in the full image of God has been called the "ultimate core of misogynism."[19] He wrote, "The woman herself alone is not the image of God whereas the man alone is the image of God as fully and completely as when the woman is joined with him."[20] He said, "We should look upon the female state as being as it were a deformity." He also promoted the idea that woman is evil. Placing the blame for the Fall squarely on her shoulders, he said, "She [Eve] was the first to be deceived and was responsible for deceiving the man." He also said, "She [Eve] . . . made her husband a partaker of the evil of which she was conscious" (*Paradise*, Chapters 4 and 6)[21] He even accused woman as being the cause of the Flood![22]

---

[16] Quoted by Schmidt, 201.

[17] Ambrose, "Commentary on the Epistle to 1 Corinthians," cica A.D. 380. Quoted by Schmidt, *Veiled and Silenced: How Culture Shaped Sexist Theology* (Macon, GA: Mercer Univ. Press, 1989), 123.

[18] Schmidt, 43.

[19] Rosemary Ruether, *Liberation Theology: Human Hope Confronts Christian History and American Power* (New York: Paulist, 1972), 100.

[20] Augustine, "On the Trinity, 7, 7, 10," in *Later Works*, ed. John Burnaby (Philadelphia: Westminster, 1955); Schmidt, 83.

[21] Quoted by Schmidt, 43.

[22] Augustine, *The City of God* 15:22, quoted by Schmidt, 43-44.

"Women Are Inferior."

Cyril of Alexandria (d. 444), patriarch of Alexandria, believed that women are inferior and are not to teach men. Hypatia, a female mathematician and philosopher, contradicted his beliefs about women, particularly by teaching men mathematics and philosophy. Consequently in A.D. 415, his monks murdered her in the church and then burned her flesh as they tore it from her bones.[23]

"Woman Taught Once and Ruined All."

Chrysostom (A.D. 347-407), patriarch of Constantinople, is considered the greatest expositor and preacher of the Greek Church.[24] He said, "The woman [Eve] taught once, and ruined all" (Homilies on Timothy 9).[25] Like Augustine, Chrysostom believed that women do not possess the image of God. He writes, woman did not possess the "image of God" (Gen. 1:26) as man did, and he linked her subordinate status to this deficiency. Her secondary, inferior status, in other words, was not simply a result of the Fall, as some had surmised, but was an inferior one even at the moment of her creation. He argues his case in *Discourse 2 on Genesis* against those who claim that both the man and the woman have the "image of God." He adds, "The 'image' has rather to do with authority, and this only the man has; the woman has it no longer. For he is subjected to no one, while she is subjected to him."[26] He says that for a man to go to a woman for advice is like going to "irrational animals of the lower kind."[27] Ruth Tucker and Walter Liefeld note,

---

[23] Schmidt, 74, 123; Philip Schaff, *History of the Christian Church*, vol. 3 of 8 vols., (Grand Rapids: Eerdmans, 1910, reprinted 1994) 3:67.

[24] Schaff, 937.

[25] Quoted by Schmidt, 43.

[26] Chrysostom quoted by Clark, 35.

[27] Chrysostom, "Homily 7 on Matthew, 6," quoted by Tucker and Liefeld, 125.

Although Chrysostom attempts to argue for an "equality of honor" between Adam and Eve, he makes a point of Paul's comment on man being the image of God, while woman is (only) the glory of man. The man is "skilled at the greater things" but he is "downright inept and useless in the performance of the less important ones, so that the woman's service is necessary. . . God maintained the order of each sex by dividing the business of human life into two parts and assigned the more necessary and beneficial aspects to the man and the less important, inferior matters to the woman."[28]

"Woman Are Miserable, Sin-Ridden Wenches."

Jerome (A.D. 340 - 420), recognized as the ablest scholar of the ancient Western Church, said, "Woman is a temple built over a sewer."[29] He popularized the belief in Mary's perpetual virginity and also gave the Church the Latin Vulgate.[30] He once acknowledged that two women co-authored the Vulgate, but later theologians in the church erased the names of these women and substituted the words 'venerable brothers.'"[31] Jerome strongly opposed women speaking, singing, praying, and teaching in public (*Against the Pelagians* 1.25). He said, "It is contrary to the order of nature and of the law that women should speak in a gathering of men" (*In Priman Epistolam Ad Corinthios* 14).[32] He also said that "women, especially those who assumed leadership roles in religion were 'miserable, sin-ridden wenches'" (*Epistola* 132).[33] It was his opinion that if a woman wanted to serve Christ, "she will cease to

---

[28] Chrysostom, "Homily XX and Discourse 4 on Genesis 12," quoted by Ruth Tucker and Walter Liefeld, *Daughters of the Church: Women and Ministry from New Testament Times to the Present* (Grand Rapids: Zondervan, 1987), 125.

[29] Quoted by Storkey, 48. She notes that because of this statement and attitude, Jerome "might today be recommended for therapy."

[30] W. Walker, *A History of the Christian Church* (New York: Charles Scribner, 1920), 173; Schmidt, 152.

[31] Schmidt, 153.

[32] Schmidt, 157.

[33] Quoted by Schmidt, 65.

be a woman and will be called a man" (*Commentarius in Epistolam and Ephesios* 3).[34]

Conclusion

The church fathers who laid the foundations of orthodox theology did so from the perspectives of Platonic and Aristotelian philosophy. They interpreted the writings of Paul through the eyes of pagans who lived five hundred years before Jesus and Paul! This problem intensified when Thomas Aquinas (1125-1274) systematized Roman theology using Aristotelian philosophy. Thus, the male superiority/female inferiority, male rulership/and female subjugation, male dominance/female silence formula was established in the root system of orthodox theology. These sexist presuppositions now permeate theology and provide a misogynous starting point for biblical interpretation regarding women even today among Spirit-oriented believers.

[34] Schmidt, 201.

6

The Dark Ages
and Dark Days for Women

Medieval Misogyny

Life was especially difficult for women in the Middle Ages. They were valued only as "wombs," "workers," and objects of male gratification in a highly patriarchal society. The attitude of the institutional Church contributed to this hardship. As the institution exercised increasing authority, it imposed celibacy on its clergy and their wives were suddenly cast out and demonized. The witchcraft craze led to innocent old peasant women and midwives being burned at the stake for alleged witchcraft.

Bold Women of Spirit

Despite prevalent discrimination and oppression, courageous women of faith did their best to live for God. The Beguines, for example, were religious women in a movement that originated in the Netherlands in the twelfth century.[1] They did not live cloistered lives but moved about Europe feeding the hungry and caring for the sick. Not having the sanction of the papacy, however, they were condemned by the Church. They were charged with a number of deviations from orthodoxy including refusal to make confessions to a priest and to respect "the host." They were also "guilty" of preaching and theologizing, but their greatest "crime"

---

[1] Caroline W. Bynum, *Jesus as Mother: Studies in the Spirituality of the High Middle Ages* (Berkeley: Univ. of California Press, 1982), 14-15; Schaff, *History of the Christian Church*, 5:490.

was their translating of the Bible![2] As victims of the Inquisition, they were among those who were burned at the stake.[3]

The Angelic Doctor?

Thomas Aquinas (d. 1247), the "Angelic Doctor," was a Dominican monk appointed in 1286 by Pope Leo XIII to the post of authoritative teacher of Roman theology. Aquinas, more than anyone else, systematized Christian beliefs and harmonized them with Greek philosophy. In this process, Aquinas drew heavily from Augustine and Aristotle, and so "the Greek deprecation of women became solidly infused within Christian theology."[4]

Aquinas believed that a woman does not possess the image of God in the same way that a man does, and therefore, is spiritually inferior.[5] He also believed that woman is both biologically and intellectually inferior to man. He said, "Woman is defective and misbegotten." He also said, "Woman is naturally subject to man, because in man the discernment of wisdom predominates."[6] He said that women are not sufficiently wise, and therefore, must not be allowed to teach publicly (*Summa Theologica* 2a-2ae, 177,2).[7] In his opinion, a wife is lower than a slave because a slave may be freed, but a "Woman is in subjection according to the law of nature, but a slave is not."[8] His hatred of women so dominated the scene that Schaff writes,

> If the horrible beliefs of the Middle Ages on the subject of witchcraft are to be set aside, then the bulls of Leo XIII and

---

[2] Robert E. Lerner, *The Heresy of the Free Spirit in the Later Middle Ages* (Berkeley: Univ. of California Press, 1972), 46.

[3] Schaff, 5:532.

[4] Torjesen, 4; Bristow, 29; Schaff, 6:518.

[5] See Schmidt, 84.

[6] Patricia Gundry, *Woman Be Free!* (Grand Rapids, Zondervan, 1977), 11.

[7] Quoted by Schmidt, 74.

[8] Quoted by Walker, 593.

Pius X pronouncing Thomas [Aquinas] the authoritative guide of Catholic theology must be modified.[9]

Aquinas was not alone in his belittling of women. Odo of Cluny, in the twelfth century, wrote, "To embrace a woman is to embrace a sack of manure."[10] Bonaventura was willing to concede that woman is "man's equal in nature, grace, and glory," but he agreed with Aristotle in saying,

> Woman is an embarrassment to man, a beast in his quarters, a continual worry, a never-ending trouble, a daily annoyance, the destruction of the household, a hindrance to solitude, the undoing of a virtuous man, an oppressive burden, an insatiable bee, man's property and possession.[11]

"Scold Her Sharply. Bully and Terrify Her."

The Medieval Church sanctioned the beating of wives, calling it "chastisement" and basing it on the "headship" supposedly espoused by 1 Corinthians 11:3.[12] Because it was believed that woman had sinned more than man, it was taught that men were doing God's will when they made women suffer. "Men were exhorted from the pulpit to beat their wives and wives to kiss the rod that beat them." In the 13th century, the Laws and Customs of Beauvais advised men to beat their wives "only within reason" since an excessive number of women were dying of marital chastisement.[13] The Decretum of 1140 said, "It is right that he whom woman led into wrongdoing should have her under his direction

---

[9] Schaff, 6:518.

[10] Quoted by E. Storkey, "Nuns, Witches and Patriarchy," *Contributions to Christian Feminism* (London: Christian Impact, 1995) 32.

[11] Emma T. Healy, *Woman According to Saint Bonaventure* (New York: Georgian, 1956), i-ii, 46.

[12] Barbara G. Walker, "Marriage," *The Woman's Encyclopedia of Myths and Secrets* (San Francisco: Harper and Row, 1983), 591. The primary sources for the following information and quotations are found in the text and endnotes on pp. 591-592, 597.

[13] Will Durant, *The Age of Faith* (New York: Simon and Schuster, 1950), 505.

so that he may not fail a second time through female levity." Friar Cherubino's 15th century *Rule of Marriage* said,

> Scold her sharply, bully and terrify her. And if this still doesn't work . . . take up a stick and beat her soundly, for it is better to punish the body and correct the soul than to damage the soul and spare the body. . . . Then readily beat her, not in rage but out of charity and concern for her soul, so that the beating will redound to your merit.[14]

In the thirteenth century, "'the Laws and Customes of Beauvias' bade a man beat his wife 'only in reason.'"[15] And in Russia, a pope recommended that a husband should beat his wife, not with wood or iron that might cripple or kill her, but with a whip. He said, "Keep to a whip and choose carefully where to strike: a whip is painful and effective."[16]

The Witchcraft Frenzy ... a Sexist Atrocity

The Roman Church had been struggling from the fourth to the twelfth centuries to impose celibacy on the clergy.[17] In its bid, it increasingly demonized female sexuality by attributing the power of sexuality to demons. "When sexuality was defined as demonic, a new concept of woman was invented—the medieval witch."[18] The resulting persecution, "the witchcraft frenzy of the late Middle Ages, was one of the most sexist atrocities to have occurred in all of history."[19]

A series of papal reforms intensified the persecution of women. By the eleventh century, Pope Gregory VII condemned the marriage of priests, even condemning as fornicators those priests who

---

[14] Durant, 592.
[15] Durant, 505.
[16] Walker, 592.
[17] Torjesen, "Clerical Celibacy and the Demonization of Female Sexuality," *When Women Were Priests*, 224-233.
[18] Torjesen, 224.
[19] Tucker and Liefeld, 166.

were already married. In 1089, Pope Urban II allowed for the wives of priests to be made slaves. Some suffered imprisonment and public whippings. In 1139, Pope Innocent III annulled the marriages of priests, condemning their wives as concubines, whores, and adulteresses. Papal couriers traveled from town to town proclaiming the evils of female sexuality. One church leader declared that "the wickedness of women is greater than all other wickedness, . . . that the poison of asps and dragons is more curable than the familiarity of women." He vowed "to avoid them like poisonous animals."[20] In 1322, a synod forbade them church burial. As Torjesen says, "It was a short step from the idea that female sexuality was dangerous and an instrument of the devil to the idea that female sexuality itself could be a demonic power."[21]

The absolute hatred of women, fear of female sexuality, and disdain for marriage can hardly be imagined in our minds. It is most clearly articulated, however, in a volume called *The Witches' Hammer* (1486).[22] Written by Jakob Sprenger and Heinrich Institoris (Krämer), two German theologians, it is a landmark document about witches, womanhood, and the unspeakable torture that was ordered to be used against them. In it, female sexuality is portrayed as demonic and women, in general, as evil, inferior, and deceitful. It alleges that the word describing woman, *femina*, came from *fe minus* or *fides minus* meaning "less in faith."[23] As a result of this document and the persecution that it inflamed, it has been estimated that more than a million women were tried for the heresy of witchcraft and were burned at the stake.[24]

---

[20] A. Erens, "Les Soeurs in l'ordre Prémontre, analect Praemontratensia," 1929, v. 6-26, trans. R. Southern, *Western Society and the Church in the Middle Ages* (New York: Penguin, 1970), 314.

[21] Torjesen, 228.

[22] Jakob Sprenger and Heinrich Institoris, *Malleus Maleficarum (The Witches' Hammer)*, trans. Montague Summers (New York: Benjamin Blom, reprint 1970); Torjesen, 229.

[23] Schaff, 6:524.

[24] Torjesen, 229.

Were They Witches or Charismatic Christians?

Another aspect of the persecution of women during this time may have to do with their operating in the legitimate gifts of the Holy Spirit, including speaking in tongues. In the *Roman Ritual* (1000 A.D.), the Roman Church had designated speaking in tongues as the chief evidence of demonic possession among the common folk. In fact, any supernatural phenomena among the common people was looked upon as sorcery and witchcraft. Of course, during the centuries following this decree, as true believers sought the Lord, they were no doubt baptized in the Holy Spirit and developed an intimate relationship with the Spirit, spoke in tongues, experienced an anointing above that of the professional clergy, and experienced the manifest gifts of the Spirit. Then, too, with all of this intimacy with the Lord, came a Holy boldness that released them from unwarranted fear and submissiveness to the tyrannical, authoritarian lordship of the institutional Church. In fact, Rome had to make a concerted effort to control the people, a control that reached its apex in the Inquisition.

As a Spirit-oriented woman, my question is this: Were those thousands of women who were burned at the stake as witches, really *witches*? Perhaps some were, but I suspect that perhaps thousands of those abused and executed women were Spirit-filled women who spoke in tongues and exercised other gifts of the Holy Spirit. I say this in light of the ruling of the Roman Church in A.D. 1000, in light of the spiritual hunger of the common people, in light of the spiritual nature of true Christianity, and in light of the push for celibacy and the demonization of female sexuality by the Church. Definitely, the Albigensian, Waldensian, and Catharis— all charismatic groups—were targets of intense persecution for alleged witchcraft.

In 1484, just four years after Pope Sixtus IV approved the Spanish Inquisition, the papacy turned northward to use the same inquisitional machinery against other unassimiable elements. . . . The Dominicans and the Franciscans carried the inquisition into the Alpine regions and the Pyrenees, where they had little difficulty identifying aspects of witchcraft with vestiges of the Albigensian and Waudensen heresies. In Lyonnais and in Flanders witches were known as *Waudenses* and their gatherings as *Valdesia* or *Vauderyr*; and in the Pyrenees, they were described as Gazarri or Cathars, both names being synonyms for Albigensians.[25]

Elaine Storkey of the Institute for Contemporary Christianity also suspects that many of the women accused of witchcraft "could have been expressing what we today call 'charismatic gifts'—healing, prophesying." Storkey's concerns go beyond this probable charismatic connection, however. She says that some of these women "were clearly 'old wives' whose days of childbearing were over." She is convinced that many were "simply being punished for knowing more than the men knew about gynaecology." She writes, "Because women's sexuality was threatening and mysterious, those who were associated with it in an intimate way were regarded also as threatening." She also notes, Childbirth, blood and the uterus were all part of the fascination with the unknown and were the object of many superstitions.[26]

Conclusion

The thinking of the men who shaped medieval theology and practice was, to put it mildly, hostile toward women and toward the charismatic activity of the Holy Spirit. These influential men held a chain-of-being perspective which purported that men were of higher substance and greater value than women. In fact, they

[25] Clyde L. Manschreck, "The Occult Tradition in the Reformation," *Spiritual Frontiers* (Evanston: Spiritual Frontiers Fellowship, Autumn, 1974, and Winter, 1975): 104; H. R. Trevor-Roper, *The European Witch-Craze* (New York: Harper & Row, 1967), 103..

[26] Storkey, 37-38.

viewed women as evil and inferior to men in every way. Thus the pattern of male supremacy and female subjugation in Church and society was firmly secured as a theological premise.[27] Biblical interpretation and theology were warped by a medieval church that merged pagan philosophy, misogyny, and hierarchical worldview. As a result, theology about women was highly unbiblical and unchristian, yet much of it still provides the context in which we interpret the Bible today.

---

[27] Morton Kelsey, *Tongues Speaking: The History and Meaning of Charismatic Experience* (New York: Crossroads, 1981), 186-87.

7

Respect for Women? Not Yet!

Some have charged that the Reformation (1517-1648) only "pretended to return to Christian origins."[1] Certainly, it did little to revive Jesus' regard for womanhood. The chain-of-being perception, which attributed superiority to man and inferiority to women, prevailed. And the conviction that only the male can represent Jesus in institutional church offices remained firmly intact.[2] A sexist bias continued to skew biblical interpretation against women, and Scottish Reformer, John Knox states this position: "Woman in her greatest perfection was made to serve and obey man."[3]

Did "Priesthood of All Believers" Include Women?

The main concern of the Reformers, after breaking free of the control of Rome, was to determine what should constitute legitimate authority. In this process, Martin Luther (1483-1546) appealed to the Bible as the locus of authority and has, in fact, been accused of turning the Bible into a "paper pope." He proposed three vital theological principles in establishing this new locus of authority. They are *sola scriptura (Scripture alone), sola fide (faith alone),* and the priesthood of all believers.

How to interject the biblical principle of the priesthood of all believers into a society and ecclesiastical system that rejected the principle of biblical equality of women was problematic. Did "all believers," in fact, include women—or just men? In 1516, Luther

---

[1] Peters, 133
[2] Peters, 133-34.
[3] John Knox, "The First Blast of the Trumpet Against the Monstrous Regiment of Women" (1558) in Laing, ed., *Works*, 4:365. Quoted by Tucker and Liefeld, 177.

excluded women from leadership in worship and from preaching. This is not surprising, since he had been an Augustinian monk, and would have been indoctrinated with ideas of woman's inferior and evil nature. He believed that "woman was much more liable to superstition and occultism," and he appealed to the apparent rule of female silence (1 Cor. 14:34; 1 Tim. 2:11). Furthermore, he held women responsible for the Fall, and therefore retained the concept of female subjugation.[4] In 1522, no doubt confronted by the obvious inconsistency between his espoused doctrine and his practice, he made concessions. He decided, "If it happens that no man is present a woman can take charge and preach before others as far as she is able."[5] Although women were no longer excluded, men still ruled.

Sola fide declared the biblical truth that salvation is by grace through faith. This relieved believers of the heavy and vain burden of salvation by works. This doctrine posed no problem when confined to men only, but what were the consequences for women? Was there equal redemption available for all? Were women wholly human and could they be wholly saved? If so, what were the implications in practice?

Sola scriptura, as refreshing and noble as it is, also raises problems. Formulated to make the Bible—rather than tradition or the rulings of the institutional Church—authoritative for faith and practice, it seemingly provided a safe locus of authority outside the individual believer. But here is the problem: authority was not derived from Scripture itself, but from interpretation of Scripture. And it must be noted that interpretation continued to be skewed by misogyny, hierarchical worldview, and the perennial influence of Greek philosophy. In other words, the starting point for interpreting the Bible continued to be biased against women.

---

[4] Martin Luther, "Lectures on Genesis," Gen. 2:18, in *Luther's Works*, ed. Jaroslav Pelikan (St. Louis: Concordia, 1958), 1:115.

[5] Peters, 133.

A description of the marriage ritual between Luther and Katherine von Bora, a former nun, illustrates the humiliation and degradation of womanhood even in the Reformed church in the sixteenth century.

> On the evening of 13 June 1525, according to the custom of the day, he appeared with his bride before a number of his friends as witnesses. The Pomeranian (Johann) Begenhagen blessed the couple, who consummated the marriage in front of the witnesses. [Justus] Jonas reported the next day: "Luther has taken Katrina von Bora to wife. I was present yesterday and saw the couple on their marriage bed. As I watched this spectacle I could not hold back my tears."[6]

"Let the Woman Be Satisfied with Her State of Subjection."

John Calvin (1509-1564), too, inherited the prevailing view of women derived from the church fathers and common in the medieval church. It is not surprising, then, that he would say, "Let the woman be satisfied with her state of subjection, and not take it amiss that she is made inferior to the more distinguished sex."[7] He wrote,

> As the woman derives her origin from the man, she is therefore inferior in rank . . . as the woman was created for the sake of the man, she is therefore subject to him . . . God's eternal law . . . has made the female subject to him . . . God's eternal law . . . has made the female subject to the authority of men. On this account all women are born, that they may acknowledge themselves as inferior in consequence of the superiority of the male sex.[8]

---

[6] Richard Friedenthal, *Luther*, 438. Quoted by Tucker and Liefeld, 180.
[7] John Calvin, *Commentary on the Epistles of Paul the Apostle to the Corinthians* (Calvin Translation Society, 1848), 361.
[8] Calvin, 357-58.

It is said that he did not derive his system of theology from Augustine, but from the Bible. Nevertheless, it is admitted that he allowed the writings of Augustine to confirm his theology. There is no reason to suppose, then, that he did not share Augustine's misogynous perspective. In fact, his teaching on sovereignty, predestination, and government simply reinforces authoritative male headship/female subjugation, predetermined roles based on gender, and institutionalism with its hierarchical/patriarchal model. Calvin "forbade woman to baptize, speak or teach in the Church. He ruled that women can have "no public function apart from the diaconate."[9]

According to Calvin, God governs by delegated authority, which, some erroneously say, is observable in the Godhead.[10] This pattern of delegated authority is to be emulated in temporal institutions (i.e., civil government, the church, and the home). The idea of a subordination in the Godhead, of course, is a heresy, but it, unfortunately, seems to be widely accepted without question among many Spirit-oriented believers today.

The idea of delegated authority that is stamped on the minds of most Christians goes in this descending order: God, Jesus, Holy Spirit, man, woman. Added to this is the idea that God is male and the metaphor of God as "Father." In the minds of most people, this means that a man, who is a father, represents God and therefore has authority of the highest order. This means, of course, that a woman can never ascend to this kind of authority since she can never be "father." It also implies that woman is not made in the image of God. This falls short of what the Bible teaches and of Who God really is. The truth is that God is Spirit and, ultimately, is not gender-defined. Jesus' purpose in calling Him *Abba* and *Father* was not to teach the gender of God but to

---

[9] Peters, 134.

[10] For a refutation of the idea of hierarchy and subordination in the Godhead, see Gilbert Bilezikian, "Subordination in the Godhead: A Re-emerging Heresy," audiocassette, 3rd International Conference of Christians for Biblical Equality, Wheaton, July 29-Aug. 1, 1993.

imply His personableness in opposition to the impersonable nature of the pagan gods. It was never Jesus' intention to restrict the
Great Creator to human images and cultural roles, especially to
one human role, and to think that Almighty God can be adequately defined either in terms of male and father or as female
and mother. Along this line, Professor John Yoder, outstanding
Mennonite scholar teaching at Notre Dame University, writes,

> All communication about God must use analogies from
> the human world. Yet every analogy has limits. That
> "Yahweh is King" is the central Hebrew doxology; that
> "Jesus Christ is Lord" is its Christian counterpart. Jesus
> taught his followers to call God "Father." Yet there are
> meanings of "King," "Lord," and "Father" that are inappro-
> priate, because they connote oppression. The perspective of
> the cross, of the victim, of the outsider, of the slave or the
> child or the woman is a necessary corrective to wrong uses of
> analogy, especially to such usages as might support power gra-
> dients instead of undoing them as the Gospel does.[11]

Protestant Rejection of the Activity of the Spirit

Both Luther and Calvin followed Augustine's notion of the cessation of the charismatic gifts.[12] Although Luther seems to have
made some room for miracles and the *charismata* in his personal
life, he also denounced charismatic manifestations, especially
those demonstrated among the Anabaptists and at Roman Catholic shrines.[13] And although Calvin has been called the *Theologian of
the Spirit*, his anti-charismatic stance was fed by Aristotle and

---

[11] John H. Yoder, "Thinking Theologically from a Free-Church Perspective," *Doing Theology in Today's World*, eds. J. D. Woodbridge and T. E. McComiskey (Grand Rapids: Zondervan, 1991), 260.

[12] The so-called *cessation theory* is the idea promoted by Augustine and Chrysostom that the *charismata* and miracles had ceased with the death of the last of the Twelve Apostles. For a refutation of this position, see Vinson Synan, *In the Latter Days* (Ann Arbor: Servant, 1984), 27-29; Eddie L. Hyatt, *2000 Years of Charismatic Christianity* (Tulsa: Hyatt Publishing, 1996), 46-47; 75-88.

[13] Hyatt, 75-80; Martin Luther, *The Babylonian Captivity* (Grand Rapids: Baker, 1982 reprint), 130-131.

Aquinas whose influence "left no room for the direct spiritual experience with the Holy Spirit."[14]

Following the lead of Luther and Calvin, Reformed Protestants have related to the charismatic activity of the Spirit on a scale ranging from cautious acceptance to stern rejection and violent denouncements that they are "of the devil." This rejection of the charismata—which could be defined as a restriction on the Holy Spirit—appears to coincide with a restriction on women. Where the Holy Spirit is silenced, it appears that women are also silenced. Where the Holy Spirit is secondary, it seems that women are also secondary. On the other hand, men and women who truly honor the Holy Spirit are more inclined to honor men *and* women equally. This is because the emphasis is on the real Presence of the Spirit, on dynamic relationship with the Spirit, and on yieldedness to the Spirit. Furthermore, it is the anointing of the Spirit that demonstrates God's choice, election, or selection of a person, and so, to Spirit-oriented believers, it is obvious that He does not base His choice on gender.

Thus, although Reformed Theology is to be commended for taking authority out of the hands of the institutional tradition and authority of Rome, it did little to elevate women because it did not acknowledge and regard the activity of the Holy Spirit with equal respect. J. M. Stevenson, in his 1873 book, *Woman's Place in Assemblies for Public Worship,* accurately voices the position of the Reformers when he says that Reformed interpretation "applies the law of man's official headship and woman's subordination."[15]

To the extent that the children of the Reformation follow Luther and Calvin, they promote a theology of inequality. This attitude is expressed, for example, by prominent evangelical scholar

---

[14] Morton Kelsey, *Tongue Speaking: The History and Meaning of Charismatic Experience* (New York: Crossroad, 1981), 186-87; Lindsay Dewar, *The Holy Spirit and Modern Thought* (New York: Harper and Brothers, 1959), 191.

[15] J. M. Stevenson, *Woman's Place in Assemblies for Public Worship* (New York: J, M. Sherwood, 1873), 53.

Leon Morris who has said, "Neither in her origin, nor in the purpose for which she was created can the woman claim priority or
even equality."[16] Another example comes from the pen of another
prominent evangelical scholar, Donald Guthrie, who writes, "The
idea of woman's subjection is not only ingrained in the conviction
of the mass of mankind . . . but also appears to be inherent in the
divine constitution of the race."[17] Perhaps the loudest voice proclaiming this position in our day is the Council on Biblical Manhood and Womanhood.[18] The traditional statement is found in
the CBMW *Danver's Statement.* It clearly promotes the traditional
perspective of a social order predetermined and ordained by God
in which men take the authoritarian headship position and
women, the secondary, subordinate position. It is unfortunate that
Spirit-oriented people would subscribe to and promote this position.

"An Insolent Daughter of Eve"

Although during the Reformation era, women continued to be
repressed, individual women gained a degree of prominence. Argula von Grumback (1492-1563), for example, was a highly intel-
ligent and gifted woman who debated the Catholic theologians at
the University of Ingolstadt. Rather than being applauded, however, she was condemned "an insolent daughter of Eve, a heretical
bitch and confounded rogue."[19] She was persecuted by the
Church as well as by her husband who locked her up so that he
would not be locked out of his job.

Argula was not the only prominent woman locked up by her
husband and threatened with divorce for being a threat to the
male establishment. Jeanne d'Albert (1528-1572), Queen of

[16] Leon Morris, *The First Epistle of Paul to the Corinthians* (n.p.: Tyndale, 1958), 153.

[17] Donald Guthrie, *The Pastoral Epistles*, (n.p.: Tyndale, 1957), 76.

[18] Christians for Biblical Manhood and Womanhood. P. O. Box 317, Wheaton, IL 60189. On the Board of Reference are well known people such as Jerry Falwell, D. James Kennedy, J. I. Packer, Paige and Dorothy Paterson, Adrian Rogers, as well as Charismatic, Pat Robertson. On the Council are people such as Wayne Grudem, May Kassian, Beverly LaHaye, and John Piper.

[19] Roland Bainton, *Women of the Reformation in Germany and Italy* (Minneapolis: Augsburg, 1971), 97, 100, 105.

Navarre, France, too was persecuted for her outspoken support of the French Protestants known as Huguenots.[20]

Respect for the Experience of the Holy Spirit

In addition to the Lutherans and the Calvinists, other significant groups of Reformers arose. These included those who, at first, had followed Zwingli and who became known as *Anabaptists*. The Anabaptists were charismatic Christians,[21] and for this reason, it is important to look at how they regarded women.

Felix Manz and Conrad Grebel broke with Zwingli's Reform movement in Zurich on the grounds that he was compromising. On January 21, 1525, they held their first meeting after separating from Zwingli, which marks the birth of the Anabaptist movement. Their desire was to recover New Testament Christianity "in its original purity and simplicity."[22] They held to believer's baptism (as opposed to infant baptism) and to the separation of church and state (as opposed to a state church). They also refused to take vows and to participate in war.[23]

John Yoder, a leading Mennonite scholar, says that Pentecostalism "is in our century the closest parallel to what Anabaptism was in the sixteenth."[24] It was not unusual for them to speak in tongues, fall under the power, and dance in the Spirit.[25] They believed in the active presence of the Holy Spirit including divine revelation and illumination of Scripture. They also believed in both the priesthood and prophethood of all believers. For this reason, they rejected hierarchical structure in church leadership, choosing instead a congregational-charismatic order in which the

---

[20] Tucker and Liefeld, 187-88.

[21] E. L. Hyatt, *2000 Years of Charismatic Christianity* (Dallas: Hyatt Press, 1997), 83-92.

[22] C. Henry Smith quoted by Franklin H. Littell, "The Anabaptist Concept of the Church," *The Anabaptist Vision*, ed. Guy F. Hershberger (Scottdale, PA: Herald, 1957), 121. See also E. Hyatt, 81-87.

[23] Yoder, 251-252.

[24] Kenneth R. Davis, "Anabaptism as a Charismatic Movement," *Mennonite Quarterly Review* 53, no. 3 (1979): 221.

[25] Littell, 121.

Holy Spirit was invited to flow through each member. When it was obvious to them that the Holy Spirit ministered to and through men and women both without gender distinction, women initially experienced a new freedom that broke through religious and cultural tradition.

As a result of the anointing of the Spirit on Anabaptist women, the Anabaptists were known for their women preachers. However, Anabaptism was not a utopia for women. Some, fearing the influence of women, made the husband "absolute master of the home." In some circles, in fact, wives were expected to "address their husbands as Lord, reflecting their dependence on him—analogous with man's dependence on God."[26] A radical Anabaptist leader, Bernard Rottman, decried women's elevation saying that men should exercise their God-given superiority and that one of the best ways to do so was through polygamy.[27]

Menno Simons (1496-1561), a former Catholic priest from Holland, pulled together scattered Anabaptists who became known as *Mennonites*. It was a break with tradition when he encouraged men not to beat their wives. On the other hand, he retained the traditional concept of womanhood, requiring them to function in traditional roles. He wrote:

> Remain within your houses and gates unless you have something to regulate, such as to make purchases, to provide in temporal needs, to hear the Word of the Lord, or to receive the holy sacraments, etc. Attend faithfully to your charge, to your children, house, and family.[28]

The Anabaptist sexist bias contradicted what the Spirit was doing in elevating women. Perhaps it was the pressure of culture that caused them to take refuge in the perceived patriarchalism of

---

[26] John Cairncross, *After Polygamy Was Made a Sin: The Social History of Christian Polygamy* (London: Routledge & Kegan Paul), 1974), 25, 9.

[27] Cairncross, 9.

[28] Menno Simons, *The True Christian Faith*, ed. John C. Wenger, *The Complete Writings of Menno Simons* (c. 1496-1561), trans. Leonard Verduin (Scottdale, PA: Herald, 1956), 376-83.

the Old Testament. Their interpretation of the Old Testament sanctioned the cultural custom of subjugating wives and women in general.[29] As is so often the case today among Spirit-oriented people, the Anabaptists did not develop a theology consistent with their experience of the Holy Spirit. They certainly did not develop a theology to undergird what the Holy Spirit was doing in relation to women in their midst; instead, they quenched the activity of the Spirit with "the traditions of men."

Conclusion

For women, the period of Reformation continued to be a time of great darkness. They remained at the bottom of the chain-of-command in the thoroughly hierarchical mindset of the Church. A slight ray of light pierced the darkness with the formulation of the doctrine of the priesthood of all believers. Another ray of light flickered with the Anabaptist recognition of the prophethood of all believers. Nevertheless, these doctrines were not espoused on behalf of women. Consequently, they served primarily the purposes of a patriarchal culture.

---

[29] Joyce Irwin, *Womanhood in Radical Protestantism, 1525-1675* (New York: Mellen, 1979), 490.

8

A Little Kingdom and a Little Church

"Where Two or Three Are Gathered ...."

Ideas do not develop in isolation. They develop in real historical settings among real people. This is true regarding the popular notion that the Christian home is the basic unit of the Church, and socially it might be true. But it is not a Biblical principle as we currently proclaim it to be. Think about it.

Did Jesus Himself say that the home is the basic unit of the Church? What He said was, "Where two or three have come together in my Name, there I am in the midst of them (Mt. 18:20, Author's translation). It could be argued that when a believing man and woman marry, the home meets Jesus' definition of Church. But that is not the inherent meaning of Jesus' words. If, for instance, an unbeliever lives in that home, is it still a little church?

Irenaus affirmed Jesus' teaching about what constitutes the Church of which Jesus spoke. It, indeed, is where the Presence of the Lord is. Irenaeus said, "Where the [true] church is, there is the Spirit; and where the Spirit of God is, there is the church."[1]

How, then, did the idea that the home is the basic unit of the Church evolve? And how did the idea develop that the man is the "high priest" of the home? A primary avenue for the evolution to this notion was the period of the English Reformation in the 1600s. During this era of great cultural upheaval, the English

---

[1] John Lacy, *The General Delusion of Christians Touching the Ways of God's Revealing Himself to and by the Prophets, Evinced from Scriputre and Primitive Antiquity*, ed. H. Drummond (London: Republished by R. B. Seeley and W. Burnside, MDCCCXXXII), p. 257.

kings and Puritan leaders used the idea as a means of imposing hierarchical order on a seemingly chaotic society.

The English Reformation

The Reformation Period fragmented Christendom politically. As opposing groups contended for dominance and absolute control, a series of religious conflicts ensued known as the Thirty Years' War (1618-1648). This struggle inflamed the European continent and spread to England where, under the Stuart monarchs, the state Church of England swayed between Roman Catholicism and Protestantism. Henry VIII (1509-47), had already severed the English church from the papacy by the Act of Supremacy of 1534, an act declaring the king "the supreme head of the church of England."[2] This reflected an austere, hierarchical worldview, and it reinforced, in the English-speaking world, an institutional form of church government patterned after hierarchical state government. In addition, the Stuarts held to the "divine right of kings," that is, the God-ordained right of the monarch to ultimate authority.[3] It is interesting to note that it was in such a climate that the Authorized King James Version of the Bible (1611) was translated.

A Well-Known King Who Hated Women

King James I (b. 1566, ruled 1603-25) commissioned the 1611 version of the Bible. Having alienated both the Puritans and the Catholics, he had to find a way to rally support and consolidate his power base. In this context, to pacify the Puritans, he authorized the translation of the Bible, the King James Version, 1611,

---

[2] Henry Bettenson, *Documents of the Christian Church* (New York: Oxford University Press, 1963), 261-63.

[3] Earle E. Cairns, *Christianity Through the Centuries*, rev. ed. (Grand Rapids: Zondervan, 1981), 338-341; Lars P. Qualben, *A History of the Christian Church* (New York: Thomas Nelson and Sons, 1933), 350-363; George L. Mosse, "Puritanism," *Twentieth Century Encyclopedia of Religious Knowledge, An Extension of the New Schaff-Herzog Encyclopedia of Religious Knowledge*, ed. Lefferts A. Loetscher (Grand Rapids: Baker, 1955), 931-933.

still used by millions of Christians today.

Unfortunately, James I was no friend of women. Selma Williams says, "The moment James had the crown placed securely on his head, he gave notice that . . . he would take every opportunity to trample women into permanent invisibility."[4] He also refused to upgrade female education and remarked that "to make women learned and foxes tame had the same effect: to make them more cunning."[5]

The writings of James and others of this period show a prevailing hostility toward women. James, in fact, made a concerted attack on "witchcraft," declaring it a crime punishable by hanging. (Again, as in the earlier discussions of witchcraft, it is indeed questionable as to what constituted "witchcraft.") Persecution was intense and the king himself published his *Daemonologie* sanctioning the execution of convicted witches. According to this decree, guilt and punishment could be established by mere hearsay without the normal process of English justice. In his estimation, most witches were women because women, like Eve, he contended, are more susceptible than men to the devil. James would, it appears, agree with Joseph Swetnam, who in 1615, published a tract declaring that "women spring from the Devil."[6]

The King's Influence on the Version that Carries His Name

In such a climate, is it possible that the King James Version (KJV) could have been influenced by misogynous sentiments? A couple of examples clearly illustrate that such tampering did, in fact, occur.

- In Acts 18:26, the KJV translators reverse the order of Priscilla and Aquila. In the Greek text, Priscilla comes first.

---

[4] Selma Williams, *Divine Rebel: The Life of Anne Marbury Hutchinson* (New York: Holt, Rinehart and Winston, 1981), 35.

[5] Antonia Fraser, *The Weaker Vessel* (New York: Knopf, 1984), 122.

[6] Joseph Swetman, *The Arraignment of Lewd, Idle, Froward, and Unconstant Women* (n.p.: n.p., 1615), n.p. Quoted by Tucker and Liefeld, 208.

In the KJV, however, Aquila comes first, a reversal that shows deference to the husband.

- The KJV translation of the Greek word *hesychia* also reveals evidence of anti-woman sentiments. 1 Tim. 2:11 reads, "Let the women learn in silence." 2 Thes. 3:16 reads, "with quietness they work and eat." The phrases "in silence" and "with quietness" are translations of the same Greek word *hesychia*. In a context referring to women, the KJV translators used "in silence," but in a context referring to men, they used "in quietness."

- Phoebe (Rom. 16:1), Paul (1 Cor. 3:5), Timothy (1 Tim. 4:6), Epaphras (Col. 1:7), Tychicus (Col. 4:7; Eph. 6:21), and Apollos (1 Cor. 3:5) are all referred to as *diakonos* in the Greek text. The KJV translates *diakonos* as "deacon" and "minister"—except on one occasion! In the case of Phoebe, *diakonos* becomes "a servant" instead of a "deacon" or "minister."[7]

These are only examples of this sort of influence present in the KJV. An easy-to-understand exposure of this action on the part of translators of the KJV and various other translations is presented by Alvera and the late Berkeley Mickelsen in "Does Male Dominance Tarnish Our Translations?" (*Christianity Today*, Oct. 5, 1979: 23-27).

Home: A Little Kingdom and A Little Church

The low estate of women was further entrenched as the cultural norm through Puritan and Anglican efforts to bring order out of chaos. As both groups attempted to force their perspectives on society, the rulers increased their political power over the masses by using the power of religion in their personal lives. In this, both

---

[7] Some other translations of *diakonos* in Rom. 16:1 are: Revised Standard Version and Phillips read "deaconess," a word that does not exist in Greek; and Living Letters reads, "a dear Christian woman from the town of Cenchreae."

Anglicans and Puritans contributed to the notion that the home was to be considered a little church where patriarchal rule was to be enforced.

An additional irritant that both groups were attempting to eradicate, especially between 1640 and 1660, was the host of powerful women preachers who had arisen among groups such as the Friends. Thus, they reasserted with great intensity the idea of authoritative male headship in the home. The man was called upon to manage his wife, his children, and his workers. His authority was sanctioned with enthusiasm and urgency by both the state and the church. A family was, in fact, described as a "little church and a little commonwealth," and was to serve as a school for training servants and women in subjugation."[8]

The Puritans, following Calvin, established human government on the basis of what they believed were three divinely ordained institutions: the state, the church, and the home. Each institution was divinely ruled by means of delegated authority: that is, in the same way that the *head-of-the-state* allegedly derived authority from God, the *head-of-the-church* derived authority from God, and the *head-of-the-home* derived authority from God. And the *head* (meaning "ruler") of each of these had to be a man because, according to their theology, God had predestined man to rule! The apex of this Puritan thinking in England came under Oliver Cromwell who had deposed the monarchy on May 16, 1649.

When the monarchy was reinstated in 1660, the throne had the ongoing task of stabilizing society, and the idea of the divine right of kings remained in tact. This doctrine intensified the sense of authority already inherent in the head-of-state/head-of-church concepts. The English king was now authoritative in the state as king, that is, as God's designated ruler of the earthly kingdom, and as high priest, that is as God's representative earthly ruler of

---

[8] William Gouge, *Of Domesticall Duties* (London: John Haviland, 1662). See quotation in Jeanette Carter Gadt, "Women and Protestant Culture" (Ph.D. diss., University of California, 1974) 32.

the Church. No where in Scripture is this taught.

Nevertheless, this convenient notion of *divine order* was extended to the home. According to this teaching, the home was to be seen as a little kingdom where the man was to rule as king of "his castle" in the same way as the King of England was to rule the state. Furthermore, the home was also to be seen as a little church where the man was to rule as high priest in the same way that the King was to rule the Church of England. So the man was now king and priest of the home with woman as subject both politically and religiously.

This is probably the first time that the link was made between the two separate "roles" of *head-of-home* and *priest-of-the-home* so commonly taught among Pentecostal/Charismatics today. Yet nowhere in the New Testament are these roles taught. And nowhere in the New Testament are they linked. And nowhere in the New Testament is the male given responsibility to dominate the female.[9]

Conclusion

It is expedient for us to understand that the formulators of the prevailing, traditional theology about women maintained the pagan ideas that women are evil, inferior, unclean, and unequal. It is equally important to realize that Jesus taught, by precept and example, a theology of womanhood that was totally opposite to this. It is, however, exciting to observe an elevation of women by the Holy Spirit beginning with great force among the Friends in the 1600s and continuing in recognizable dimensions among the early Methodists (1700s), the Holiness people (1800s) and the early Pentecostals (1900s). Indeed, in the midst of great darkness, the Light would shine.

---

[9] This statement will be substantiated in Part 6, "Agreement of Spirit and Scripture."

Restoration of Truth

9

Biblical Equality And the Friends

At the same time that political and religious leaders were at work strategizing for social and political control, God was also at work bringing forth a different order. In His plan, oppression and control of one person over another would be seriously challenged and a remarkable pattern of equality, respect, and mutuality would be modeled. It would be the beginning of a new day for women. This plan of God was—and still is—orchestrated by the Spirit.

Who Were These People?

The strategy of the Spirit surfaced with serious consequences in England in about 1650 through George Fox and the Religious Society of Friends. By 1660, their numbers had ballooned to 60,000, and despite unimaginable persecution, they became the fastest growing movement in the Western world. Empowered by the Spirit, in only forty years, they proclaimed the Gospel of an intimate relationship with God from Turkey in the east to the English Colonies of the New World in the west.[1] Who were these people and how did their hunger for God promote a tendency toward biblical equality?

---

[1] William C. Braithwaite, *The Beginnings of Quakerism* (London, n.p., 1912); Frank C. Huntingdon, "Quakerism during the Commonwealth : The Experience of the Light," *Quaker History* 71, no. 2 (Fall 1982): 69-88; Phyllis Mack, *Visionary Women: Ecstatic Prophecy in Seventeenth-Century England* (Berkeley: University of California Press, 1992), 1; Elton Trueblood, *A People Called Quakers* (New York: Harper and Row, 1966), 2, 16; Charles L. Cherry, "Enthusiasm and Madness: Anti-Quakerism in the Seventeenth Century," *Quaker History* 74, no. 2 (Fall 1984): 1; William Penn, "The Preface, Being a summary account of the divers dispensations of God to men, from the beginning of the world to that of our present age, by the ministry and testimony of his faithful servant George Fox, as an introduction to the ensuing Journal," vol. 1., *The Works of George Fox,* 8 vols. (1706; reprint, New York: AMS Press, 1975), i-xlviii; Margaret Hope Bacon, *Mothers of Feminism, The Story of Quaker Women in America* (San Francisco: Harper and Row: 1986), 18, 24-26; Bonnelyn Young Kunze, *Margaret Fell and the Rise of Quakerism* (Stanford: Stanford University Press, 1994), x-xvii.

Their name of choice, *Friends,* was the abbreviated form of the group's official title, "The Religious Society of Friends." This came, first of all, from Jesus' words, "I have called you friends" (Jn. 15:15). It also occurs in Acts 27:3 where the Centurion gave Paul the freedom to go to the friends to refresh himself. A third time it occurs is in 3 John 14, "Peace to you. The friends greet you. Greet the friends by name."[2]

Reflecting their deep desire to experience and proclaim New Testament Christianity, the Friends had initially referred to themselves as "Children of Light." They referred to their itinerant preachers as "First Publishers of Truth," and to their movement as "Primitive Christianity Revived."[3] Their adversaries, however, called them "Quakers," a slur by which the Friends refused to be offended. In fact in 1678, Robert Barclay responded by saying, "We are not ashamed of it [the name], but have rather reason to rejoice therefore, even that we are sensible of this power that hath oftentimes laid hold of our adversaries, and made them yield unto us, and join with us, and confess to the truth."[4]

These Spirit-oriented, revival people were the first advocates of biblical equality since Jesus Himself walked the earth. [5] They demonstrated a biblically-based, egalitarian lifestyle that was revolutionary in its day. To the chagrin of many, the Quaker women interpreted the Scriptures and preached.[6] Quaker men and women were equal partners in marriage. This egalitarian lifestyle was the fruit of a high degree of biblical literacy and an intense dependence on the indwelling Holy Spirit.

---

[2] William Sewel, *The History of the Rise, Increase, and Progress of the Christian People Called Quakers* (Philadelphia: Friends Book Store, 1774), 419.

[3] George Fox, *A Journal or Historical Account of the Life, Travels, Sufferings, Christian Experiences in the Work of the Ministry of that Ancient, Eminent, and Faithful Servant of Jesus Christ, George Fox, vol. 1, The Works of George Fox,* 8 vols. (1706; reprint, New York: AMS Press, 1975), 105; Henry J. Cadbury, *Quakerism and Early Christianity* (London: n.p., 1957), explores the parallels between early Quakerism and early Christianity.

[4] Robert Barclay, *An Apology for the True Christian Divinity: Being an Explanation and Vindication of the Principles and Doctrines of the People Called Quakers* (1678; reprint, Philadelphia: Joseph James, 1789), 359.

[5] Bacon, 87.

[6] Bacon, 6.

"He exercised no authority but over evil."

The Friends, perhaps because of the egalitarian nature of their society, had no star performers or organizational heads. Nevertheless, during the formative period, George Fox (1624-1691) was the itinerant preacher who seemed to inspire its style and is, therefore, regarded by most historians as its founder.[7] Born in Drayton, Leicestershire, England, in 1624, in a Presbyterian/Puritan home that stressed honesty and integrity, Fox, as a child, was inherently "religious, inward, still, solid, and observing, beyond his years." This nature matured under the watchful eye of his father, "Righteous Christer" Christopher Fox, a weaver by trade, and his mother, Mary Lago Fox "a woman accomplished above most of her degree in the place where she lived." As a young man, in addition to gaining a thorough knowledge of the Bible, George learned sound business practices as a cobbler's apprentice and enjoyed solitude tending his employer's sheep.[8]

Fox's spiritual quest began in earnest when he was nineteen. Dissatisfied with the spiritual help offered by esteemed clergymen of the official church and "prompted by God," on September 9, 1643, he left all behind and traveled throughout England in search of someone who could tell him how to satisfy his yearning for a genuine relationship with God.[9] He visited "the most retired and religious people . . . who waited for the consolation of Israel night and day, as Zacharias, Anna, and good old Simeon did of old time."[10] In addition, many of his early associates were Anabaptists; in fact, in 1648, a dissolved Anabaptist congregation in Nottingham rallied around him.[11]

---

[7] See Cecil W. Sharman, "George Fox and His Family I," *Quaker History* 74, no. 2 (Fall 1985): 1-19; "George Fox and His Family II," *Quaker History* 75, no. 1 (Spring 1986): 1-11.

[8] George Fox, *George Fox: An Autobiography*, ed. Rufus M. Jones (Philadelphia: Ferris and Leach, 1903), 65-67; Penn, xxix-xxx, xliv; Lars P. Qualben, *History of the Christian Church* (New York: Thomas Nelson and Sons, 1933), 358; Bacon, 9.

[9] Fox, *Autobiography*, 68-69, 72.

[10] Penn, xxx.

[11] Qualben, 358-359.

Fox's spiritual passion generated encounters with God that helped define his lifestyle and ministry. In 1647, for example, he reports hearing a voice say to him, "There is one, even Christ Jesus, that can speak to thy condition." He writes, "When I heard it, my heart did leap for joy . . . and this I knew [God] experimentally."[12]   He began urging his listeners to turn from "self-performance," and instead, to heed the leading of "the light of Christ within."[13] He writes,

> I was sent to turn people from darkness to the Light, that they might receive Christ Jesus; for to as many as should receive Him in His Light, I saw He would give power to become the sons of God; which power I had obtained by receiving Christ. I was to direct people to the Spirit that gave forth the Scriptures, by which they might be led into all truth, and up to Christ and God, as those had been who gave them forth.[14]

Then in 1652, while in prayer high atop Pendle Hill in Yorkshire, Fox had a second vision. In it, he saw a great work of God in the earth and his part in it. Concerning this event, William Penn writes,

> He [Fox] saw people as thick as motes in the sun, that should in time be brought home to the Lord, that there might be but one shepherd, and one sheepfold in all the earth. There his eye was directed northward, beholding a great people that should receive him and his message in those parts. Upon this mountain he was moved of the Lord to sound out his great and notable day, as if he had been in a great auditory, and from thence went north, as the Lord had shown him. And in every place where he came, if not

---

[12] George Fox, *The Journal of George Fox*, ed. by John L. Nickalls (Cambridge: University Press, 1952), 11; Fox, *Autobiography*, 82.

[13] Penn, xxx.

[14] George Fox, *Autobiography*, 102-103.

before he came to it, he had his particular exercise and service shown to him, so that the Lord was his leader indeed; for it was not in vain that he traveled, God in most places sealing his commission with the convincement of some of all sorts, as well publicans as sober professors of religion."[15]

Fox's itinerant ministry consisted of visiting churches and of preaching in markets, fairs, streets, and by the highway.[16] He traveled extensively in England, Scotland, Holland, and America (1667-70), "calling people to repentance, and to turn to the Lord with their hearts as well as their mouths, directing them to the light of Christ within them." William Penn, a first-hand witness to these events, recalls, "God was pleased so to fill them with his living power, and give them such an open door of utterance in his service, that there was a mighty convincement over those parts."[17] Among those who accepted Fox's message at this time were erudite leaders from among England's elite as well as the masses of nameless people. [18]

In 1652, Fox's ministry in Lancashire was particularly fruitful with vast numbers accepting his teaching. At this time, the Society of Friends began to take shape. Also at this time, a convert of profound influence, a former Anglican gentry named Margaret Askew Fell, joined the company of Friends. The Fell estate, Swarthmoor Hall, quickly became the heart of Friends' activity in the north, and in 1669, eleven years after her husband's death, Margaret Fell and George Fox married. Fox believed his marriage was a symbol of the true Church coming out of the wilderness, and of "the redemption of all marriages out of the Fall."[19]

Fox endured severe religious persecution as did thousands of

---

[15] Penn, xxxi.

[16] Fox, *Autobiography*, 49; Qualben, 359.

[17] Penn, xxxi.

[18] Fox, *Autobiography*, 49.

[19] Fox, *Journal, Works of George Fox*, 8 vols., 557. Also see Penn's "Preface," iii, where he delineates Fox's understanding of the stages in God's relation with humanity. The tenth stage involved the flight of the true church into the wilderness.

other sincere Quakers. A period of particularly severe persecution occurred during the reign of Charles II in conjunction with the Conventicle Act (1660) whereby Charles sought to destroy all nonconforming churches. As many as 15,000 Friends were incarcerated at one time. Of these at least 450 died as a result. They were imprisoned for refusing to pays tithes to support local priests, refusing to remove their hats in the presence of their social superiors, refusing to take oaths, refusing to be married by the priests, interrupting church services, and refusing to serve in the army.[20] Fox was imprisoned numerous times, but the most appalling was his time served in Launceton Castle in Cornwall, in 1656, where he was put into Doomsdale Dungeon. Fox describes it as "a nasty stinking place where they said few people came out alive; . .

where the prisoners' excrement had not been carried out for scores of years, as it was said. It was all like mire, and in some places at the top of the shoes."[21]

Fox, although poorly educated, practical, and unphilosophical, was a prolific writer.[22] Over the years, he wrote letters of instruction and encouragement and epistles of instruction to Friends on both sides of the Atlantic. He compiled his *Journal* between 1674 and 1676 primarily during a period of rest at Swarthmoor. *The Works of George Fox,* consisting of his *Journal, Epistles*, and *Doctrinal Writings*, are currently available in an eight volume set.[23]

What kind of person was George Fox? In the famous "Preface" to Fox's *Journal*, William Penn paints a character portrait of the man.[24] Apparently he was "a discerner of others' spirits, and very much a master of his own." He had "an extraordinary gift of opening the scriptures," and "above all he excelled in prayer." He was "an incessant labourer," and one who showed great sympathy

---

[20] Bacon, 17.

[21] Fox, *Journal*, ed. Nickalls, 252.

[22] Larry Ingle, "George Fox, Historian," *Quaker History* 82, no. 1 (Spring 1993): 28.

[23] George Fox, *The Works of George Fox*, 8 vols. (1706, reprint; New York: AMS Press, 1975).

[24] Penn, xxxii-xxxiv, xxxi.

and compassion for those who were suffering. Even-tempered, he "was no more to be moved to fear than to wrath." Penn writes,

He was of an innocent life, no busy-body, nor self-seeker, neither touchy nor critical; what fell from him was very inoffensive, if not very edifying. So meek, contented, modest, easy, steady, tender, it was a pleasure to be in his company. . . . A most merciful man, as ready to forgive as unapt to take or give an offense.[25]

He was also a man of considerable influence. In fact, Penn notes, "Some erroneously accused him of seeking dominion over people's consciences . . . because he was held in high esteem by many.[26] Penn reports, however, "He exercised no authority but over evil."[27]

This attitude extended to his understanding of the status of women. A number of experiences, in fact, had influenced him to work toward equality. Whenever he encountered people who believed that women had no souls, "no more than a goose,"[28] he reminded them of Mary's words: "My soul doth magnify the Lord." A woman preacher named Elizabeth Hooten (c. 1600-71/72), whom he first met in 1647 and with whom he became friends, impressed him with her ability and effectiveness as a preacher.[29] Then, in 1648, in a meeting in a "steeplehouse," he observed a woman ask a question only to be told by the priest that he did not permit women to speak in church. Fox defended her right to speak, arguing that a church is "a spiritual household," not a building made of "lime, stones, and wood," and that in the true church, of which Christ was the Head, a woman might prophesy

---

[25] Penn, xxxiv.

[26] Penn, xxxiv-xxxv.

[27] Penn, xxxiv.

[28] Bacon, 10. Bacon makes this quotation but gives no source.

[29] Fox, *Autobiography*, 79-80.

and speak.[30] Fox notes, "It broke them into pieces and confused them, and they all turned against me into jangling."[31]

Margaret Fell, A Remarkable Woman of God

Traditional Quaker history stresses Fox's primary leadership position, flanked by William Penn and Robert Barclay, with Margaret Fell (1614-1702) cast only in a secondary role.[32] This view has been challenged, however, especially within the last decade, by Margaret Hope Bacon in her book *Mothers of Feminism: The Story of Quaker Women in America* (Harper and Row, 1986) and by Bonnelyn Young Kunze in her book *Margaret Fell and the Rise of Quakerism* (Stanford University Press, 1994). Kunze says, "Fell's role as an idealogue has been seriously underestimated."[33] Both Kunze and Bacon agree that Fell was a major player who helped assure stability in the Society.[34]

Born Margaret Askew near Dalton, England, in 1614, she married Judge Thomas Fell (1598/9-1658) in 1632, and subsequently gave birth to eight children. In 1652, when George Fox first visited Fell's Swarthmoor Hall, Margaret and her seven daughters were converted. Although an only son and Judge Fell never became Quakers, the Judge served as a true friend to the Quakers keeping persecution from the priests at bay in his jurisdiction. In addition, the Fell estate, "became a haven for George Fox, a clearing house for Quaker correspondence, and an important center for the organizational activities of men and women in the rise of Quakerism."[35]

---

[30] Fox, *Journal*, ed. Nickalls, 24; Bacon, 11.

[31] *Journal*, 24.

[32] Kunze, 4-6. Margaret Askew Fell Fox (1614-1702) is best known by the name of her first husband, Judge Thomas Fell (1598-1658). Throughout this paper, I will refer to her as Margaret Fell, although in 1669, she married George Fox (1624-1691).

[33] Kunze, 9.

[34] Kunze, 230.

[35] Kunze, 143; Penn, xxxi-xxxii.

Margaret Fell, the matriarch of Swarthmoor, demonstrated both authority and benevolence. "A powerful, dominant, and somewhat aloof authority figure," she was more a "mother superior" than a "nursing mother of Quakerism," as she has sometimes been called.[36] In some ways, she was representative of highly motivated, religious, gentry women of her day, yet she was far more than that. Her fifty years of effective leadership "as a literate, independent, wealthy, and widely traveled religious leader placed her among a tiny minority of women who may claim some degree of historical influence."[37] She was "a model of powerful female public ministry whose authority went far beyond that of the seventeenth-century female sectarian prophet."[38] In the opinion of Fell biographer, Isabel Ross, she was

> an outstanding woman, a pioneer in thought, with grace of body and mind. . . . She had the spiritual qualities which revealed to her profound religious truths and in addition she had the practical ability which enabled her to manage a large household and estate and to help organize the growing body of Friends into a coherent whole, resilient against the troubles of the time.[39]

Fell enjoyed certain privileges and held some values that were class-defined rather than gender-defined. She enjoyed, for example, the privileges of wealth, education, social connections, leisure time, and high visibility and recognition in the public sphere. These factors together with a strong sense of self-esteem destined her to become "a powerful leader and [to] pierce through traditional gender constraints."[40] Several times, she had audiences with

---

[36] Kunze, 230; See also Isabel Ross, *Margaret Fell, Mother of Quakerism* (London: Longmans, Green, and Co., 1949).
[37] Kunze, 3.
[38] Kunze, 229-230.
[39] Ross, v.
[40] Kunze, 3, 231-232.

the British monarchs on behalf of the Friends. She was also an authoritative public apologist for Quaker doctrine and polity.[41]

Like Fox and her other colleagues, Margaret Fell believed in this harmony between the Holy Spirit and the Holy Scriptures. In an unpublished manuscript (1660), she explains her understanding of how the Spirit and Word collaborate in communicating truth to humanity.[42]

> We received this Spirit . . . not by Man, but by the immediate Power and Revelation of Jesus Christ, according to the work and operation of it in us; . . . Now though these Scriptures bear testimony to the Truth of this, yet these Scriptures are not our Testimony only, for we have our Testimony in the same Spirit as was in them that spoke forth the Scriptures; and these Scriptures bears Testimony with us and we to them, and so are in unity with the same Spirit which gave them forth.[43]

Fell's major contribution to the movement may have been the stabilizing of the Women's Meetings. These separate meetings were necessary when women began to exercise their new-found equality in the Society, and it quickly became apparent that they had neither the education nor the experience to exercise that equality. The Women's Meetings served as a forum for the development of their abilities and the skills vital to leadership.[44] In these gatherings, the women functioned with the knowledge of their equality, and took responsibility for overseeing marriages, regulating the conduct of their members, relieving the needs of the poor, and keeping good accounts and records.[45]

---

[41] Kunze, 232-33.
[42] Kunze, 206.
[43] Kunze, 206; Kunze quotes from "An Unpublished Paper of Margaret Fell," 446.
[44] Kunze, 208.
[45] Kunze, 5; Bacon, 23.

Fell wrote and published voluminously, a fact that gave her high visibility and recognition. "Her public letters and theological writings," writes Kunze, "are very useful in defining primitive Quaker thought and practice from a woman's perspective, not only within the seventeenth-century movement, but within the wider range of Protestant hermeneutics.[46] In 1655, she wrote two letters to Oliver Cromwell on behalf of the Friends. In 1660, she was the first to publish a statement regarding the peaceful principle of Quakerism clarifying for the political authorities and the public the fact that the Friends could be counted on to uphold the government while not necessarily agreeing with all policies.[47] In 1666, she wrote *Women Speaking Justified*, the first Quaker woman to write in favor of a female public ministry. Fell was among the first of the Quaker leaders to correspond with the Jewish leader Menassah Ben Israel and other Jews of Holland regarding Jewish reentry to England during the Commonwealth period.[48] Fell's tracts were translated into Latin, Dutch, and Hebrew and were carried to the Netherlands by Quaker missionaries. [49] Many of her writings are available in *A Brief Collection*.[50]

Rejecting Symbols, Regarding Substance

Fox knew the hollowness of outward religion. It did not satisfy the inner craving of a person for intimacy with the Creator. He therefore denounced all outward mediatory elements such as the priesthood, the church buildings, the sacraments, and regalia.

---

[46] Kunze, 9.

[47] Margaret Fell, "A Declaration and an Information from us the people of God called Quakers, to the present Governors, the King and both Houses of Parliament, and all whom I many concern," *A Brief Collection of Remarkable Passages and Occurrences Relating to the Birth, Education, Life, Conversation, Travels, Services, and Deep Sufferings of that Ancient, Eminent, and Faithful Servant of the Lord, Margaret Fell; But by her Second Marriage, Margaret Fox. Together With Sundry of Her Epistles, Books, and Christian Testimonies to Friends and Others; and also to those in Supreme Authority , in the several late Revolutions of Government* (London: J. Sowle, 1710), 202-10.

[48] Kunze, 3, 5-6, 7.

[49] Kunze, 9.

[50] Margaret Fell, *A Brief Collection* (London: J. Sowle, 1710). This is available in the Rare Book Collection at the Goddard Memorial Library at Gordon-Conwell Seminary, Hamilton, MA. See also Margaret Fell, *Womens Speaking Justified* (1979, reprint by the Augustan Reprint Society; London, 1667). This is available in the Huntingdon Library (Shelf Mark: 94232; Wing F-643).

Through these, the Church had controlled its members, but Fox believed that Jesus Christ was the only legitimate Mediator (1 Tim. 2:5; Heb. 8:6; 9:15; 12:24). He, therefore, upheld personal, individual responsibility for a direct and intimate relationship with God. This biblically-based, Spirit-oriented Christianity severely threatened the rigid hierarchical social pattern promulgated by the state church and Puritans who held to a medieval, hierarchical worldview.[51] It threatened the authority by which these religious systems controlled people.

Out of Fox's belief system came the notion that women were equal with men in God's sight. Women were, therefore, to function without regard for gender but in response to relationship with God. The concept of women speaking in public and of any other expression of equality stirred up a major persecution against the Friends. "The idea of women inspired by the Holy Spirit and acting in an authoritative public role was anathema to most Protestants."[52]

But this understanding of what it meant to be a Christian did not appear suddenly out of nowhere. It was, in certain respects, a product of the theological climate of the day. Rufus Jones, in his "Introduction" to *George Fox: An Autobiography,* observes, "There is hardly a single truth in the Quaker message which had not been held by some one of the many sects of the time." Fox was unique, however, in this respect:

> He saw the spiritual and eternal element which was almost lost in the chaos of half truths and errors. In his message these scattered truths and ideas were fused into a new whole and received new life from his living central idea (i.e. the Inner Light).[53]

---

[51] Kunze, 169; James W. Sire, *Scripture Twisting: Twenty Ways the Cults Misread the Bible* (Downers Grove: IV Press, 1980), incorporates "worldview" in his discussion of interpretation. Essentially "worldview" is a set of presuppositions a person holds about the basic make-up of the world.

[52] Kunze, 20.

[53] Jones, 24.

Some scholars have, nevertheless, identified Fox as a right-wing Puritan. After all, he grew up in a devout Puritan family, and it "should not be forgotten that George Fox came to his spiritual crisis" under Calvinist theology, a format whose "linked logic might compel intellectual assent," but which ultimately fails to satisfy inner longing for God because "there is something in a man as real as his intellect, which is not satisfied with this clamping of eternal truth into inflexible propositions."[54] Historians Geoffrey Nuttall and Hugh Barbour see more similarities than differences between the early Quakers and the Puritans, while Henry J. Cadbury and Howard H. Brinton believe the differences dominate.[55] Melvin Endy, in his 1986 article, "Puritanism, Spiritualism, Quakerism,"[56] notes critical divergence. Puritans, for example, "de-emphasized outward mediatory religion in terms of clergy, sacraments, and saints, while Quakers rejected all three."[57] Further, Quakers believed that the work of the Holy Spirit at work in the believer was necessary for rightly dividing and understanding the Scriptures.[58]

Some scholars consider early Quakerism to be an offshoot of continental mysticism.[59] Rufus Jones says that "The consciousness of the presence of God is the characteristic thing in George Fox's religious life ... it is this experience which puts him among the mystics.[60] Jones would call him a "positive" mystic, one who experiences God's presence in relating to life, not in withdrawing from it. [61]

---

[54] Fox, *Autobiography*, ed. Jones, 17-18.

[55] Kunze, 282-83; For development of this idea, see Hugh Barbour and Arthur O. Roberts, eds. *Early Quaker Writings: 1650-1700* (Grand Rapids: Eerdmans, 1973).

[56] Melvin Endy, "Puritanism, Spiritualism, Quakerism, *The World of William Penn*, ed. by Richard S. Dunn and Mary Maples Dunn (Philadelphia: University of Pennsylvania Press, 1986), 281-301, especially 284.

[57] Kunze, 197.

[58] Kunze, 198.

[59] Bacon, 5-7; Fox, *Autobiography*, ed. Jones, 30-31; Elbert Russell, *The History of Quakerism* (Richmond: Friends United Press, 1979), 48.

[60] Jones, 30-31.

[61] Jones, 31-32.

Perhaps, as Eddie L. Hyatt points out, the experience of Fox and Fell was simply an expression of charismatic Christianity.[62] H. J. Cadbury presents weighty evidence to this end.[63] Among the characteristics that would sustain this view was their practice of singing in the spirit.[64] In fact, biblical *charismata* were common in their midst, as Fox discloses in his *Journal* and *Book of Miracles*. He writes, for example, "The Lord gave me a spirit of discerning, by which I many times saw the states and conditions of people, and could try their spirits."[65] His associate, Edward Burroughs, writes, "Our tongues were loosed and our mouths opened, and we spake with new tongues, as the Lord gave utterance."[66]

Fox had a thorough knowledge of the Scriptures. His "mystical" experiences, in fact, were always rooted in Scripture and could be validated by the Bible. They were revelatory in nature, never disconnected from Scripture itself.[67] Fox's strict Puritan upbringing, his reported pious nature as a child, his search for an experiential relationship with the Lord on the basis of Scripture, and his remarkable integration of Scripture in his voluminous writings all point to Fox's biblical literacy. His associates used to say, "Though the Bible were lost, it might be found in the mouth of George Fox."[68] He writes, "I had no slight esteem of the Holy Scriptures. They were very precious to me; . . . and what the Lord opened in me I afterwards found was agreeable to them."[69]

How Fox related Scripture and Spirit is also important. He explains,

---

[62] Eddie L. Hyatt, *2000 Years of Charismatic Christianity* (Chicota, TX: Hyatt International Ministries, 1996).

[63] Henry J. Cadbury, *George Fox's Book of Miracles* (Cambridge: n. p., 1948) and *Quakerism and Early Christianity* (London: n. p., 1957).

[64] Kenneth L. Carroll, "Singing in the Spirit in Early Quakerism," *Quaker History* 73, no. 1 (Spring 19840: 1-13.

[65] Fox, *Autobiography*, edited by Jones, 185.

[66] Kelsey, 55.

[67] M. R Austin, "Bible and Event in the Journal of George Fox," *The Journal of Theological Studies*, ed. H. Chadwick and G. B. Caird (Oxford: Clarendon Press, 1981), 82-100

[68] Fox, *Autobiography*, 30; Penn, xxxix.

[69] Fox, *Autobiography*, 101-103.

I saw, in that Light and Spirit which was before the Scriptures were given forth, and which led the holy men of God to give them forth, that all, if they would know God or Christ, or the Scriptures aright, must come to that Spirit by which they that gave forth were led and taught. [70]

His mission was to point people "to the Spirit that gave forth the Scriptures, by which they might be led into all truth, and up to Christ and God, as those had been who gave them forth."

The Inner Light

It has been said, "Quakerism was fundamentally a way of life, not a system of thought or doctrine."[71] Its associates were not required to subscribe to a creed. Its distinctive factors were the belief in the "Inner Light," the necessity of intimate relationship with God, and respectful, practical concern for all people.

The definitive theological principle of Quakerism is "Inner Light." Medieval scholars had believed light to be the supreme symbol of God so it was not an isolated, purely creative revelation. Fox, however, seeing the biblical reality, internalized this outward symbol so that the supreme outward symbol of authority became his new supreme inner symbol of authority, the *Inner Light*.

Early Friends did not give this "Inner Light" exact theological definition, "for it represented an experience rather than a theological 'notion.'"[72] Those who gave heed to the Inner Light became new creatures in Christ, and received the "Seed of Promise," the Lord Jesus Christ, and were part of the converted community. In his "Preface" to Fox's *Journal*, William Penn says, "the light of Christ within" is God's gift by which He draws people to salva-

---

[70] Fox, *Autobiography*, 101-103.
[71] Frederick B. Tolles, *Quakerism and the Atlantic Culture* (New York: Octagon Books, 1960) 88; Russell, 46.
[72] Russell, 48-49.

tion.[73] Fox understood the spirit of a person to be the candle of the Lord (Prov. 20:27), and with David, believed, "thou wilt light my candle; the Lord my God will enlighten my darkness" (Ps. 18:28).[74]

Fox may have related to the Light more on the basis of what it did rather than from the perspective of actual definition, and the light, indeed, does many things. For example, everyone who has "turned to the light, turned to Christ" sees Jesus Christ, Who is the One by Whom the world was made and Who is the end of the prophets. Also everyone who has "turned to the light . . . with the light sees Christ, the gift of God, the promise of the Father," and is able to distinguish between those things that are of God from those things that are not of God.[75]

A key text regarding this issue is John 1:1-14.

1:1   In the beginning was the Word, and the Word was with God, and the Word was God.

1:2   The same was in the beginning with God.

1:3   All things were made by him; and without him was not any thing made that was made.

1:4   In him was life; and the life was the light of men.

1:5   And the light shineth in darkness, and the darkness comprehended it not.

1:6   There was a man sent from God, whose name was John.

1:7   The same came for a witness, to bear witness of the Light, that all men through him might believe.

1:8   He was not that Light, but was sent to bear witness of that Light.

1:9   That was the true Light, which lighteth every man that

---

[73] Penn, xiii.

[74] George Fox, "The Spirit of Man the Candle of the Lord: the Candle of the Wicked often put out," vol. 2, *Doctrinal Books*, 3 vols., *The Works of George Fox* (1706; reprint, New York: AMS Press, 1975), 291.

[75] George Fox, "The Women Learning in Silence," 110.

cometh into the world.

1:10 He was in the world, and the world was made by him, and the world knew him not.

1:11 He came unto his own, and his own received him not.

1:12 But as many as received him, to them gave he the power to become the sons of God, even to them that believe on his name:

1:13 Which were born, not of blood, nor of the will of the flesh, nor of the will of man, but of God.

1:14 And the Word was made flesh, and dwelt among us, (and we beheld his glory, the glory as of the only begotten of the Father,) full of grace and truth (Authorized King James Version -1611).

On the basis of verse 9, in particular, Fox believed that "'there was that of God,' . . . in all men and women everywhere." This is the key to Fox. This is what gave him confidence in evangelism, for it meant that the potential to respond to the Gospel was inherent in every person. This is what gave him an egalitarian worldview, as well, for it indicated that God was no respecter of persons.

The Inner Light had a democratizing or leveling social effect. It was the basis of a Christian community in which no one was to dominate another.[76] Gender was not the determining factor in responsibility and spiritual function; rather, the primacy of inner experience verified by the community was.[77] Fox and his Friends, therefore, "stoutly defended the ministry of women . . . and maintained that the Pauline prohibitions were only 'local and temporary conditions which have passed away."[78] William Penn wrote, "Sexes made No Difference; since in Souls there is none: and they are the Subjects of Friendship."[79]

---

[76] Kunze, 6, 20; Bacon, 10.

[77] John Wesley Chilcote, *John Wesley and the Women Preachers of Early Methodism* (Metuchen: Scarecrow, 1991), 10.

[78] Chilcote, 9-11.

[79] William Penn, *Fruits of Solitude* (London: Northcott, 1693), 33.

A Way of Life

William Penn, in his "Preface" to Fox's *Journal*, gives the following three effects of the "Blessed Light." First, it gives awareness of sin, of the spirit of the world, and of the fallen nature of humanity. Second, it conjures a genuine sorrow for sin, revealing not only the awful nature of sin but also the saving work of Jesus Christ on the Cross. Third, it alerts the redeemed of the Lord to walk in holiness in thought, word, and deed, and in love of God and others. He writes,

> Now you come to be Christ's indeed, for you are his in nature and spirit, and not your own. And when you are thus Christ's, then Christ is yours, and not before. And here communion with the Father and with the son you will know, and the efficacy of the blood of cleansing, even the blood of Jesus Christ, that immaculate Lamb, which speaketh better things than the blood of Abel, and which cleanseth from all sin the consciences of those, that, through the living faith, come to be sprinkled with it from dead works to serve the living God."[80]

From these points, according to Penn, flow three essential doctrines.[81] The first is repentance from dead works to serve the living God. This repentance leads to justification and sanctification. The second is perfection from sin, "a redeemed state, regeneration, or the new birth, teaching everywhere, according to their foundation, that unless this work was known, there was no inheriting the kingdom of God." By perfection from sin "they never held a perfection in wisdom and glory in this life, or from natural infirmities or death, as some have with a weak or ill mind imagined and insinuated against them." The third doctrine is the acknowledgment of eternal rewards and punishments. These three

---

[80] Penn, xlviii.
[81] Penn, xiii-xiv.

doctrines deal with an individual's past life, present life, and future life.

Finally, Penn delineates at least twelve practical implications of the Inner Light for the believer.[82] The goal of these principles, he explains, is "to bring things back into their primitive and right order again."[83] In greatly abbreviated form, they are:

1. To commune with and love one another.

2. To love enemies, taking no revenge for wrong inflicted, but forgiving.

3. To speak the truth at all times and obey the prohibition regarding oaths (Mt. 5).

4. To use energy to fight sin and Satan, not people, and to be willing to suffer if necessary.

5. To refuse to pay tithes but instead to follow Christ's command: "Freely you have received, freely give."

6. To treat all people with equal respect, not using flattering titles nor vain gestures and compliments.

7. To use plain language in addressing all people so as not to elevate one person above another by means of titles.

8. To value silence and solitude, but when in company to be careful to keep discussion brief and profitable.

9. Neither to drink to people nor to pledge by oath-taking.

10. To make marriage coincide with the biblical mandate of equal meet-helps.

11. To avoid pomp, ceremonies, and festivals in relation to births and naming children.

12. To keep burials simple and to avoid outward symbols of mourning in dress and ceremony.

---

[82] Penn, xiii-xix.
[83] Penn, xix.

Marriage Style Among the Friends

For the purposes of our study, we should hear Item 10 in greater length. Speaking of marriage, it reads as follows:

Their way of marriage is peculiar to them, and shows a distinguishing care above other societies professing Christianity. They say that marriage is an ordinance of God, and that God only can rightly join man and woman in marriage. Therefore they use neither priest nor magistrate, but the man and woman concerned take each other as husband and wife in the presence of divers credible witnesses, 'promising unto each other, with God's assistance to be loving and faithful in that relation till death shall separate them,' But antecedent to this, they first present themselves to the Monthly Meetings for the affairs of the church where they reside; there declaring their intentions to take one another as husband and wife, if the said meeting have nothing material to object against it. They are constantly asked the necessary questions, as in case of parents or guardians, if they have acquainted them with their intention, and having their consent, &c. The method of the meeting is to take a minute thereof, and to appoint proper persons to inquire of their conversation and clearness from all others, and whether they have discharged their duty to their parents or guardians, and make report thereof to the next Monthly Meeting; where the same parties are desired to give their attendance. In case it appears they have proceeded orderly, the meeting passes their proposal, and so records it in their meeting book. And in case the woman be a widow and hath children, due care is there taken, that provision also be made by her for the orphans before the said marriage; advising the parties concerned to appoint a convenient time and place, and to give fitting notice to their relations, and such friends and neighbours as they desire should be the witnesses of their marriage: where they take one another by the hand, and by name promising reciprocally love and fidelity after the manner before expressed. Of all which proceedings a narrative, in a way of certificate, is made, to which the said parties first set their hands, thereby making it their act and deed; and then divers of the relations, spectators, and auditors set their names as witnesses registered in the record belonging to the meeting where the marriage is solemnized. Which regular method has been, as it deserves, adjudged in courts of law a good marriage, where it has been disputed and contested for want of the accustomed formality of priest and ring, &c. Which ceremonies they have refused, not out of humour, but conscience reasonably grounded, inasmuch as no scripture example tells us, that the priest had any other part of old time than that of a witness among the rest, before whom the Jews used to take one another: and therefore this people look upon it as an imposition to advance the power and profits of the clergy. And for the use of the ring, it is enough to say, that it was an heathen and vain custom, and never in practice among the people of God, Jews, or primitive Christians. The words of the usual form, as 'With my body I thee worship,' &c. are hardly defensible. In short, they are more careful, exact, and regular than any form now used, and it is free of the inconveniences other methods are attended with: their care and checks being so many, and such as no clandestine marriages can be performed among them."[84]

Christ, The Only Head

George Fox wrote extensively. Whether that writing was in letter or tract form, it always was biblical commentary and applica-

---

[84] Penn, xvii-xviii.

tion. In several of these writings, he revealed an egalitarian understanding of the biblical word *head*. By the Spirit, he understood that only Christ could stand above, and by principle found from Genesis to Revelation, he found biblical evidence of what he believed the egalitarian activity of the Holy Spirit demonstrated. Examples of his writings express his perspectives.

Christ in Us, The Great Mystery

Fox wrote a tract in 1656 during a period (1640 and 1660) when women preachers were jailed and ruthlessly persecuted by Puritans and Anglicans. He entitled it, "The Woman Learning in Silence, or the Mystery of the Woman's Subjugation to Her Husband. As also the Daughter prophesying, wherein the Lord hath fulfilled and is fulfilling what he spake by the Prophet Joel: 'I will pour out my spirit upon all flesh,' &-c."[85] In this tract, Fox makes a careful, comprehensive statement affirming the Friends and attempting to convert the Puritans and Anglicans regarding women speaking in church. He boldly commands, "Now hear you magistrates, priests and people, which do put into prison sons and daughters for prophesying. . . ."[86]

To launch his case, Fox selected 1 Thessalonians 5:19-20, "Quench not the Spirit. . . . Despise not Prophesying." Thus, he immediately identifies both the Spirit as the locus of authority and prophecy as the Spirit-authorized, human activity. He contends that ultimate authority does not reside in the Scripture, the individual, nor the activity, but in the Spirit of Christ. The same Holy Spirit who gave Scripture now resides in the believing man or woman (Joel 2), and to quench that Spirit is to err. He asks,

---

[85] George Fox, "The Woman Learning in Silence, or the Mystery of the Woman's Subjugation to Her Husband. As also the Daughter prophesying, wherein the Lord hath fulfilled and is fulfilling what he spake by the Prophet Joel: 'I will pour out my spirit upon all flesh,' &-c.," vol 1, *Doctrinal Books*, 3 vols. *The Works of George Fox*, 8 vols. (1706; reprint, Philadelphia: Marcus T. C. Gould, 1831), 104-1109.

[86] For an interesting discussion of the literary activity of the early Quaker women, see Judith Scheffler, "Prison Writings of Early Quaker Women," *Quaker History* 74, no. 2 (Fall 1984): 25-37.

"What? came the word of God out from you, or came it unto you only."

Fox says that the believer can escape incorrect and potentially destructive interpretations of Scripture by growing in the grace and knowledge of the Lord Jesus Christ. Thus, he points the reader to Jesus Christ, the One Who is Truth, to acquire truth (Jn. 14:6). He points out that the Spirit of Christ was the One Who inspired the Old Testament prophets and the One Who was poured out on the believers in the New Testament. This latter activity of the Spirit ended the external law, instituting instead the teaching of truth by His own indwelling presence.

Fox then tackles a critical issue in this whole matter—the problem of authoritative male headship. It was at this time that the State Church was teaching the idea that the man was ordained by God to be the high priest and authoritative, spiritual head of the home. How then, could a woman possibly prophecy if she does not have direct access to the Spirit and the Spirit to her because of male spiritual headship? Fox responded to this difficulty by stating that the indwelling Christ is the Husband figure in all believers, male and the female without distinction. This liberates believers in Christ from any and all restrictions previously imposed by the law on the basis of gender. Furthermore, all believers symbolically become the Wife or Bride of Christ.

With this in place, Fox deals with Paul's writings in Ephesians 5:23-32. This is the pivotal paragraph in his tract, a fact that is reflected in his alternate title, "Mystery of the Woman's Subjection to Her Husband." He insists that Paul's intended meaning is bound up in verse 32, "This is a great mystery, but I speak concerning Christ and the church." Fox proposes that Paul's purpose is not to compare the patriarchal marriage relationship with the relationship of Christ and the Church; but rather, his purpose is to illustrate the mystery of Christ's relationship with the Church. Paul explains this great mystery, Fox says, by means of the metaphor of Christ as the male and the Church as the female. All members of the true Church enjoy this symbolic spiritual marriage relationship with Christ. The person who is not ignorant of the Lord's workings and of the voice of His prophets recorded in Scripture, understands this mystery.

At this point in his discussion, Fox links the Ephesians 5 passage with the prophetic voice of Joel 2:28:

And it shall come to pass afterward that I will pour out of My Spirit upon all flesh: and your sons and your daughters shall prophesy, and your young men shall see visions, and your old men shall dream dreams: and on My servants and on My handmaidens I will pour out in those days of My Spirit and they shall prophesy (KJV).

The reason for this linking is that the mystery of the relationship between Christ and the church is contingent upon the outpouring of the Spirit, and this outpouring is on sons and daughters alike. Fox explains that the fulfillment of this end-time event is, indeed, the key that unlocks the great mystery of Ephesians 5.

Having proposed this principle, Fox then scrutinizes the Bible from Genesis to Revelation to determine if it is, in fact, a biblical reality. By means of example after example, he establishes the existence of a pattern and thus validates his position. He concludes that the Joel 2:28 prophecy was initially fulfilled in Acts 2 when the Spirit of Christ came for the first time to abide in believers. At that point, the men and women both, without distinction, experienced the phenomenon and thereby received the mystery (Eph. 5:32), "Christ in you, the hope of glory" (Col. 1:27).

He also points to Paul's imperative, "Despise not prophesying" (1 Thess. 5:20), and the Scriptural commands, "Touch not mine anointed, and do my prophets no harm" (1 Chron. 16:22). To reject and persecute the women who prophesy, claims Fox, is to reject the biblical mandate. Those who despise prophecy and imprison the prophets and prophetesses show by such action that they are outside the apostles' doctrine, are "strangers to the spirit the scriptures were given forth from," and "are ignorant of the church the apostles speak of." True church order facilitates the activity of the Spirit through both sons and daughters. Fox concludes, "You that forbid a woman to speak that hath the spirit of the Lord, you forbid scripture." In that Paul endorses women prophesying and ministering according to the Spirit, he charges that those who hinder them are disobedient to the apostles' doctrine.

Fox speaks with intensity, building upon the notion of the lunacy of imprisoning women in whom Christ dwells and through whom Christ acts. He concludes with the probability of "punishment prepared for the devil and his angels" awaiting those professors of religion who imprison these women (Mt. 25:31-46). Their treatment of these women, in reality, is their treatment of Christ Who dwells in them by His Spirit. In addition, Fox argues that the Spirit of Christ who indwells men is the same Spirit of Christ who indwells women. Christ "is one in all, and [is] not divided." "Who is it," he demands, "that dare stop Christ's mouth?" "Who is it that dare limit the holy one of Israel?" That person is a reprobate who does not acknowledge that the same One who created the world now reigns, rules, and speaks in the female as well as the male. That person is a reprobate who would, like the Pharisees, "have scripture, but would not have Christ to reign," who profess words but do not show forth the fruit of true religion.

From his vast knowledge of the Bible, then, Fox leaves no stone unturned in affirming the equality of men and women in Christ. He points to the significance of the outpouring of the Spirit on all flesh, the indwelling Holy Spirit, the authority of the Spirit, the Spirit as Christ within, the pattern of Scripture, the egalitarian attitudes and actions of Jesus toward women, the precedent of equality set by Paul. With such overwhelming evidence of equality, he has no problem with the use of symbolism in understanding Ephesians 5:22-24, which when studied in isolation without regard for the other factors, might be misconstrued to oppress women. Thus, in his dealing with female subjugation (Eph. 5:23) and female silence (1 Cor. 14), Fox is unwilling to succumb to cultural mores and prevailing religious codes. He reaches beyond both.

Christ the Only Spiritual and Holy Head[87]

During the summer, 1673, Fox records having had many wonderful meetings. In addition to the ongoing persecution from the state church, however, serious new opposition began "from some who had set themselves against women's meetings."[88] Once again, Fox found it necessary to justify the equality and gospel activity of women. This time, he approaches the issues from the perspective of the Headship of Christ.

The truly revolutionary nature of this treatise is obvious only when it is contrasted against the backdrop of intense power struggles that pervaded the political and religious spheres at the time. In these struggles, "headship" was defined as "rulership." It was considered a position of ultimate power and authority. The Pope was the "Head" of the Roman Catholic Church. The King of England reigned as "Supreme Head" of the Church of England, according to the Supremacy Act of 1534. Likewise, each man was supreme "head" of the family unit. With this in mind, the title of this treatise takes on greater significance: "Concerning Christ the Spiritual and Holy Head of his Holy Church."

The revolutionary nature of this treatise is also clear when it is seen in the light of prevailing theological perspectives on woman-

---

[87] George Fox, "Concerning Christ the Spiritual and Holy Head over his Holy Church, and his Church's steadfastness, and confidence, and unity and oneness in him," vol. 2, *Doctrinal Books*, 3 vols., *The Works of George Fox*, 8 vols. (1706; reprint, New York: AMS Press, 1975), 291-234.

[88] Fox, *Autobiography*, edited by Jones, 536-537.

hood. Fox recommended to the Friends, for the benefit and advantage of the Church of Christ, that faithful women be respected as equal human beings, filled with the same Spirit of Christ as the men, and therefore, that they be facilitated in ministry. The following statement is, indeed, remarkable given the cultural climate in which Fox formulated his ideas. He writes,

> Faithful women, who were called to the belief of the Truth, being made partakers of the same precious faith, and heirs of the same everlasting gospel of life and salvation with the men, might in like manner come into the possession and practice of the gospel order, and therein be helpmeets unto the men in the restoration, in the service of Truth, in the affairs of the Church, as they are outwardly in civil, or temporal things; that so all the family of God, women as well as men, might know, possess, perform, and discharge their offices and services in the house of God, whereby the poor might be better taken care of, the younger instructed, informed, and taught in the way of God; the loose and disorderly reproved and admonished in the fear of the Lord; the clearness of persons proposing marriage more closely and strictly inquired into in the wisdom of God; and all the members of the spiritual body, the Church, might watch over and be helpful to each other in love.[89]

Such counter-cultural views so forcefully stated, so enthusiastically pursued, and so powerfully instituted aroused much animosity. At this time, through an enthusiastic woman in Worcester who wanted time off from her employment as a domestic to attend Fox's meeting, the local authorities learned of his visit to their town. The local justice, accompanied by an Anglican priest, arrested him "although he had nothing to lay to our charge."[90]

---

[89] Fox, *Autobiography*, edited by Jones, 537.
[90] Fox, *Autobiography*, 540.

Subsequently, Fox spent over a year in the Worcester jail, and following his release, physically weakened, he spent most of the next fourteen years at Swarthmoor and Kingston, near London, writing. It was during this period that he composed the treatise "Concerning Christ the Spiritual and Holy Head . . .," dated the fifth day of the tenth month, 1676.[91]

Fox appeals to Scripture to uphold the sole Headship of Christ over his Church individually and corporately. Refusing to accept the legitimacy of priests, church, and sacraments as legitimate mediators—a foundation he has already laid and reiterated on many other occasions—he makes this treatise a positive, biblical statement of Christ as the sole Head of the church. That Headship is mediated only by the Light of Christ which gives God direct, inner access to every person, and conversely. which gives each person direct and equal access to God. This gives men and women the potential to embrace the saving work of Christ when they hear the gospel. When any person turns to the Light within, the Holy Spirit reciprocates by taking up residence in the believer, mediating the life and lordship of Christ, the Head.

Authority is the central issue in this treatise. From the first statement, Fox leaves no doubt as to where he places the locus of that authority. Referring to Christ's prayer in John 17, he writes, "Christ prayed for his church. . . ." It was <u>His</u> Church, not the pope's Church, nor the king's Church, nor the man's Church.

Of utmost importance in understanding Fox's interpretation of Scripture, and in this case, his interpretation of "headship," is the defining role of the "mystery" of "Christ in you." That each believer has this direct access to God is critical in Fox's interpretive process. In his opinion, no other mediator can legitimately intervene between the believer and God.

---

[91] Fox, *Autobiography*, 544-45; *Doctrinal Books*, vol. 2, 341.

So being built in him, in whom all the building fitly framed together, groweth up a holy temple in the Lord, in whom you also are built together, [mark, are,] for a habitation of God through the spirit.

So all such as know what is the fellowship of the mystery from the beginning of the world, that hath been hid in God, who created all things by Jesus Christ; to him be glory in the church through Jesus Christ, throughout all ages, world without end.[92]

Fox speaks again of the mystery of the spiritual relationship between the members of His Body and Christ's own position as Head. In doing so, he reiterates his exegesis of Ephesians 5:23 explicated in "Women Learning in Silence." Christ is the Husband figure and the believers, the Wife figure. "Christ is the head of the church, and Saviour of the body; . . . and we are many members, yet one body, and of his flesh and his bone." Fox says, Paul "speaks figuratively, 'for this cause shall a man (said he,) forsake father and mother and cleave unto his wife, this is a great mystery, but I speak concerning Christ and his church.[93]

Fox again employs the symbolism of Christ as the Husband and the members, as one, his Wife, in interpreting Christ's Headship in Hebrews 1.

For God who hath spoken to us, to wit, his church, by his Son, who was the speaker to Adam and Eve in paradise, and was the speaker by his Son to the church in the primitive times, is the speaker to his church now.

But since the apostles' days, that the whole world has worshipped the beast, and drank the whore's cup, they have gone from this speaker; but now his church is come and

---

[92] Fox, "Concerning Christ the Spiritual and Holy Head," vol. 2, *Doctrinal Books*, 3 vols., 294.

[93] Fox, vol. 2, *Doctrinal Books*, 295.

coming out of the wilderness, which is the bride, the wife of Christ the Lamb.

And so Christ is the speaker again unto his church, and who should speak unto his wife, his church, but himself? being members of his body, of his flesh, and of his bone, and they are in him, and he in them, according to his promise and prayer.[94]

Fox seeks biblical patterns to validate His understanding of individual passages. He therefore examines the Old Testament for affirmation of Christ's Headship, and he is persuaded that the Old Testament reveals the sole headship of the One Who would come, Christ. In investigating the Gospels, Fox is satisfied that they declare Christ's saving work and position as Head of His Church. Those who believe and are sealed with the Spirit of Promise "are the living members of the living head, Christ Jesus, who is the head of the church." Finally, he looks for the sole "Headship of Christ" rubric in Acts, the Epistles, and Revelation. He also looks for the unity of the members of the body with each other and with the Head. He summarizes this lengthy section, saying,

So Christ is the head of his church, and he walks in his church, and he feeds his church, as he is a shepherd; and he opens to his church, as he is a prophet; and oversees his church, as he is a bishop; and sanctifies and offers up his church, as he is a priest; and he commands his church, as he is a captain and commander, he commands and leads his church; and as he is a heavenly counsellor, he counsels his church; and purifies his church, as he is a purifier; and baptizeth his church, as he is a baptizer; and he is a Mediator, he makes their peace betwixt them and God, and gives them

---

[94] Fox, vol. 2, *Doctrinal Books*, 300.

one faith, who is the author and finisher of it, by which he rules in their hearts.[95]

Fox concludes his treatise with an evangelistic appeal. Switching to the second person pronoun, he extends to his readers a personal challenge to walk in obedience to the light and spirit, so to experience new life, salvation, and unity

For Fox, biblical headship is an attribute solely of Christ. He refuses to take his cues for interpretation from the prevailing cultural or religious climate. To circumvent the weight of cultural and religious factors, he employs a number of interpretive techniques including recognition of the authority of Christ, use of symbolism, identification of the biblical pattern, articulation of the sameness of Christ, and the recognition of authority of the Holy Spirit over the law, over culture, and over prevailing patriarchal theology.[96]

The First Book on Equality for Women

Margaret Fell's writings contributed to her prominence and helped imprint her name in a lasting way on the corridors of time. She was, for example, the first Quaker leader to write to the Jewish leader, Menassah Ben Israel, and to the other Jews of Holland at a time when Jewish reentry into England was a hotly debated issue in the Cromwellian government.[97] In 1666, Fell published a

---

[95] Fox, vol. 2, *Doctrinal Books*, 303.

[96] See also the following two examples. (1) George Fox, "An encouragement to all the faithful women's meetings in the world, who assemble together in the fear of God, for the service of the truth. Wherein they may see how the holy men encouraged the holy women, both in the time of the law, and in the time of the gospel; though selfish and unholy men may seek to discourage them. But go on in the name and power of Christ, and prosper, CCCXX. (1676)," vol. 2, *A Collection of Many Select and Christian Epistles, Letters and Testimonies . . .*, 2 vols., *The Works of George Fox*, 8 vols. (1706; reprint, New York: AMS Press, 1975), 94-116. Fox wrote this lengthy epistle at Marchgrainge on the sixteenth day of the ninth month, 1676. (2) George Fox, "God made them in his image of righteousness and holiness, and how Christ restores man up into his image again, and how that male and female are all one in him, and of the increase of Christ's government and peace there is no end," vol. 3, *Doctrinal Books*, 3 vols., *The Works of George Fox*, 8 vols. (1706; reprint, New York: AMS Press, 1975), 356-359. Fox appears to have written this tract at the home of one of Margaret Fell's daughters at Kingston upon Thames near London, probably on or about the seventh day of the tenth month, 1687. Written, then, when Fox was sixty-three years old and within about three years of his death, this treatise represents the reflections of the mature Fox. See Henry J. Cadbury, "George Fox's Later Life," *The Journal of George Fox*, ed. John L. Nickalls (Cambridge: Cambridge University Press, 1952), 749.

[97] Kunze, 5-7.

treatise called *Women's Speaking Justified*.[98] Written while she served a four-year stint in Lancaster prison (1665-8), this small book has been esteemed as a milestone in women's history, being the first book of its kind written by a woman since the Reformation.[99] It was the first apology written by a Quaker woman defending the right of women to speak publicly, prophesy, teach, or preach.[100]

Fell's argument takes the form of a Bible study in which she profiles twenty-four women, thereby demonstrating the existence of a biblical model that permits women to speak in church. In addition, she asserts that the inherent authority of both the Gospel and the indwelling Holy Spirit overrules any purported Old Testament gender prohibitions of the law or alleged New Testament gender prohibitions presented by Paul. She also argues that both men and women who respond to the call of the Holy Spirit are the true ministers of Christ.

Fell's purpose in writing this treatise was to refute the objections raised by "clergy, ministers, and others," to women speaking in the church. These objections are based on 1 Cor. 14:34-35 and 1 Tim. 2:11-12. Fell argues that Paul's true intent in these passages was not a general banning of women speaking, and that his true intention of a specific restriction becomes clear when the reader is willing to allow the context to contribute to the meaning.

---

[98] Margaret Fell, "Women's Speaking Justified, Proved, and Allowed of by the Scriptures, All such as speak by the Spirit and Power of the Lord Jesus. And how Women were the first that Preached the Tidings of the Resurrection of Jesus, and were sent by Christ's own Command, before he Ascended to the Father, John 20:17," *A Brief Collection of Remarkable Passages and Occurrences Relating to the Birth, Education, Life, Conversion, Travels, Services, and Deep Sufferings of the Ancient, Eminent, and Faithful Servant of the Lord, Margaret Fell; But by her Second Marriage, Margaret Fox Together With Sundry of her Epistles, Books, and Christian Testimonies to Friends and Others; and also to those in Supreme Authority, in the several late Revolutions of Government* (London: J. Sowle, 1710), 331-350.

[99] Ross, 200.

[100] Kunze, 20; Abbreviated versions of *Women's Speaking Justified* are included in most source books of religious sectarianism. See Joyce L. Irwin, *Womanhood in Radical Protestantism, 1525-1675* (New York: Edwin Mellen Press, 1979), 179-88. Early tracts written by Quakers in defense of women preaching include Richard Farnsworth, *A Woman Forbidden to Speak* (1655); George Keith, *The Woman Preacher of Samaria* (1674); Anne Whitehead and Mary Elson, *An Epistle of True Love, Unity and Order* (1680); see also William Mather, an erstwhile Quaker who wrote against women's meetings and ministry, *A Novelty, or Government of Women* (1694?). For some further comment, see Elaine Hobby, *Virtue of Necessity; English Women's Writings* (Ann Arbor: University of Michigan Press, 1989), 43, 45; David Latt, ed. *'Women's Speaking Justified'* (Margaret Fell 1667), *Epistle from the Women's Yearly Meeting at York* (1688), *A Warning to All Friends* (Mary Waite, 1688), Los Angeles, 1979.

To support her argument, Fell presents her understanding of the general principle of Scripture concerning women which she believes occurs in the Creation/Fall/Redemption motif. She points out that in creation, God made no distinction in the impartation of His image to male and female. In the fall, both Adam and Eve sinned; however, Adam blamed Eve, while Eve, told God the truth. Genesis 3 indicates that enmity would henceforth exist between the serpent and the woman, and between the serpent's seed and the woman's Seed (Gen. 3). Those who speak against woman, Fell alleges, are speaking out of the enmity and envy of the serpent's seed. Through His Son, born of a woman, God fulfilled His promise that the Seed of the woman would bruise the head of the serpent (Gal. 4:4-5). Thus, woman, an instrument of the devil in the fall became an instrument of God in redemption.

Fell maintains that those who denounce and prohibit woman's voice on the basis of gender, are speaking against the Spirit of the Lord in that woman. They are speaking against Christ and His church. They are, in fact, of the seed of the Serpent, "wherein lodgeth Enmity."

Fell states that the Church of Christ is represented figuratively in Scripture as a woman (Is. 54; Jer. 31:22; Ps. 45; Song of Sol. 1:8; 5:9; Rev. 12). This fact must be brought to bear in interpretation. Also it is a fact that illustrates God's esteem of women.

Fell declares that the opposition to women speaking comes from the bottomless pit and from the spirit of darkness and apostasy that had been prevailing in the church for twelve hundreds years. During this period of apostate rule, the false church figuratively represented in Scripture by the woman of Rev. 13, has spoken and ursurped authority over Christ in His true church, the Bride of Christ, the Lamb's Wife. Fell proclaims the rise of the true church. She is the free Woman, shining throughout the whole earth and bringing perfect redemption, unity, and liberty to her seed. The apostate church is as the bond-woman who brings only strife and bondage to her offspring. The seed of the true church are born of the Spirit; the seed of the apostate church, of the flesh.

Christ in the male and in the female is one and the same. The true church, therefore, consists of males and females who are indwelt by the same Christ. Figuratively speaking, this Church is the Wife of Christ, and He is Her Husband. This principle lifts any possible, prior restriction from believing women.

Even though the law would seem to forbid women from speaking, women who have come to Christ, who are led by the Spirit of God, are free from the law. Christ in the male and in the female is one, and Christ chooses to express himself through both male and female without distinction.

Fell reaches to the apocryphal writings for additional support. The reason for this is unclear, unless it is a deliberate challenge to the authority of the official church and its role related to canonical literature. Whatever her reason, Fell notes that the Book of Judith records the noble words and deeds of a woman. Perhaps in Judith, Fell finds one with whom she identifies. Fell, like Judith, spoke to the elders of her nation who commended her and requested that she pray for them. The political elders of England and Israel, contrary to the blind priests of Fell's day, were willing to give at least some degree of respect to a women.

Jezebel, the woman figuratively representing the false church, the great whore, along with the unlearned women and busybodies, are forbidden to speak by the true church of which Christ is the Head. On the other hand, the true church is the Wife and Christ is her Husband. In this sense, Christ is the Husband of both male and female believers who constitute the true church. This true church correctly forbids the speaking of the Jezebel women and busybodies; however, she encourages her sons and daughters to prophesy and women to labour in the Gospel. Continuing to project Christ as Husband, Fell notes that the only Husband from whom a widow can learn is Christ the Husband. Also, she asserts that Christ was the Husband of Philip's four prophesying daughters. Contrariwise, Jezebel, the whore, and the tattlers are not permitted to speak, for they are not the Wife of Christ. Those who will not learn of Christ and who are out of the Spirit of Christ, are ignorant of the Scriptures and forbid women from speaking.

In Fell's economy, the Pope is the Head of the false Church and the false Church is the Pope's wife. Both the Pope and the false Church are called "Woman" in Rev. 17. This Woman would usurp authority over the Man Christ Jesus and his Wife, the True Church. Christ is the Head of the true Church, and in it, daughters prophesy. Christ is the Head of the male and the female who together constitute his true Church, and both prophesy. Furthermore, the Church is called a royal priesthood; therefore, women and men are both priests and are therefore both responsible to offer priestly sacrifices.

In Rev. 22:17, the Spirit and the Bride appear to be one, saying, "Come." The Bride is the Church; the Church consists of both men and women; therefore, the Bride consists of both. The false Church attempts to silence the Bride, but cannot because the Bridegroom, Christ, is with the Bride and He opens her mouth and gives victory.

Biblical Interpretation

Fox's approach to understanding God's Written Word is important. He held the Bible in highest regard and approached it prayerfully. But what role did the Spirit, the Word itself, reason, and tradition play in his interepretation of what he read?

1. The Holy Spirit. Fox's starting point in biblical interpretation is the ability of the indwelling Spirit of Christ to reveal God's truth to the reader. The Holy Spirit was that aspect of Himself which

God had deposited in humanity. It was the vital link between God and humanity. The Spirit was, therefore, the only valid Mediator between God and a human being in the various aspects of life, including the interpretation of Scripture. Fox attributed to the Spirit of Christ the position of ultimate authority. The Spirit was not subject to the law, culture, or gender; rather, the Spirit was the One by whom the law had come. The Spirit was the One by whom all Scripture had been given. The Spirit was the One by whom prophetic activity would come upon both sons and daughters.

2. The Holy Scriptures. Fox's belief in the ultimate authority of Christ expressed in the substance of the indwelling Spirit, did not signify disrespect for the authority of Scripture. In fact, from childhood, George Fox had held the Bible in high esteem. Yet the Written Word itself had not met the deepest need of his heart for God. On the other hand, the Written Word did provide authoritative parameters for Fox in his quest for a meaningful, experiential relationship with God. He accepted, for example, the creation/fall/redemption motif revealed in Scripture as the historical context for God's dealing with humanity. He also accepted both Old and New Testaments as authoritative receptacles for the patterns by which God expected humanity to live. Fox sought these paradigms as a chief means of testing the inner leadings and revelations arising in the inner person. He also employed biblical patterns in seeking the true meaning of difficult passages that seemed to contradict the Spirit (e.g. 1 Tim. 2:11-12; 1 Cor. 14:34-35; and Eph. 5:22-24).

3. Human Reason. The early Post-Reformation period in which Fox lived encouraged the use of reason. The power of both reason and skepticism flourished, and propositions that could not be proved by sense experience were subject to criticism.[101] Fox seems com-

---

[101] A. Berkeley Mickelsen, *Interpreting the Bible* (1963; reprint, Grand Rapids: Eerdmans, 1991), 41-43.

fortable with this framework in which "reason, systems, and abstract formulations ruled in theology." But as Berkeley Mickelsen explains, "Theology often controlled exegesis." Fox's key theological principle of the Inner Light seems to fit in this general milieu.

The role of reason enabled Fox to develop his Spirit christology. Christ was "God with us" (i. e., Emmanuel), the One in whom all authority dwelt. This One was now the Risen Christ, the One Fox could link him with the eschatological mystery of "Christ in you, the hope of glory" (Col. 1:27). He could talk about the same Christ being one, undivided, and the same in men and women.

According to Fox, the best means of avoiding erroneous interpretation, that is, interpretation which does not coincide with the original intent of the passage, was to grow in grace and the experiential knowledge of the Lord Jesus Christ Who Himself is Truth. Examples from the life of Jesus recorded in the Gospels also served as authoritative lenses through which to look at other Scriptures, and were expected to be incorporated into the process of reasoning toward Truth.

4. Church Tradition. In his interpretations, Fox does not lean on the writings of church fathers, the determinations of the church councils, or the definitions of sacred creeds. He obviously is of the opinion that the ruling church is the false church of Revelation. He sees the move to a pure and spiritual relationship with God of thousands in his day as the true Church coming out of the wilderness.

Biblical Values Threaten Church and Precipitate Persecution

The impact of the Friends' lifestyle was signficant and far-reaching. The idea that God would take up residence in each person meant that each person could gain a new sense of his or her worth in the sight of God. Since God was no respecter of persons and since the same Christ dwelt in each one, believers were to treat all human beings with equal dignity and respect. The words of Jesus in Matthew 25:40 came alive, "I say to you, inasmuch as you have done it to one of the least of these My brethren, you did it to Me." This had revolutionary social implications.

Further, the inner connection with God through the indwelling Spirit of Christ shifted the locus of authority from external religious symbols to direct, internal relationship with God. This threatened the authority of the institutional church which had depended on outward symbols such as priesthood, clerical robes, church buildings, and the sacraments to control the masses. Since religion was the business of the state, this defiance of the law by the Friends resulted in severe persecution.

Thousands of Quakers, men and women alike, went forth motivated by evangelistic zeal in spite of severe persecution. In New England, persecution from the Puritans reached savage heights. Much of this arose because of the Quaker threat to Puritan patriarchal structures and a theocracy that combined the authority of church and state.[102] The possibility of women preachers was most alarming, and consequently, anti-Quaker propaganda published in Boston linked Quakerism with witchcraft, the common element being the empowerment of women.

On July 11, 1656, Mary Fisher and Ann Austin sailed into Boston harbor. The first Quakers to arrive in the Massachusetts Bay Colony, they had come from England on a preaching mission. They were immediately denounced as heretics and unsubmissive women, and the deputy governor, Richard Bellingham, "ordered that they not be allowed to land until they were stripped naked, searched for signs of witchcraft, and all their tracts confiscated." They were then isolated for five weeks in prison and extradited.[103]

---

[102] Bacon, 28; Gadt, 147, gives a full exposition on this subject in Ch. 3, "Attitudes Toward Women in the New World: The Opposites of Quaker and Puritan."

[103] Bacon, 24-25.

This was only the beginning of the savage persecution inflicted on Quaker men and women in New England.

Quaker women were also hung publicly by Puritans in Boston, convicted of insubordination and possible witchcraft. When Mary Dyer visited Boston in 1659 to comfort imprisoned Quakers, she was sentenced to death and, to the beating of a drum, was led through the streets to the gallows. Already bound and noosed for execution, she was suddenly released. In the spring of 1660, however, feeling she could not accept this stay of execution, she returned to Boston, where, this time, the Puritan authorities sentenced and hanged her. Her statue now stands on the grounds of the Boston State House as a symbol of freedom of conscience.[104]

Quakers were also subjected to public whippings and beatings. In 1653, for example, Mary Fisher and Elizabeth Williams confronted young theologians at Cambridge about their beliefs. When taunted by the scholars, the women denounced Cambridge as a "Cage of Unclean Birds," whereupon the mayor of Cambridge had the women whipped until the blood ran down their backs.[105]

The Good Fruit of an Egalitarian Perspective

Perhaps the best measure of a method of biblical interpretation is the fruit it produces. Is it biblical fruit? Does it look like the fruit of the Spirit (Gal. 5:22-23)? Does it coincide with the fruit of Jesus' life? Does it last? A brief survey of the fruit in the lives of the early Friends and the later Friends would help to answer these questions.

The "first business in their view, after the example of the primitive saints, was the exercise of charity, to supply the necessities of the poor. . . . Wherefore collections were early and liberally made for that and divers other services in the church. . . ."[106]

---

[104] Bacon, 24-26.
[105] Bacon, 18.
[106] Penn, xxv.

"They were also very careful, that every one that belonged to them answered their profession in their behaviour among men upon all occasions; that they lived peaceably, and were in all things good examples."[107]

In spite of persecution, the Quakers flourished in America especially during the formative colonial period. Their legacy remains strong in a number of areas. They were trailblazers, for example, in the abolition movement, prison reform, Indian affairs, government policy, co-education, and women's rights.[108]

The Abolition Movement. Quakers were champions of abolition. Sixty years before the Emancipation Proclamation, there was not one Quaker slave-holder in America. They were the first to make a direct assault against slavery, and in the mid-nineteenth century conducted the underground railroad, providing for the safe conduct of escaped and freed slaves to the Canadian border.[109].

In 1657, Fox wrote an important epistle entitled, "To Friends beyond sea, that have Blacks and Indian Slaves."

"Dear friends,—I was moved to write these things to you in all those plantations. God, that made the world, and all things therein, giveth life and breath to all, and they all have their life and moving, and their being in him, he is the God of the spirits of all flesh, and is no respect of persons; but 'whosoever feareth him and worketh righteousness, is accepted of him.' And he hath made all nations one blood to dwell upon the face of the earth, and his eyes are over all the works of his hands, and seeth every thing that is done under the whole heavens; and the 'earth is the Lord's and the fullness thereof.' And he causeth the rain to fall upon the just and upon the unjust, and also he causeth the sun to shine

---

[107] Penn, xxv.

[108] Bacon, 1. According to Bacon, It has been estimated that Quaker women compromised thirty percent of the pioneers in prison reform, forty percent of women abolitionists, and fifteen percent of suffragists born before 1830.

[109] Trueblood, 4.

upon the just and the unjust; and he commands to 'love all men,' for Christ loved all, so that he 'died for sinners.' And this is God's love to the world, in giving his son into the world; 'that whosoever believeth in him should not perish.' And he doth 'enlighten every man that cometh into the world,' that they might believe in the son. And the gospel is preached to every creature under heaven, which is the power that giveth liberty and freedom, and is glad tidings to every captivated creature under the whole heavens. And the word of God is in the heart and mouth, to obey and do it, and not for them to ascend or descend for it; and this is the word of faith which was and is preached. For Christ is given for a covenant to the people, and a light to the Gentiles, and to enlighten them, who is the glory of Israel, and God's 'salvation to the ends of the earth.' And so ye are to have the mind of Christ, and to be merciful, as your heavenly Father is merciful."[110]

Friends in Germantown, Pennsylvania, had spoken out against slavery as early as 1688, and in various American Quaker communities, the issue of slavery had been debated in the early 1700s. By the 1770s and 1780s, the yearly meetings began to make it unacceptable for any Quaker to own slaves.[111] As early as 1775, Quakers lobbied against slavery in state governments and in the new American Congress.[112] When the Northwest Territory opened in 1787 as a land forever free from slavery, many Quakers moved to that area.[113]

Quaker women were actively involved in abolition. In 1788, Sarah Harrison, a traveling Quaker minister, "prayed with the owners of some fifty slaves until they were persuaded to set them

---

[110] George Fox, "To Friends beyond sea, that have Blacks and Indian Slaves," *Epistles*, vol. 7, *Works*, 8 vols., 144-145.

[111] Bacon, 78.

[112] Bacon, 77-79.

[113] Bacon, 86.

free."[114] Through the efforts of Rebecca Jones, another traveling minister and educator, as early as 1796, Quakers of Northern New York State began accepting blacks as members of their societies.[115] Probably the most famous Quaker abolitionists were in the 1830s were the Grimke sisters. Sarah Grimke, in commenting on equality for women, writes,

> I ask no favors of my sex. I surrender not our claim to equality. All I ask of our brethren is that they will take their feet from off our necks, and permit us to stand upright on the ground which God has designed for us to occupy.[116]

Prison Reform. Quaker women had been active in prison reform ever since 1655 when Elizabeth Hooten wrote a letter to the English King protesting prison conditions. Elizabeth Guerney Fry (1780-1845),[117] another English Quaker preacher, is commonly acknowledged as the founder of prison reform.[118] Trueblood writes, "Her Quaker conscience made her feel the sufferings of prisoners." He adds, "The essence of Mrs. Fry's approach was to treat the prisoners as persons, because she could so easily imagine herself in their place.[119]

Quakers in America also initiated important steps in prison reform. In 1787, for example, Quakers in Philadelphia organized the Society for Alleviating the Miseries of the Public Prisons. Their first effort was "to convert the Walnut Street prison into a penitentiary, a place where prisoners had the opportunity to meditate upon their sins and repent, while being given moral instruction by a group of friendly visitors."[120]

---

[114] Bacon, 77-79.

[115] William J Allinson, comp., *Memorials of Rebecca Jones* (Philadelphia: Longstreth, 1849) quoted by Bacon, 85.

[116] Sarah Grimke, "Letters on the Equality of the Sexes and the Condition of Women," quoted by Gerda Lerner, *The Grimke Sisters From South Carolina: Pioneers for Woman's Rights and Abolition* (New York: Schocken Books, 1971), 192.

[117] See Janet Whitney, *Elizabeth Fry, Quaker Heroine* (Boston: Little, Brown, and Company, 1936). Quoted by Bacon, 138-144.

[118] Bacon, 35.

[119] Trueblood, 177.

[120] Bacon, 79.

Indian Affairs. In America, Quakers were trusted by the Indians. Knowing the Pennsylvania Quakers were their friends, they asked them to represent their interests when they made treaties with the new American government. In 1794, four Quakers went to Canandaigua, New York, to protect the interests of the Six Nations in a treaty signing with the United States. Various yearly committees established centers where farming and other skills were taught to Indians on reservations. In the nineteenth century, women began to serve on some of the Indian committees."[121]

Government Policy. William Penn (1644-1718), the most noted of Quaker political reformers, played a key role in American colonization. In 1682, he and eleven other Quakers bought northern New Jersey, and later he received the grant of Pennsylvania from the British Crown. Elton Trueblood says," Penn exerted an undoubted influence on the entire American development by means of his suggestions, presented to the Royal Commission in 1697, that there be a union of the colonies." It seems he helped prepare the plan for the United States Senate a hundred years in advance by proposing "that two representatives be elected from each colony in a 'congress.'"[122]

Co-education. George Fox had been interested in the education of both boys and girls and had recommended the founding of a school in Shacklewell, England, "for instructing girls and young maidens in whatsoever things are civil and useful in the creation." Fox also wrote a primer for the instruction of Quaker children of either sex.[123] George Fox insisted on equal education for both boys and girls.[124]

In 1825, Jonathan Dymond, a Quaker moralist and essayist, wrote:

---

[121] Fox, *Works*, vol. 7, 144-145. See Bacon, 79-80;144-146.
[122] Trueblood, 57-58; Bacon, 146-150.
[123] Bacon, 59.
[124] See Bacon, 81-85.

There does not appear any reason why the education of women should differ in its essentials from that of men. The education which is good for human nature is good for them. They are part--and they ought to be in a much greater degree that they are, a part--of the effective contributors of the welfare and intelligence of the human family.

He went on to say that qualities such as intelligence, sound sense, considerateness, and discretion generally characterized Quaker women in a degree "not found in any other class of women as a class."[125] Quakers helped pioneer higher educational opportunities for women in the fields of education, science, and the professions.[126]

The Good Fruit Remains

From humble beginnings in a culture hostile to women—especially to women speaking in public and leading—Quaker women developed confidence and leadership skills.[127] Much credit must go to George Fox and Margaret Fell for promoting an approach to biblical interpretation which made this possible. What they started and nurtured created an egalitarian trend still apparent in contemporary American culture. The experience Quaker women had accumulated in public speaking and conducting business in public prepared them for leadership roles when the time was ripe for a women's rights movement to emerge.

Four movements, the Suffrage Movement, early Pentecostalism, and women's rights among Evangelicals, and the Vineyard Fellowship of Churches have a direct Quaker heritage. These four movements, in varying degrees, reflect the dynamic egalitarianism initiated by George Fox and Margaret Fell. Indeed, the trend to-

---

[125] Jonathan Dymond, *Essays on the Principles of Morality* (New York: Collins and Brother, 1825), 251-52.
[126] Bacon, 151-165.
[127] Bacon, 2.

ward an egalitarian lifestyle still apparent three hundred and fifty years later, originated in the Friends' devotion to the Lord Jesus Christ, to the indwelling Spirit of Christ, and to their interpretation of the authoritative Written Word.

Suffrage Movement.[128] Quaker women led the seventy year-long struggle that gave American women the right to vote. This struggle gained corporate identity at Seneca Falls, New York on July 13, 1848, through the leadership efforts of four Quaker women Lucretia Coffin Mott, Martha Coffin Wright, Jane Hunt, Mary Ann McClintock, and a Quaker sympathizer, Elizabeth Cady Stanton.[129] Formulated by these Quaker women, the Declaration of Women's Rights was ratified by one hundred delegates. It should be noted that this movement was born in the hearts of Spirit-oriented, Bible-believing women. These women faced persecution, incarceration, suffering, and defamation not unlike that of their seventeenth-century Quaker forerunners.[130]

Early Pentecostalism.[131] An important religious forum for egalitarianism was the early Pentecostal Revival (1901-1907).[132] The initial outpouring occurred at the 1900 Watchnight Service of Bethel Bible School in Topeka, Kansas, a Bible school operated by Charles Parham, Sarah Thistlethwaite-Parham, and Lillian Thistlethwaite. Although Bethel is commonly considered a Holiness institution, it should be remembered that the Thistlethwaite sisters were Friends, and that Parham himself had spent many hours modifying his Methodist-Holiness theology in dialogue with his wife's Quaker grandfather, David Baker, in Tonganoxie, Kansas. While the Parham-Thistlethwaite leadership prevailed (1900-1907), egalitarianism and a Quaker dignity characterized the Re-

---

[128] This will be dealt with in greater detail in a later chapter.

[129] Bacon, 1, 114.

[130] Doris Stevens, *Jailed for Freedom: American Women Win the Vote*, Carol O'Hare, ed. (Troutdale, OR: NewSage press, 1996).

[131] This will be dealt with in greater detail in a later chapter.

[132] Sarah Parham, *The Life of Charles Fox Parham* (Baxter Springs: Sarah Parham, 1930), 11-29.

vival.[133] This was the case in the Tri-State area of Kansas-Oklahoma-Missouri, in South Texas, in Zion City, Illinois, and from these regional revivals thousands of men and women carried the message around the world. As the revival spread beyond the Parham-Thistlethwaite influence, especially at Azusa Street, among the Southern Holiness groups, and among Baptistic and Reformed people, however, hierarchicalism pushed out egalitarianism, and other Quaker characteristics gave way to cultural and denominational practices.[134]

Conservative Evangelical Feminist Movement. A third movement with a Quaker connection is the Evangelical feminist movement. Perhaps the most effective group is Christians for Biblical Equality, begun in the 1980s among conservative Evangelicals.[135] Chief catalyst and organizer of C.B.E. is Catherine Clark Kroeger. Dr. Kroeger did her undergraduate studies at Bryn Mawr College, a prestigious Quaker women's school.[136] C.B.E. boasts a strong contingent of egalitarian scholars,[137] and is gaining influence through local groups, conventions, and publications including a periodical, *The Priscilla Papers,* currently edited by Presbyterian, Gretchen Gaebelein Hull. *The Priscilla Papers* was the name of the publication of women belonging to the evangelical wing of Quakerism. Having developed great interest in Quaker women's history, they formed a Task Force on Women and helped expose modern Friends to their egalitarian heritage.

Vineyard Ministries and the Third Wave Movement. A Spirit-oriented, Biblically-based movement that has helped to facilitate

---

[133] Parham, 51-68 and 161-170 provide evidence of this.

[134] Susan Hyatt, *Your Sons and Your Daughters* (Dallas: Hyatt Int'l Ministries, 1994). Hyatt traces the development of this phenomenon.

[135] Bacon, 227-28.

[136] In 1885 a group of Gurneyite Quakers established Bryn Mawr College for women a few miles from another famous Quaker school, Haverford College (est. 1833), in Haverford, Pennsylvania. Bacon, 98.

[137] A few of these include the following: Millard Erickson, W. Ward Gasque, Vernon Grounds, Roberta Hestenes, Rufus Jones, Roger Nicole, Lewis Smedes, Timothy Weber, James R. Beck, Alvera Johnson Mickelsen, Gilbert Bilezikian, and Stanley N. Grundy. See brochure entitled "Christians for Biblical Equality," 380 Lafayette Rd. S., Suite 122, St. Paul, MN 55107-1216. See also flyer entitled "Men, Women and Biblical Equality," from the same C.B.E. source.

the current revival is Vineyard Ministries International. Founded by John Wimber (1934-1997), this movement spread quickly among conservative evangelicals who were hungry for intimacy with God and for the activity of the Spirit in evangelism. Wimber grew up in a non-Christian environment but had a dramatic conversion in 1963. He entered full-time ministry, graduated from Azusa Pacific University, and co-pastored the Yorba Linda Friends Church from 1970-75. In an effort to see a true expression of New Testament Christianity, Wimber developed prayer-team ministry approach in which members of a congregation serve together in praying for others. In this approach, the ministry of the Spirit is facilitated in and through men and women alike. As a result of Wimber's Spirit-focus, hosts of conservative evangelical women have experienced a new freedom to minister in Vineyards and among most groups influenced by Wimber.[138]

Conclusion

A friend recently asked what ever happened to the Quakers. The implication was that since they are not visible in terms of great cathedrals or well-known denominational organizations that they had, in fact, been of little consequence and had ultimately and quietly passed from the scene. This is hardly the case. In fact, the opposite is true. As the evidence shows, the Spirit of the Lord on whom they depended, without regard for earthly reward or honor, has allowed their influence to be immeasurable, incredibly significant, and ongoing. The Early Friends truly represented the most significant historic turning point for women since the time of Jesus. Through a people yielded to the Holy Spirit, God accomplished far more than the politics and policies of an institutional church ever could.

---

[138] See John Wimber, *Power Evangelism* (San Franciso: Harper and Rowe, 1986); C. P. Wagner, "John Wimber," *Dictionary of Pentecostal and Charismatic Movements*, ed. S. M. Burgess and G. B. McGee (Grand Rapids: Zondervan, 1988), 1889

10

A Breakthrough for Women
in Early Methodism

The early Methodist Revival in England (1739-1760) was a charismatic revival,[1] and as is normally the case in such a revival,
women experienced significant elevation. In the opinion of one
scholar, early Methodism "represented the ultimate manifestation" of the liberation of women based on spiritual enthusiasm
[i.e, the activity of the Spirit].[2] Another scholar suggests,
"Emancipation of womanhood began with John Wesley,"
Methodism's founder.[3] Although it is true that the Methodist
Revival played a major role in elevating women within institutional Christianity, such remarks may be an overstatement since
Methodism was, in fact, *inclusive* but not *egalitarian*.

John Wesley was an ordained Anglican minister and he retained Anglicanism's hierarchical social structure in his Methodist
societies. Consequently, Methodism did not facilitate a model of
biblical equality with the purity demonstrated by George Fox and
the early Friends in the previous century. Welsey, in fact, maintained a patriarchal posture, and as late as 1777, he made a clear
statement indicating the difference between his position and that
of the Friends regarding women in ministry.

---

[1] Eddie L. Hyatt, *2000 Years of Charismatic Christianity*, 2nd. ed. (Dallas: Hyatt Int'l Ministries, 1998), 107.

[2] Ronald A. Knox, *Enthusiam: A Chapter in the history of Religion with Special Reference to the Seventeenth and Eighteenth Cen-turies* (Osford: Oxford University Press, 1950), 140, cited by Paul Wesley Chicote, *John Wesley and the Women Preachers of Early Methodism* (Metuchen: Scarecrow Press, 1991), 4.

[3] Robert Wearmouth, *Methodism and the Common People of the Eighteenth Century* (London: Epsworth, 1945), 223; E. Douglas Bebb, Welsey, A Man with a Concern (London: Epworth Press, 1950), 140; See also Walter Lyon Blease, *The Emancipation of English Woman* (London: Benjamin Blom, 1910).

The difference between us and the Quakers is manifest. They flatly deny the rule itself excluding women from preaching, although it stands clear in the Bible. We allow the rule; only we believe it admits some exceptions.[4]

Nevertheless, arising in the more stable era of the 1700s, early Methodism elevated women within a more socially acceptable structure than did the early Friends in the tumultuous 1600s. Albeit not characterized by true gender equality, Methodism was characterized by an important inclusivism of women. Methodist women enjoyed respect, recognition, and freedom to minister not afforded them in the state Church. Perhaps this was because influences other than Anglicanism helped mold Wesley's thinking. His mother Susanna played no small part in this. In addition, his central theology of holiness had a levelling or democratizing effect not inherent in Anglicanism. As well, the Holy Spirit anointed and so gifted women that Wesley could not, with integrity, deny their divine mandate. He refused to ignore both the manifest success of these women and the witness of the Spirit in his own heart validating the Spirit-led activity of these women.[5]   Essentially, then, the early Methodist revival facilitated the elevating, equalizing activity of the Holy Spirit.

The Good Fruit of the Holy Spirit's Manifest Power

The Power of Godly Knowledge. Susanna Annesley Wesley (1669-1742), mother of John Wesley, grew up in the tumultuos England of the 1600s. Although it was a time when girls and women were deprived of any formal education, Susanna was both .a remarkably liberated and learned woman. As the youngest of twenty-five children, she spent much time with her Puritan father,

---

[4] John Wesley, Letter v.vi, *Letters of John Wesley*, 8 vols., ed. J. Telford (London: Epworth Press, 1931), 290-91.
[5] Earl Kent Brown, *Women in Mr. Wesley's Methodism, Studies in Women and Religion*, vol. II (Lewiston/Wueenston: Edwin Mellen Press, 1983), 28.

"the Saint Paul of Nonconformity," and his knowledgeable friends who spent their time debating theological issues. In this environment, she was "schooled in solid piety,"[6] and while still in her teens, Susanna taught herself Hebrew, Greek, and Latin so that she could read the Bible and early Christian literature in the original languages. This equipped her to grapple with theological issues, to teach the Bible proficiently, and to educate her children in those things suited to their gifting and beneficial to the furtherance of the Kingdom of God.

The Power of Spirit-Led Motherhood. Susanna married Samuel Wesley, an Anglican minister. Of their nineteen children, only seven reached adulthood. Quite a remarkable mother, she considered parental responsibility a divine mandate. In a letter to her son John, she reflected on this, saying,

> There's few (if any) that would entirely devote above twenty years of the prime of life in hope to save the souls of their children (which they think may be saved without much ado); for that was my principle intention, however unskillfully and unsuccessfully managed.[7]

Because Susanna believed that God had uniquely gifted each child, she nurtured each one with puprose. One method she used was to spend an hour each week alone with each child. As she interacted with each one during this time, she discerned and developed those precious talents.

In her son Charles (1707-1788), for example, she noticed a special aptitude for words, rhythm, and music. So she provided activities and encouragement to cultivate this dominant feature of his personality. It was not by chance, then, that Charles became

---

[6] Frank Baker, "Susanna Wesley:Puritan, Parent, Pastor, Protagonist, Pattern," *Women in New Worlds* (Nashville: Abingdon, 1982), 113; John Wesley Chilcote, *John Welsey and the Women Preachers of Early Methodism* (Metuchen, NJ: Scarecrow, 1991), 17; Frank Baker, "Salute to Susanna," Methodist History 7 (April 1969): 3-12; John Haggai, "Women in the Lead," *Charisma*, Nov. 1987, 25-32.
[7] Chilcote, 18

the great hymn writer of the Wesleyan Revival. It was by divine design and human cooperation! The result? The Church still enjoys his magnificent hymns.[8]

Son John (1703-1791), she observed, had an unusual sense of destiny and was especially enthusiastic about the Bible. So she not only coached him in the biblical and theological languages but also required extensive memorization of Scripture. She writes,

> [I determined] to be more particularly careful of the soul of this child that thou hast so mercifully provided for, than ever I have been, that I may do my endeavour to instill into his mind the principles of the true religion and virtue.[9]

The Power of the Spirit. In this manner, then, Susanna's pastoral gifts were developed first at home. Then they found expression in public. This happened when her husband was thrown into debtor's prison. In his absence, a curate filled the parish pulpit. Susanna and the children continued to live in the Epworth rectory, where, on Sunday evenings, she conducted family devotions. Everyone was welcome, and soon crowds of 300 were jamming into the residence. At the same time, Evensong, conducted by the curate in the sanctuary, drew only twenty-five or thirty parishioners.

Riled by the enthusiastic response to Susanna's family devotions, the curate charged her with "conducting a clandestine conventicle and usurping the authority of her husband."[10] When Samuel confronted her with the curate's charges, she boldly defended her right to continue the meetings. She pointed to both the numerical and spiritual success of her endeavors. She appealed as well to the positive social effect of her ministry, noting the "improved relationships among the townspeople and increased

---

[8] *The Methodist Hymnal*. Nashville: The Methodist Book Concern, 1939. See Hymn numbers 25, 32, 84, 137, 154, 155, 162, 169, 171, 183, 186, 189, 191, 200-203, 208, 211, 217-18, 229, 282, 287, 290, 299, 309, 311, 338, 339, 343, 356, 370, 371, 372, 373, 377, 400, 402, 403, 404, 417, 419, 422, 444, 500, 518, 522, 536, 538, 540.

[9] Chilcote, 20.

[10] Chilcote, 20.

fervor and desire for the things of God."[11] She confounded her husband with a sobering thought:

> If you do, after all, think fit to dissolve this assembly, do not tell me that you desire me to do it, for that will not satisfy my conscience: but send me your positive command, in such full and express terms as may absolve me from all guilt and punishment for neglecting this opportunity of doing good when you and I shall appear before the great and awful tribunal of our Lord Jesus Christ.[12]

Samuel responded by supporting Susanna. The evidence in her favor was overwhelming indeed, and her bold insistence was obviously not motivated by misguided self-importance or stiff-necked rebellion. In defiance of cultural restrictions based on gender, she continued to minister and the parish flourished in her husband's absence. Without the titles, regalia, training, liturgy, or sanction of the State church, Susanna got the job done! Despite her lack of formal education, she exhibited superior theological skills and biblical knowledge as well as effective leadership skills and pastoral ability.

In accomplishing this, Susanna Wesley did an amazing thing. While remaining loyal to the Anglican Church, at least politically, she was in fact practicing the theological persuasions of the Nonconformists among whom she had developed her own informed theology. For all practical purposes, she ignored the mediatoral position maintained by the Anglican church and the Anglican priesthood. She opted, in practice, for "the sanctity of the inner conscience and the present activity of the Holy Spirit"[13] in the life of the believer. In other words, she believed it was her personal responsibility to obey, first and foremost, the Holy Spirit when this proved contrary to the dictates of the State church.

---

[11] Chilcote, 20.

[12] Chilcote, 20.

[13] Chilcote, 19.

This determination to obey the Holy Spirit was grounded in Biblical literacy, theological reflection, and personal experience. It produced in her a dependence on God that permitted a healthy detachment from the need for human approval and hence from the control of human opinion. Evidence of this appears in her writings. For example, in a letter to Lady Yarborough written in 1702, Susanna says,

> I value neither reputation, friends, or anything, in com-
> parison of the simple satisfaction of preserving a con-
> science void of offense towards God and man.[14]

This position, coupled with a God-directed sense of responsibility and caring for people, made Susanna a remarkable person indeed. In a letter to her husband during his stint in prison, she writes, "I cannot but look upon every soul you leave under my care as a talent committed to me under a trust by the great Lord of all the families."[15] This statement highlights Susanna's integrity. That is to say, the Susanna who nurtured her children was the same Susanna who nurtured the people of the parish. She saw each child and parisioner as a special trust from God. In each one, she sought that unique gifting divinely deposited by the Creator God for His service and glory. Whereas in the State church, ritual provided the construct for righteous religious behavior, for Susanna, relationship with God and with others constituted true piety. Given the restrictions of her day, Susanna Wesley was a remarkable woman.

The Lasting Fruit. Although traditional history regards Susanna's son, John Wesley, as the "Father of Methodism," Susanna may, indeed, be considered its founder. Her perceptive, conscientious guidance during her son's formative years equipped him with biblical tools, theological perspectives, and a God-centered lifestyle.

---

[14] Chilcote, 19.
[15] Chilcote, 19.

Her family devotions served as pattern for the Methodist societies he instituted as cells to nurture spiritual life within the existing structure. Furthermore, as a result of his mother's counsel and example as a teacher, Wesley began appointing women as class leaders in 1739, and between 1761 and 1791 he appointed women as local preachers and itinerant ministers. Furthermore, throughout her life, Susanna was, in fact, her son's most trusted and most influential counselor.

Various researchers have recognized Susanna's importance in Methodism. For example, John Chilcote, in his 1991 work, *John Wesley and the Women Preachers of Early Methodism*, writes,

> In her style of life, spiritual and intellectual disciplines, theological acumen, and ecclesiastical sensibility she was set forward as the paradigm of the Methodist woman for years to come.[16]

Wesleyan scholar, Frank Baker, notes in his article, "Susanna Wesley, Apologist for Methodism," that Susanna was Methodism's instigator, initial theologian, and apologist.[17] Significant literature of the nineteenth century Holiness Movement concurs, and Benjamin St. James Fry, writing in 1892, remarks,

> If I were asked to name the beginning of the present revival of the spirit and practice of the first century . . . I should name Susanna Wesley . . . persisting in her conviction of duty against the advice of rector and curate, prompted no doubt, by the Holy Spirit.[18]

Also writing in 1892, Charles Wesley Rishell notes, "From the beginning Methodism has granted to women a large liberty in public dress, beginning with Susanna Wesley."[19]

---

[16] Chilcote, 18.

[17] Frank Baker, "Susanna Wesley, Apologist for Methodism," Wesley Historical Society 35 (Sept. 1965): 68-71.

[18] Benjamin St. James Fry, *Woman's Work in the Church* (New York: Hunt and Eaton, 1892), 1.

[19] Charles Wesley Rishell, *The Official Recognition of Woman in the Church* (New York: Hunt and Eaton, 1892), 62-63.

Susanna was also highly acclaimed by women of the 19th century Holiness Movement. Mrs. Jennie Fowler Willing, an editor of the prestigious Holiness periodical, *The Guide to Holiness*, spoke highly of her. In an 1898 article, she said that Susanna was, "the founder of a religious organization that ... girdled the globe with a grand gospel of salvation from sin, a holy inspiration to millions of souls."[20] Regardless of the degree of recognition granted Susanna Wesley, the fact remains that "in her life, spiritual and intellectual disciplines, theological acumen, and ecclesiastical sensibility she was set forward as the paradigm of the Methodist woman for years to come."[21]

The Centrality of Holiness

Historically, the church recognizes John Wesley (1703-1791) as the founder of Methodism and John Fletcher (1729-1785) as its initial systematic theologian.[22] Wesley provided the major theological distinctive by democratizing holiness through his doctrine of sanctification. Fletcher introduced Spirit-oriented terminology, such as *baptism of the Holy Spirit*, and the idea of a crisis experience in relation to sanctification.[23] Both agreed that the believer should pursue sanctifying experience subsequent to conversion.

Wesley's revolutionary view of holiness was based on Hebrews 12:14: "Pursue peace with everyone, and sanctification [holiness], without which no one will see the Lord" (Heb. 12:14). He rejected the notion prevalent in the Church that holiness was reserved for the clergy-class. He insisted, instead, that biblical holiness is the life-long pursuit of a lifestyle pleasing to God enabled

---

[20] Mrs. Jennie Willing Fowler, "Woman Under the Pentecostal Baptism," *The Guide to Holiness* 69 (Sept. 1892): 84.

[21] Chilcote, 18.

[22] Vinson Synan, "Lecture 3," *The Holiness-Pentecostal Movement*, Tulsa, Spring 1991. Fletcher's idea of the subsequent experience being the Baptism of the Holy Spirit and empowerment for service were adopted by Phoebe Palmer, the chief theologian of the Holiness Movement.

[23] Donald Dayton, *Theological Roots*, 183-184.

by the Spirit and required by every person regardless of ecclesiastical office, social, economic or academic status, or gender.

According to Wesley, holiness held two requirements. The first was an intimate relationship with the Spirit of God. The second was accountablility through public testimony of one's personal spiritual state. These two requirements thus brought about a new era of personal and social responsibility for every man and every woman. For the first time in the Methodist societies and the state Church, women were not only permitted to speak publicly, but, in fact, were expected to do so!

"Who am I that I should withstand God?"

Wesleyan theology had a profound effect on British society. Socially it reformed a degenerate English culture by igniting an evangelical Revival. Ecclesiastically it brought the importance of the experience of the Holy Spirit to the forefront, a factor which promoted charismatic leadership and inevitably challenged the patriarchal system of the institutional church which elevated and protected an all-male clerical class.[24] It brought about a socially acceptable inclusion of women in public life that had not existed prior to this time.

The eminent Holiness scholar Donald W. Dayton identifies three features of the Wesleyan Revival which opened important new possibilities for women.[25] These include "an implicit egalitarianism, a turn toward Christian experience, and a certain pragmatism that encouraged experimentation with new cultural patterns."

1. **Implicit Egalitarianism.** Dayton believes that the Wesleyan Revival was fundamentally egalitarian because it was motivated "by the conviction that the most important fact about any person is human sinfulness and the need of transforming grace." This re-

---

[24] Chilcote, 6, 238.
[25] Donald W. Dayton, "Evangelical Roots of Feminism," Photocopy, n.d., 2-4.

ligious conviction disrupted old social patterns producing "social fluidity." Dayton concludes that as a result of religious experience, people looked at Scripture and discovered that "some of those elements that had been assumed to be part of a Christian view of life were more assumed cultural patterns than essential features of the Faith."

2. Heartfelt Experience. The second critical feature identified by Dayton was Wesley's emphasis on heart experience over cold, dead, religious orthodoxy. With spiritual experience as the new point of reference for spiritual authority, positions of authority depended on "spiritual maturity and insight" rather than on "theological training or ecclesiastical ordination." In such a milieu, women "may more easily qualify for positions of leadership. . . . In fact, women, whose socialization has perhaps contributed to greater sensitivity to feelings and the emotional life, may even excel in these new patterns."[26]

3. Social Experimentation. Dayton's third point is that the Wesleyan openness to experimentation with new patterns of ministry, together with the willingness to "let the validity of these new forms be judged by the results that they produced," opened new avenues for women. A case in point was Wesley's recognition of results as the validation of the divine call as he observed many of his female class leaders advancing in their public speaking from giving simple testimonials to explicating Scripture in an expository manner. Obvious results, he decided, superseded gender, formal education, and institutional ordination as criteria for leadership. When asked why he encouraged women preachers, Wesley replied, "Because God owns them in the conversion of sinners, and who am I that I should withstand God."

---

[26] Dayton, "Evangelical Roots," 4.

Growing into God's Plan

Wesley grew toward a position that allowed him to facilitate gifted women within Methodist leadership. This was possible, first of all perhaps, because of the example of the gifted ministry of his mother. In addition, he knew of the nontraditional status and ministry of women among the Friends, other charismatic groups, and to a lesser extent among the Puritans.[27]

When Wesley attended Oxford, he fellowshipped with a group of religious women at the Stanton rectory in Cotswold. He was particularly close friends with Sally Kirkham who inspired him to read the devotional classics of Thomas à Kempis and other mystics.[28] This exposure alerted him to the power of the indwelling Spirit out of which biblical equality ultimately emerges.

As a young man on his sea journey to do missionary work in Georgia, Wesley made the acquaintance of Moravian missionaries also enroute to the New World. He was tremendously impressed with these German Lutheran descendents of John Huss (1373-1415). Under the leadership of Count Zinzendorf (1700-60), these devout believers had experienced a tremendous charismatic renewal in 1727 at *Herrnhutt*, their home in Saxony.[29]

Socially, the Moravians were strictly divided according to gender. This gave Moravian women the oppotunity to serve one another in various capacities, and in so doing, many women developed leadership and pastoral skills. The "chief eldress" maintained a position of considerable influence in the community. Anna Nitschmann, who became Zinzendorf's wife, functioned in this post with great diligence from the age of fifteen until her death. Having observed the effectiveness of this Moravian model, Wesley

---

[27] See Chilcote, 4-11.

[28] Chilcote, 22, cites Richard P. Heitzenrater, "John Welsy and the Oxford Methodists, 1725-1735," (Ph.D. diss. , Duke University, 1972), 67-68.

[29] See Hyatt, 103-106; Edward Langton, *History of the Moravian Church* (London: George Allen& Unwin, 1956), 63; John Greenfield, *When the Spirit Came* (Minneapolis: bethany, 1967), 25.

was inspired to integrate the help of women in his ministerial activities.[30]

Welsey speaks of a conversion experience at a Moravian meeting at Aldersgate in London on May, 14, 1738. About this time, he shows outspoken support for women. In fact, when some attempted to exclude the contributions of women in the meetings, he bolted, saying, "I do very exceedingly disapprove of the excluding of women when we meet to pray, sing, and read the Scriptures."[31]

As Methodism developed under Wesley's leadership, the list of women preachers grew in number and influence. He eventually extended preaching rights to women under his supervision. One event, in particular, marked the inauguration of women as preachers in Methodism: Wesley approved when Mrs. Sarah Crosby's (1739-?) class attracted two hundred and the numbers alone demanded that she stand to lead and to testify.[32]

The Co-Pastors of Madeley Woods (1782-85)

Representative of early Methodist women leaders was Mary Bosanquet Fletcher (1739-1815), wife of Welsey's colleague, John Fletcher. Concerning her ministry, she writes, "My call is so clear and I have such liberty in the work [public and private ministry], and such sweet encouragement among the people."[33] It was not unusual for her to preach to crowds of two to three thousand people, and she inspired many women to follow her dynamic example in life and ministry.[34]

During their brief life together, the Fletchers served "for all practical purposes, as co-pastors" of the parish of Madeley

---

[30] See Chilcote, 23 and footnotes 109-112 for extensive sources.
[31] Chicote, 24, citing John Wesley to J. Hutton and Mr. Fox, November 24, 1738, Welsey, *Oxford Edition*, 25:588.
[32] Chilcote, 121; Dayton and Dayton, 3.
[33] Henry Moore, *The Life of Mrs. Mary Fletcher, Consort and Relict of the Rev. John Fletcher* (London: J. Kershaw, 1824), 164-156.
[34] Chilcote, 182-186, 199; Dayton and Dayton, 3.

Woods.[35] When he died prematurely in 1785, she continued regular preaching services in the parish and extended her influence to surrounding villages where she was well received.[36] Commenting on her prowess and popularity, one man who regularly attended her meetings remarked,

> Tribes were seen going up from all the neighboring places early on the Sabbath morning, for Mrs. Fletcher's nine o'clock meeting, full of joy, or of joyous expectation of having gracious manifestations from their Lord.
>
> On a week-day evening service, it was not unusual to see the room crowded with attentive and delighted hearers, while this blessed woman was expounding, generally, some historic portion of Scripture. . . . The effect produced was often truly astonishing. . . . It was not uncommon to see two, three, or more Clergymen, pious and able men, from neighboring and even distant parishes, among the congregation at these evening lectures.[37]

Conclusion

Early Methodism was, indeed, an important revival in many respects, not the least of which was its accommodation and elevation of women. Welsey's doctrine of holiness was egalitarian. He did, however, stop short of the gender equality practiced apparently by the more Spirit-oriented Fletchers. Perhaps, in practice, Wesley's approach to ministry and women could be more correctly termed *inclusive* rather than *egalitarian*. This inclusivism was important, however, in establishing a new dignity and place hitherto denied women in institutional religion. This elevation of women gained momentum in nineteenth century America.

---

[35] Chilcote, 184; Luke Tyerman, *Wesley's Designated Successor: The Life, Letters, and Literary Labours of the Rev. John William Fletcher* (London: Hodder and Stoughton, 1820), 502.

[36] Moore, 164-65.

[37] William Tranter, "Methodism in Madeley," *Wesleyan Methodist Magazine* 60 (1837): 901-2.

11

STRATEGIC ADVANCES IN 19TH CENTURY AMERICA

Nineteenth century America saw a powerful convergence of elements that elevated women. Motivated by the Holy Spirit, these elements loosened—and in some cases, broke—the cultural restraints that had chained women for centuries. They can be divided into two main historical categories: pre-Civil War (to about 1860), and post Civil War (after 1865).

During the first half of the century, at least five elements helped establish the trend. The Quakers remained a force in American culture, and continued, at least to some extent, to stand for women and equality in a way that other groups did not. Methodism, with its inclusivism of women, had come to America in 1760 where it had become the nation's largest denomination.[1] Early in the century, the revivalism of Charles Finney and Asa Mahan had brought social reforms that included the elevation of women. America's special sense of divine destiny helped produce a social conscience that called for an end to social sins, especially slavery. This trend progressed through the Abolition Movement and culminated in the Civil War (1861-65).

Following this war, five more important movements arose and contributed to a further loosening of restraints on women and a trend toward gender equality. These movements were the Holiness Movement, the Temperance Movement, the Missionary Movement, the Suffrage Movement, and the Healing Move-

---

[1] Glen Miller, "Methodism in the United States," *Dictionary of American Methodism*, 4 vols. ed. L. Ketz (New York: C. Scribner and Sons, 1976), 4:318-319; Vinson Synan, "Lecture," *The Holiness-Pentecostal Movement*, Tulsa: Oral Roberts University, Spring, 1991).

ment. These movements, although individually identifiable, were also interwoven through people who participated in more than one of the movements. The Quaker women, ideally being women of Spirit-led lifestyle rather than women with denominationally-defined commitments, were a major force in all of these movements.

Fuel for Reform Before the Civil War

During the first half of the 1800s, Methodism was a major force in America. Blending with Quakerism and other forces already at work, it awakened the social conscience of the young nation. In this, women began to take a more active public role.

This more active public role by women provoked a reaction that led to the development of the theory of spheres of authority. Although women could no longer be ignored, they were held in check by the notion that they were to operate only in the domestic sphere. Men, it was theorized, were the only legitimate authorities in the public sphere. These spheres were simply social means of keeping alive the doctrine of male headship and authority while pacifying women by giving them some sense of self-respect and limited control. To break this code was to invite shame, and this in itself, served—and still serves—as an unspoken social reprimand for women who do not comply with what is socially acceptable. Nevertheless, women made—and continue to make–great strides toward both inclusivism and equality.

Methodist Holiness and American Revivalism. The overlapping of Methodist-Holiness theology and American Revivalism, especially that of Charles Finney (1792-1875) and Asa Mahan (1799-1889), helped to elevate women.[2] In fact, possibly the most controversial of Finney's "new measures" during the Second Great Awakening (1800-1840) was Finney's practice of allowing

---

[2] Dayton and Dayton, 4.

women to pray aloud and testify in mixed gatherings.[3] His, was however, a measured inclusivism of women, not an egalitarian view.[4]

In his bold move to facilitate women, Finney was influenced both by Wesley's writings[5] and by Quaker perspectives. A Quaker abolitionist, Theodore Dwight Weld (1803-1895), had been converted to Christ in his meetings in Utica, New York, in 1825-26.[6] Weld constrained Finney to facilitate women. Weld tells of his own experience in helping women participate in public meetings. He says,

> The very week that I was converted . . . and the first time I ever spoke in a religious meeting–I urged females both to pray and speak if they felt deeply enough to do it, and not to be restrained from it by the fact that they were females. . . . The result was that seven females, a number of them the most influential female Christians in the city, confessed their sin in being restrained by their sex, and prayed publickly in succession at that very meeting. It made a great deal of talk and discussion, and the subject of female praying and female speaking in public was discussed throughout western New York.[7]

Weld married Angelina Grimké (1792-1873), who, with her sister Sarah (1805-1879), had shaken New England in the 1930s by public anti-slavery activism which included lecturing and writing.[8]

Finney and Mahan helped establish Oberlin College (1833), the first coeducational college in the world, for the purpose of

[3] Dayton, "Evangelical Roots," 6.

[4] Tucker and Liefeld, 251-52.

[5] Finney and Mahan spent the winter of 1836-37 in New York City reading Welsey's works and other books concerning holiness." Hardesty, Dayton and Dayton, *Women of Spirit*, 231.

[6] Bormann, 6-12; C. Stockwell, "Thomas Weld," *Dictionary of Christianity in America*, 1240-1241;.Donald W. Dayton, "Evangelical Roots," 6.

[7] Theodore Weld to Angelina and Sarah Grimké, New York, Aug. 26, 1837, in *Letters to Theodore Dwight Weld, Angelina Grimké Weld and Sarah Grimké, 1822-44*, ed. Gilbert Barnes and Dwight Dumond (New York: Appleton-Century-Crofts, 1934; reprint ed., Gloucester, MA, Peter Smith, 1965), vol. 1, 432.

[8] Dayton: 7; Harold Smith, 73.

perpetuating Finney's "blend of revivalism and reform."[9] Mahan, Oberlin's first president, suggested the following epitaph for his tombstone:

> The first man, in the history of the race, who conducted women, in connection with members of the opposite sex, through a full course of liberal education, and conferred upon her the high degrees which had hitherto been exclusive prerogative of men.[10]

Methodist Holiness and American Optimism. Fuel for egalitarian reform also came from the fusion of Methodism and the American idea of its divine destiny: It was a nation ordained by God for His purposes. It was important, then to be a society imbued with holiness. The young nation, then, must purge itself of social sins, the most glaring of which was slavery. Thus abolition became the chief cry of the Christian reformers of the day.[11]

In the Abolition Movement, competent Christian women, especially Quaker women such as Sarah and Angelica Grimké, spoke publicly against slavery.[12] This public display by women shocked the Calvinist-Puritan status quo which upheld the idea of strictly predestined social roles based on gender and color. In this way of thinking, both women and people of color were to be silent and to serve. The intense hostility toward the biblical message of equality and the Spirit-led messengers—women—only served to illustrate that both women and slaves were captives of culture.[13]

---

[9] R. Green, "Oberlin College," *Dictionary of Christianity in America*, ed. Daniel G. Reid (Downers Grove: IVP, 1990), 833-834; Dayton, "Evangelical Roots," 6.

[10] Asa Mahan, *Autobiography, Intellectual, Moral and Spiritual* (London: T. Woolmer, 1882), 169.

[11] Ernest G. Bormann, ed., "Female Antislavery Speakers," *Forerunners of Black Power: The Rhetoric of Abolition* (Englewood Cliffs, NJ: Prentice-Hall, 1971; Synan, *The Holiness-Pentecostal Movement.*

[12] Harold Ivan Smith, "A Time to Speak Out: The Grimke Sisters Challenged Slavery in the Early 1800s," *Charisma and Chritian Life*, March 1988, 73; Sarah Grimke, *The Letters on the Equality of the Sexes* (Philadelphia: G. Donohue, 1839); Bormann, 183-192.

[13] For a thorough discussion in favor of the subjugation of women in ministry and in marriage, see J. M. Stevenson, "Woman's Place in Assemblies for Public Worship," (New York: J. M. Sherwood, 1873). For a thorough discussion in favor of the pro-slavery/abolitionist debate, see Jonathan Blanchard and N. L. Rice, *A Debate on Slavery* (Cincinnati: Wm. H. Moore, 1846); Albert Barnes, *An Inquiry into the Scriptural Views of Slavery* (Philadelphia: Parry and MacMillan, 1855).

The interpretation of Scripture that sanctioned this captivity was based on selected passages arbitrarily pieced together. (This method of biblical interpretation is known as *proof-texting*.) Since this approach produced a futile war of words, it soon became obvious to the abolitionists that they would have to discard this method.[14] In its place, they made an important step forward in correctly interpreting the Bible by developing a method of biblical interpretation that embraced broad scriptural principles and that set the pertinent passages in their legitimate contexts. For their so-called *abolitionist hermeneutic,* or approach to understanding the meaning of Scripture, they chose Galatians 3:28 as their starting point and guiding principle.

There is neither Jew nor Greek, there is neither slave nor free, there is neither male nor female; for you are all one in Christ Jesus.

Not only did this, taken in context, address the heart of the issue, but it also harmonized the writings of Paul with the evidence of equality found in Luke-Acts.

The struggle to abolish slavery eventually climaxed with the American Civil War (1861-65). The victory of the northern Union States fighting against slavery led to the legal demise of racial slavery. This bloody confrontation together with the Spirit-driven social changes that were in motion helped break the back of hyper-Calvinism in America. It was an important step in a the trend toward racial equality.

The victory was important to women for a number of reasons. First, it brought women into the public arena. Second, it strengthened the public speaking skills of those women who were bold enough to preach, speak, and debate on behalf of the slaves. Third, it challenged the idea of predestined social roles based on skin color, thereby opening the possibility that God did not, in fact, have predestined social roles dictated by skin color

---

[14] Dayton, "Evangelical Roots," 9.

or gender. (Perhaps the notion of women's and men's spheres was, after all, a hoax intended to keep women "in their place.") Fifth, it called forth an approach to biblical interpretation that led to a more accurate reading of the text which helped advance the biblical truth of women's equality.

The Nineteenth Century Holiness Movement

When Methodism came to America in the 1760s,[15] it flourished. In fact, by 1900 its four million adherents made it the nation's largest denomination. About half of these held to the Wesleyan view of sanctification or holiness, and so they were known by the *holiness* designation. By the final decade of the century, controversy arose regarding the doctrine of holiness and other issues such as the place of women. About 100,000 Holiness people left the Methodist ranks. Known as "come-outers," many formed new holiness denominations, many of which gave women a more inclusive and egalitarian place.

Throughout the course of the entire century, Methodist ideas helped mold American society. Its most influential ideas were the same ideas that had characterized the Methodist Revival in England during the previous century. These were Wesley's ideas of a life-changing experience subsequent to conversion and the accompanying need to testify publicly to ones spiritual state. As in Wesley's day, most of this occurred outside the sanctuary in such informal settings as parlors, and this gave women a greater opportunity to participate.

So vital was this approach that it produced a state of Christian influence throughout the nation, even among non-Methodists, known as the Holiness Movement. Non-Methodists referred to the sanctification experience in terms compatible

---

[15] Glen Miller, "Methodism in the United States," *Dictionary of American Methodism,* 4 vols., ed. L. Ketz (New York: C. Scribner Sons, 1976), 4:318-319; Vinson Synan, *The Holiness-Pentecostal Movement in the United States* (Grand Rapdis: Eerdmans, 1971), 19-23; Vinson Synan, "Lecture," *The Holiness-Pentecostal Movement_,* Tulsa: Oral Roberts University, Spring 1991.

with their theological perspectives: Oberlin revivalists, for example, pursued "Christian perfection";[16] Keswickians aspired to the "deeper Christian life;"[17] Presbyterians pursued the "higher Christian life;" and Baptists promoted the "rest of faith."[18]

As in Welsey's day, and as in the early part of the century in America, the idea of personal holiness brought remarkable results. It caused individuals to draw near to God and He, in turn, drew near to them. In this intimacy, He inspired and empowered people to accomplish His purposes. Men and women challenged the cultural status quo through courageous acts of faith. And culture began to yield.[19]

Biblical Themes for Equality

Within the Holiness Movement, the idea of equality developed around three main themes. The first theme, based on Galatians 3:28, had come to the forefront through the fight to free the slaves. The second theme was based the fall/redemption/sanctification theme. The third theme emphasized the importance of the End-Time and was based on the outpouring of the Spirit on the Day of Pentecost (Joel 2:28 and Acts 2:16-18).

1. The Galatians 3:28 Theme. This passage had become the rallying cry for those who would honor the Bible and free the slaves. Once that battle had been won, those who would free women from similar oppressive subjugation made it their own special cry.[20] Commenting on this verse, Adam Clark (1760?-1832) says, "under the blessed spirit of Christianity, [women]

---

[16] Asa Mahan, *Scripture Doctrine of Christian Perfection* (Boston: D. King, 1839) and *The Baptism of the Holy Ghost* (New York: Walter C. Palmer, 1870).

[18] William E. Boardman, *The Higher Christian Life* (Boston: Henry Hoyt, 1858).

[19] A. B. Earle, *The Rest of Faith* (Boston: James H. Earle, 1876).

[20] Timothy L. Smith, *Revivalism and Social Reform in Mid-Nineteenth-*Century America (Nashville: Abingdon, 1957).

Susie C. Stanley, "Response to Klyne R. Snodgrass' 'Galatians 3:28: Conundrum or Solution,'" *Women, Authority, and the Bible*, ed. Alvera Mickelsen (Downers Grove: IVP, 1986), 183-185.

have equal rights, equal privileges, and equal blessings, and let me add, they are equally useful."[21] Rev. Luther Lee (1800-1889), a Wesleyan Methodist,[22] and Jonathan Blanchard, a Presbyterian-Congregationalist and founding president of Wheaton College, spoke boldly for equal ministry rights for women.[23] In 1891, William B. Godbey, a New Testament scholar, spoke bluntly on behalf of women's right to preach, saying, "It is the God-given right, blood-bought privilege, and bounden duty of the women, as well as the men, to preach the gospel."[24]

Women also spoke out courageously. The February-April 1892 issue of *Review of the Churches,* for example, reports comments by Mrs. Josephine Butler,[25] Mrs. Sheldon Amos, and Mrs. Bramwell Booth[26] in an article entitled "Woman's Place in the Church."[27] The language was strong and straightforward. Mrs. Butler, for example, says,

> Women themselves have been very slavish. It is humiliating to see a gifted woman, with dignity enough for a Bishop or a Prime Minister, putting herself willingly under the guidance of some inexperienced, not gifted clergy-boy."[28]

In the same article, Mrs. Bramwell Booth writes,

> When the Church, or the Churches, become more deeply humble; when they have realized, even more than they do

---

[21] Adam Clarke, *The Holy Bible Containing the Old and New Testaments* (New York: ABM Paul, 1824), 402.

[22] Dayton, "Evangelical Roots," 10. The Wesleyan Methodists began ordaining women in the 1860s.

[23] Dayton, 10-11. Both, however, were inclusive rather than egalitarian in their approach since they held to the concept of authoritative male "headship."

[24] Wm. B. Godbey, *Woman Preacher* (n.p.: n.p., n.d), 1.

[25] British reformer, Josephine Butler (1828-1906) was the wife of a Canon of Winchester Cathedral. She worked mainly for the reclamation of prostitutes and the slave trade of women prostitutes. "Behind her activities of reform lay a life of continuous prayer." E.L. Cross and E. A. Livingstone, ed., *The Oxford Dictionary of the Christian Church,* 2nd ed. (New York: Oxford University Press, 1983), 215. She started her work in Liverpool in 1866 and for forty years withstood continuous opposition and misunderstanding. John R. H. Moorman, *A History of the Church of England,* 3rd ed. (London: Adam and Charles Black, 1976), 379).

[26] She is the daughter-in-law of Salvation Army founders, William and Catherine Booth.

[27] "Woman's Place in the Church," *Reviewing of the Churches,* Feb.-April 1892, 343.

[28] "Woman's Place in the Church," 343.

now, their desperate need of the help of woman <u>as man's</u> <u>equal, absolutely</u>, in her relation to spiritual things, they will grant the freedom we ask; and then good gifts will no longer languish in a prison-house of conventialities, and women's energies will not be folded in napkins and buried under the church floor. The Salvation Army have led the way in the spiritual equality, and emancipation of woman's powers. May the Church follow![29]

B. T. Roberts (1823-1893), who founded the Free Methodist Church in 1860, eloquently debated in favor of both an egalitarian marriage relationship and the ordination of women.[30] In his 1891 book, *Ordaining Women,* Roberts provides a radical defense on the basis of Galatians 3:28.[31] He points out that the subjugation of women in any arena is heathenistic, and he says that this practice was introduced into Christianity through Classical Greek literature. He quotes Aristotle who said, "The relations of man to woman is that of the governor to his subject."[32] In a further effort to show the heathen roots of female subjugation, he contends, "In most nations, except Jewish and Christian, the condition of woman has been, from time immemorial, one of slavery."[33] He warns that the Church's oppressive teaching on women is wrong just as its position on slavery was wrong.[34] In appealing for equality, he writes,

> We must give her equal rights with men or we must reduce her to the servitude of by-gone ages. Either we must be governed by the Christian law of love and equity, or we

---

[29] "Woman's Place," 343.
[30] Dayton, 11.
[31] B. T. Roberts, *Ordaining Women* (Rochester: Earnest Christian, 1891).
[32] Roberts, 69.
[33] Roberts, 14.
[34] Roberts, 12.

must take a step back into barbarianism and be governed by the law of brute force.[35]

Roberts also stands firmly against the idea of "woman's sphere." The concept, according to Roberts, is one of several "cunning contrivances" designed to keep women "in their place." Such schemes, he contends, "are adopted to make her think that she is accorded all the liberty she wants. She suffers in consequence, but the cause of God suffers most."[36] Thus, he charges that the suppression of women is a major reason that Christianity does not "rot out all false religions! And why does it not have a more marked effect upon the lives of those who acknowledge its truth!" He continues his charge, saying,

> It is said that about two-thirds of all members of all the Protestant churches of this country are women. Yet in these churches a woman, no matter what may be her qualifications, and devotion, and zeal, is not permitted to occupy the same position as a man. The superior must, sometimes, give place to the inferior. The bungler must give direction, the adept must obey. The incompetent coward must command, if no competent man is found, while the competent woman is relegated to the rear. A Deborah may arise, but the churches, by their law, prohibit her from coming to the front. And these laws must be enforced though all others are disregarded.[37]

2. The Redemption Theme. A second theme of the Holiness Movement cites redemption as its central issue. The point is this: If woman was, indeed, under a curse through the fall, now, by virtue of redemption, the curse associated with that event has been broken by the work of the Lord Jesus Christ. Dayton clari-

---

[35] Roberts, 68.
[36] Roberts, 116.
[37] Roberts, 115-116.

fies this position in his paper *The Evangelical Roots of Feminism*. "In its emphasis on the doctrine of sanctification," he writes, the Holiness tradition "often came close to arguing that the pre-fallen state of men could be completely restored by the transforming grace of God." He observes, "Any elements of the curse laid upon women in the fall would not apply in the church, the company of the redeemed and restored."[38] Also arguing from this perspective, Seth Cook Rees declares, "as the grace of God and the light of the Gospel are shed abroad . . . woman is elevated, until at Pentecost she stands, a second Eve, by the side of her husband."[39]

3. The Pentecostal Theme. The Pentecostal theme for equality arose from the meaning of Joel 2:28 and Acts 2:17-18.

> *And it shall come to pass in the last days, says God, That I will pour out My Spirit on all flesh; Your sons and your daughters shall prophesy, Your young men shall see visions, Your old men shall dream dreams. And also on My menservants and on My maidservants I will pour out My Spirit in those days; And they shall prophesy (Acts 2:17-18).*

This outpouring was understood to be God's empowering of His people for ministry in the Last Days that had begun on the Day of Pentecost. The person most responsible for the emergence and development of this view was Phoebe Palmer.

Phoebe Palmer

Phoebe Worrall Palmer (1807-1874)[40] grew up in a devout Methodist home in New York City. Early in life, she made a wholehearted commitment to serve the Lord. She was consumed

---

[38] Dayton, 14.

[39] Rees, 41.

[40] Dayton and Dayton, "Women in the Holiness Movement," Photocopy, n.d., 5; Harold E. Raser, *Phoebe Palmer: Her Life and Thought* (Lewiston, NY: Edwin Mellen Press, 1987); Charles Edward White, "Phoebe Palmer and the Development of Pentecostal Pneumatology," *Wesleyan Theological Journal* (12 June 1990): 208.

with a hunger to know Him.

Phoebe married Dr. Walter Clarke Palmer (1804-1883),[41] a prominent New York physician. Like Phoebe, he was consumed with a passion to serve the Lord and decided that the most effective means of his doing so would be to become a medical doctor. So Dr. and Mrs. Palmer began their life together as faithful members of the affluent Methodist Church in New York City.

As children came along, Phoebe became a doting mother. Totally consumed with parenting, the time she once had given to the Lord, she was now giving to her children. What a devastating blow it was then, when her first two babies died in tragic accidents in her loving home. Filled with unbearable grief, Phoebe found herself on her knees, desperate for the answer to that nagging question, "Why?"

The answer she heard was this: *She had devoted herself to her children to such an extent that these gifts from God had actually displaced God in her life. They had become idols!*

Immediately she repented. For Phoebe, this meant turning from a life ruled by temporal concerns to a life directed by eternal values. With this established, Phoebe soon gave birth to two more precious children. This time, Mother Phoebe kept her purpose and priorities lined up with God's will. This alignment meant, among other things, sharing with nannies the care of her children. God blessed this decision and her offspring henceforth enjoyed long and prosperous lives. Perhaps it could be said that when Phoebe looked after God's business, God looked after her!

Obedience to the call resulted in Phoebe's becoming one of the most influential Christian leaders of the 1800s. She has, in fact, been recognized as the "major force behind a mid-nineteenth century reaffirmation of the Wesleyan doctrine of

---

[41] Raser, 30ff.

Christian perfection" that spawned a major revival.[42] So Phoebe was at the forefront of the great revival that ignited flames among the Methodists as they sought to recover the religious fervor of the Wesleyan Revival of the previous century.

As Phoebe sought her experience of sanctification, she struggled. The teaching of the day said that intense emotion would accompany the experience. Yet as devout, sincere, and diligent as Phoebe was, she just could not achieve that *feeling*. In this struggle, God showed her that she could—in fact, *must*—accept it by "naked faith in the naked Word."[43] She read, *For which is greater, the gift or the altar that sanctifies the gift? (Mt. 23:19)*. She understood in a new way that the altar was the place of total surrender to God where the shed blood of the Lord Jesus provided both salvation and cleansing. So with this insight and on the basis of Romans 12:1, she presented herself a living sacrifice on the altar and by faith received sanctification as an accomplished fact. If she needed experiential evidence, it came in the form of a new dimension of peace. It was July 26, 1837.

Phoebe also understood the Biblical principle of confessing what she had received by faith. She had gained this understanding from the writings of Wesley's theological colleague, John Fletcher. She writes,

> One must confess the blessing on the basis of faith alone (Rom. 10:9-10). Do not forget that believing with the heart and confessing with the mouth stand closely connected. What God hath joined together let not man put asunder.[44]

Phoebe's revolutionary approach to sanctification rapidly gained recognition among the Methodists. Before long it exerted

---

[42] Dayton, "Evangelical Roots," 13; Synan, Lectures (1991); M. Simpson, "Drew Seminary and Female College," and "Drew Theological Seminary," *Cyclopedia of Methodism* (Philadelphia: Louis Everts, 1881), 312;. Melvin Dieter, *The Holiness Revival of the Nineteenth Century* (Metuchen: Scarecrow, 1980), 26.

[43] Raser, 47.

[44] Raser, 175.

influence among the non-Wesleyan denominations as well. This *altar terminology* and *shorter way* to sanctification became standards in the revival.

Ultimately, and very much to Phoebe's credit, Pentecostal language replaced Wesleyan terminology in describing *the second blessing*. Instead of *sanctification* it became *the baptism of the Holy Ghost;* and instead of *cleansing from sin,* the blessing consisted of *an impartation of power.* These trends were important developments as the church moved toward the twentieth century and the explosion of the modern Pentecostal/Charismatic movement.

It is obvious that Phoebe was the pivotal figure in the Holiness Movement. She was, in fact, its dominant theologian, a foremost Bible teacher, a prominent evangelist, and perhaps its most influential writer and editor. This influence can be traced to 1840 when she became the leader of the *Tuesday Meeting for the Promotion of Holiness.* This meeting was conducted in the Palmer's spacious parlor and drew many prominent churchmen from both within and without the Methodism. Among those sanctified in her parlor were four leading Methodist bishops. Travelers to New York City were welcome visitors to the *Tuesday Meeting.*

For twenty years, beginning in 1841, the call to minister kept Phoebe away from home most of the time. During this period, Dr. Palmer presided over the home and vigorously supported his wife's ministry in every possible way. He cheerfully financed her travels, since she often ministered without receiving an honorarium. In addition, he went into the publishing business to increase Phoebe's reach as an author,[45] and eventually he closed his medical practice and accompanied Phoebe in ministry.[46]

Although Phoebe was in ministry full-time, she confesses to being "a reluctant preacher." Nevertheless, as she obeyed the

---

[45] Raser, 106-107.
[46] Raser, 63.

Lord, she found herself "pioneering alone in a man's world."[47]
She did not pursue official church ordination. The fruit of her
ministry stands alone as a testimony to the Divine Source and
integrity of her call. At least 25,000 people in the Northeastern
United States, in Eastern Canada, and in England were converted during her meetings that ran from a few days to several
weeks. In addition, countless hundreds were sanctified, or *baptized in the Spirit,* as she called it.

In her book, *Four Years in the Old World,* Phoebe records the
events of an extended time of ministry that she and her husband
spent in England. Describing her meetings in the City of Newcastle, Phoebe says, "The Lord was saving the people by scores
daily."[48] At the time of the report, the names of over 2000 people were already on record as having received the blessing "of
pardon or purity." God was moving through her ministry in such
a powerful manner that she remarks, "Now the entire community seems ready to acknowledge its [the revival's] power."[49] She
notes, "The power of God is sensibly felt to be present to heal."[50]
She speaks of those who "felt the girdings of almighty power in
an unusual manner," and of the "tokens of divine presence."[51]
Phoebe regarded the mighty manifestations of the Spirit as evidence of "a resuscitation of primitive Christianity and primitive
Methodism."[52]

The manifestations of the Spirit in the Newcastle meetings
were by no means isolated incidents. Revival-type manifestations
were typical in her meetings. Writing from Sunderland, England,
she says that there was such a sense of the divine presence that
"people are weeping all over the house."[53]

---

[47] Phoebe Palmer, *The Way of Holiness* (New York: W. C. Palmer, 1843, 1867), 37-38.
[48] Phoebe Palmer, *Four Years in the Old World* (Boston: Foster & Palmer, 1865), 145.
[49] Palmer, 145.
[50] Palmer, 103.
[51] Palmer, 111.
[52] Palmer, 107.
[53] Palmer, 120.

In addition to being a mightily anointed Bible teacher and revivalist, Phoebe gained considerable recognition as a theologian. Charles Edward White, in his scholarly article, "Phoebe Palmer and the Development of Pentecostal Pneumatology," published in the *Wesleyan Theological Journal* in 1990, calls Phoebe "the most influential female theologian the Church has yet produced."[54] Harold E. Raser, in his thorough study, *Phoebe Palmer: Her Life and Thought* published three years earlier in 1987, had already concluded that Phoebe Palmer, as a theologian, had given the Holiness Movement concrete identity and theological focus.[55]

In the early days of her ministry, Phoebe used Wesleyan terminology such as *sanctification* and *cleansing* when referring to *the second blessing*. However, she shifted to what has been called *Pentecostal terminology* in discussing the second blessing.[56] For example, writing from England, she says that the emphasis of the afternoon meetings is "the full baptism of the Holy Spirit, as received by the one hundred and twenty disciples on the day of Pentecost."[57]

This Spirit baptism affected a person's speech in the same manner that outpouring of the Holy Spirit had affected the speech of the hundred and twenty in the Upper Room (Acts 2:4). In describing this occurrence at one of her meetings, Phoebe says, "The baptism of fire descended; and, as in the early days of Christianity, utterance as a restraining gift was also given."[58] On another occasion, a local preacher was the first to receive this "tongue of fire," and according to Phoebe, he "spake as the Spirit gave utterance."[59]

---

[54] White, 208.

[55] Raser, 199.

[56] Donald Dayton, "Christian Perfection to the Baptism of the Holy Ghost," *Aspects of Pentecostal-Charismatic Origins*, Vinson Synan Ed. (Plainfield: Logos, 1975), 39-54.

[57] Palmer, *Four Years in the Old World*, 107.

[58] Palmer, 127.

[59] Palmer, 96.

Despite the fruitfulness of her ministry, Phoebe endured considerable rejection and criticism because she was a woman functioning in public ministry. Perhaps her most vocal critic was Hiram Mattison. In *The Christian Advocate and Journal* (29 Nov. 1855), he writes, "Are we so ignorant [of holiness] as to require a sister to travel from conference to conference to instruct us?"[60] Likewise, reacting to Phoebe and in particular, to her first book, *The Way of Holiness,* another male critic suggested Palmer would have "been better engaged in washing dishes than in writing."[61]

Prompted by criticism of this sort and by recognition of the need for a clearly articulated Biblical theology for the right of women to minister publicly, Phoebe wrote *The Promise of the Father.* Published in 1859, this 421-page book is a theological treatise validating women's right and responsibility to obey the call to public ministry.[62] She proposed the three-pronged Biblical argument explained in this chapter.

This Pentecostal argument was eschatological, that is, it had to do with prophesied events concerning the End-Times. It focused on the significance of the outpouring of the Holy Spirit in the last days and the fact that men and women were equal recipients of this outpouring. Furthermore, this outpouring was perceived as empowerment for ministry. The *gift of power* to prophesy, that is, *to herald the glad tidings to every creature* was given equally to men and women alike on the Day of Pentecost. Phoebe therefore asserts that equal right to speak and minister was to be a present reality among believers.[63]

Phoebe concludes her argument saying, "It is the intention of God that women, whom he has equipped to minister in his Church, be given the right to express their spiritual gifts."[64] She

---

[60] Hiram Mattison, *The Christian Advocate and Journal* (29 Nov. 1855): 189.
[61] Raser, 365.
[62] Phoebe Palmer, *The Promise of the Father, or A Neglected Specialty of the Last Days* (Boston: Henry V. Degen, 1859).
[63] Raser, 202; Palmer, 14, 23.
[64] Raser, 199-210.

asserts, therefore, that both men and women would be "expected and compelled to pray, prophesy and preach."[65] She reasons,

> [On the Day of Pentecost] did one of that waiting company wait in vain; or did the cloven tongue of fire appear to all, and sit upon "each" waiting disciple, irrespective of sex? Surely, this was that spoken by the prophet Joel; and thus has the Holy Spirit expressly declared through Peter [referring to the account of Pentecost, Acts 2]. . . . The dispensation of the Spirit was now entered upon,—the last dispensation previous to the last glorious appearing of our Lord and Saviour Jesus Christ. The Spirit now descended alike on all. And they were all filled with the Holy Ghost, and began to speak as the Spirit gave utterance.[66]

Phoebe seems to have limited her revolutionary proposals concerning women's right to speak and be heard respectfully to church meetings. She sidesteps the issue of equal privilege and responsibility in the domestic and civil arenas. In these, she appears to have maintained the traditional view of role based on gender with women being subordinate to men. According to Phoebe, women are to be "domestic overseers" because "woman's sphere" is the home and family, and are to be "subordinate religious foot soldiers who should function through various voluntary religious associations."[67]

Phoebe precludes this view, however, when she acknowledges that the demands of "Spirit baptized religious activism" could take a "woman largely out of the home." In fact, she acknowledges that a woman "seeking entire sanctification" might have to

---

[65] Dayton and Dayton, 6; Richard Wheatley, *The Life and Letters of Mrs. Phoebe Palmer* (New York: Palmer and Hughes, 1876), 496-497.

[66] Wheatley, 496-497.

[67] Raser, 367.

give up to God her spouse and family "attachments which may distract her from 'religious duties' God may require."[68]

Essentially, Phoebe's major concern was not change "in the social or domestic relations."[69] Instead she promoted the idea of men and women together in partnership, entirely consecrated to God, empowered through the baptism of the Holy Ghost, and free to preach the Gospel.[70] One cannot help but wonder if the apparent limits of her proposal were due, at least in part, to her own favorable domestic and marital circumstances! A woman of considerable intelligence and of elite New York City social status, she enjoyed the support of her husband in every respect.

Regardless, Phoebe's position on women's status was progressive, if not revolutionary. She indeed argues toward a position of Biblical equality. Harold Raser, in *Phoebe Palmer: Her Life and Thought* says that she instigated "a self-conscious female community of religious activism, which provided identity outside the home and a political training ground."[71] In addition, he says that she contributed

> to an expanded role for women first in the church and the eventual opening up of the very social issues Palmer herself skirted. This in turn strengthened the hand of women seeking feminine equality in the larger society.[72]

According to Donald Dayton, *The Promise of the Father* was "the fountainhead of innumerable feminist arguments developed through the remainder of the nineteenth century and into the twentieth."[73]

Phoebe's anointed ministry—her preaching, teaching, and theological writings—had wide-ranging and significant influence.

---

[68] Raser, 367; Wheatly, 597-598.
[69] Raser, 210.
[70] Raser, 210.
[71] Raser, 367.
[72] Raser, 210.
[73] Donald Dayton, *Discovering an Evangelical History* (New York: Harper and Row, 1976), 96.

Besides individual lives that were changed through her preaching, thousands who never met her were influenced by her impact
as editor of the major Holiness periodical *The Guide to Holiness*
(1864-1874). Moreover, she was a founder of prestigious Drew
University (1866/1868) in Madison, New Jersey. She was and is
both an inspiration and role model for multitudes of women.

Although Phoebe's name may have been lost for decades, her
influence did not die. Now, however, we know her by name and
are inspired by her insight and courage. Searching remarks such
as the following from *The Promise of the Father*, once read, never
leave us:

> The church in many ways is a sort of potter's field, where
> the gifts of woman, as so many strangers, are buried. How
> long, O Lord, how long before man shall roll away the
> stone that we may see a resurrection.

> *Daughters of Zion, from the dust*
> *Exalt thy fallen head;*
> *Again in thy Redeemer trust.—*
> *He calls thee from the dead.*[74]

Powerful Holiness Women

Besides Phoebe Palmer, whose imprint is everywhere, hundreds of Holiness women left their mark on the church and on
society in general. Alma White (1862-1946), for example,
founded the Pillar of Fire Church.[75] Giants of the faith such as
Catherine Booth and Amanda Smith were there, and forgotten
women of influence such as Mrs. Jenny Fowler Willing took
their place of power in God's plan.

---

[74] Palmer, *The Promise of the Father*, 14, 341, 347.
[75] Alma White, *The Story of My Life and the Pillar of Fire*, 5 vols. (Zarephath, NJ: Pillar of Fire, 1935-1943); White, "Woman's Ministry" (London: Pillar of Fire, n.d.); White, *Demons and Tongues* (Zarephath, NJ: Pillar of Fire, 1936); "Alma White," *Dictionary of American Religious Biographies*, ed. Henry W. Bowden (Westport, CT: Greenwood Press, 1977), 500-501.

Catherine Mumford Booth (1829-1890),[76] who "laid the first stone of the Salvation Army"[77] worked tirelessly for equal authority, equal rights, and equal responsibilities for women on the basis of redemption and Pentecost.[78] In the marriage relationship, she staunchly refused to be considered or treated anything but equal with her husband, William Booth (1829-1912).[79] Influenced by Phoebe Palmer, and appalled by a pamphlet "which denied the right of Mrs. Palmer and other women to preach," she wrote her own thirty-two page tract entitled *Female Ministry*.[80] In it she laments the inequality of women as "a remarkable device of the devil," but she triumphantly proclaims, "the time of her deliverance draweth nigh." Indeed, Booth was "an unfailing, unflinching, uncompromising champion of woman's rights."[81] As a result of her efforts, the Salvation Army has always ordained women and has promoted biblical equality.

Mrs. Amanda Matthews-Berry Smith (1837-1915) was born the child of slave parents in the State of Maryland.[82] Inspired by Phoebe Palmer to fulfill her call to ministry, she began preaching in 1870 and continued despite cruel racism and barbarous sexism. Smith, despite having only three months of formal schooling, was both highly articulate and wonderfully anointed. Her gift, indeed, made room for her and she gained remarkable respect from the educated and uneducated alike.[83] She ministered with great success throughout America, the British Isles, Liberia,

---

[76] Dayton and Dayton, 8-10; Deen, 237-245; Nancy Hardesty, *Great Women of Faith* (Grand Rapids: Baker, 1980), 103-109; Catherine Booth, *Aggressive Christianity* (Boston: The Christian Witness, 1899).

[77] Hardesty, 107.

[78] Hardesty, 104.

[79] Hardesty, 104.

[80] Catherine Booth, Female Ministry: Woman's Right to Preach the Gospel (New York: Salvation Army Supplies, 1975 reprint of London: Salvation Army, 1975 edition); F.Booth-Tucker, *The Life of Catherine Booth*, vol. 1 (New York: Fleming H. Revell, 1892), 348; Dayton and Dayton, 8.

[81] Booth-Tucker, 123.

[82] Amanda Smith, *An Autobiography: The Story of the Lord's Dealings with Mrs. Amanda Smith, the Colored Evangelist* (Chicago: Meyer and Brother, Publishers, 1893; Hardesty, 117-122; Dean, 251-258.

[83] Dayton and Dayton, 15.

Sierra Leone, Burma, and India where she was commended by Methodist Bishop Thoburn.[84]

Mrs. Jenny Fowler Willing was an important advocate of biblical equality. As a contributing editor of *The Guide to Holiness* in the last decade of the century, she roused her readers with a stirring proclamation of the power of Pentecost and its significance for woman. In "Woman and the Pentecost," she charges that woman is inclined to be content "with shining, like the moon, with borrowed splendor, as the mother, sister, or wife of the great so-and-so." Mrs. Fowler continues, "She has left her talent in its napkin while she has been obeying the world's dictum by helping make the most of his."[85]

In a further article on the same topic, she writes:

> In Christian England, when the light of the Pentecost had grown dim, it was believed that it would subvert the social order for women to learn more than merely to read and write.
>
> Less than a century ago, Mary Somerville was forbidden by her father to study mathematics, for which she had genius, for fear that such knowledge would ruin a woman's brain.
>
> When the Pentecostal light shines most brightly, women do the bulk of the common-school teaching. They are also principals, professors, college presidents, and are admitted to all the learned professions.
>
> Above all, they owe their spiritual opportunities to the outpouring of the Holy Spirit. In all places untouched by Christian light they are not sure that they have souls. Where the light shines clearly they have equal rights with the men by whose side they labor for God's glory. This

---

[84] Hardesty, 121.

[85] Mrs. J. Fowler Willing, "Woman and the Pentecost," Guide to Holiness, vol. 69, (Sept. 1898), 87.

being so, how ought they to do and endure to spread the Pentecostal light through all the earth![86]

Unlike Phoebe Palmer, Mrs. Fowler Willing's Pentecostal view was unapologetically egalitarian rather than more carefully inclusive in nature. In her article "Woman Under the Pentecostal Baptism," published in *The Guide to Holiness* in December 1899, she exhorts,

> The union of Aquila and Priscilla was a typical Pentecostal marriage. Each supplemented the other. The question of superiority or precedence could have no place in the adjustment of their relation to each other. Neither claimed special privilege or exemption from duty on account of sex, no matter what pagan, Hebrew or Christian friends or enemies might say or do. They were free in Christ, and each must ask, as Paul did in the hour of his conversion, "Lord, what wilt thou have me to do?"[87]

Holiness Renews Quaker Women

The convergence of Holiness and Quaker spirituality advanced the possibility of equality for women. The Holiness Revival, with its emphasis on spiritual experience, resounded with many Quakers, who, since the days of George Fox, had lost much of their spiritual vitality. Through the revival, however, many received new impetus to recover a biblical lifestyle with its egalitarian character.

The awakened Methodists, on the other hand, drew strength from the example of Quaker women. Appreciation for Quaker egalitarian thinking was expressed, for example, by Free Methodist founder, B. T. Roberts writing in 1891. Commending the Friends for their two hundred year-old practice of full equality of

---

[86] Mrs. J. Fowler Willing, "Women and the Pentecost," *The Guide to Holiness*, Jan. 1898, 21.

[87] Mrs. J. Fowler Willing, "Woman Under the Pentecostal Baptism," *The Guide to Holiness*, Dec. 1899, 52-53.

men and women, he observed that Quaker homes were models to be envied and Quaker women, pillars to be emulated.[88]

Friends in Need of Renewal. By the 1800s, Friends in America had divided into at least three main groups; Hicksites, Guerney-ites, and Wilburites. The Hicksites, with liberty of conscience as their principal tenet, represented the more liberal wing and were outspoken advocates both of abolition of slavery and of women's rights. The Guerneyites, emerging in 1837, had drifted toward an institutionalism and reflected Anglicanism, but gave greater emphasis to the Bible than did their Hicksites cousins. The Wil-burites of Rhode Island, maintaining the teaching of the Inner Light, were more orthodox than the Hicksites, but they also re-jected the Guerneyites as being too Episcopal. Many Wilburites migrated to Ohio and North Carolina after 1845. In the 1870-80s these conservative Quakers in Indiana, Iowa, Kansas kept alive the idea of spiritual equality. All three groups participated in strategic ways in the nineteenth century elevation of women.

Mobilized by the Spirit for Revolution. Especially after 1860, through the Holiness Revival, the Holy Spirit reawakened Quaker women. It was, in fact, through personal encounters and relationship with the Spirit of God that these women were in-spired and empowered for social action.[89] A leading Quaker minister, Drusilla Wilson, said, "I gave myself wholly to the Lord. . . . I was filled with the Spirit and experienced a real bap-tism of the Holy Ghost."[90] This heartfelt profession is an exam-ple of the level of commitment experienced by the Quaker women. Summarizing her extensive research on the subject, Carole D. Spencer says,

---

[88] The historical and biblical study of the origins of this egalitarian position are documented in Chapter 9. B. T. Roberts, *Ordaining Women* (Rochester: Earnest Christian, 1891), Preface.

[89] Carole D. Spencer, "Evangelism, Feminism and Social Reform: The Quaker Woman Minister and the Holiness Revival," *Quaker History: The Bulletin of Friends Historical Society*, Vol. 80 No. 1, Spring 1991: 28.

[90] Jospeh C. Wilson et al., *Brief Sketch of the Lives of Jonathan and Drusilla Wilson* (Plainfield, IN: Publishing Associa-tion of Friends, 1909) 30-31.

The women generally described their experience as either a consecration, a sanctification, a baptism of the Holy Spirit, or becoming "fully saved" and committed to God, and it usually included the dedication of their "tongue and talents" to some particular calling, moral duty, or social vision.[91]

Thus renewed with fresh, spiritual vigor, they seemed to regain the spunk of the early Quaker women (1650-1690) "who often defied convention and found themselves in the vanguard of a revolutionary movement."[92] They challenged the firmly entrenched notion that women were to operate in a "domestic sphere" while the "public sphere" was the sole domain of men. They functioned in a "side by side" relationship with men that allowed them to preach and teach, to have "equal place" and "equal voice" in the affairs of the congregation, and to experience "equality, unity, and consensus" in marriage.[93] As Helen B. Harris, a Holiness Quaker woman and close friend of Hannah Whittal Smith, wrote in 1888:

> As in the counsels between a truly united husband and wife, the one advises and suggests probably as often as the other, and nothing is ever done until both are agreed, so should it be in the church.[94]

In the same article, Harris speaks out about the tragedy of female subjugation among Christians. She says that Christian women have been

> repressed beyond what one would have thought possible, always under the rule of priestly masculine authority and often of masculine assumption and tyranny, one shudders

---

[91] Spencer, 28.
[92] Spencer, 30.
[93] Spencer, 24-25.
[94] Helen B. Harris, "Woman in the Church," *Friends' Review* 41 (1888): 739.

to think of the suppressed inspirations and quenched lights, and distressed, puzzled, agonized souls that have suffered from this false state of things down through the centuries, and in many churches are suffering still![95]

One of the most vibrant voices among the Friends was Esther Frame. Once an ordained Methodist Episcopalian, she was drawn to the Friends where "equality was an explicit principle."[96] Esther and her husband Nathan ministered as an evangelistic team, and for them an inherent part of the Gospel of Christ was equality. Addressing the Friends in Richmond, Indiana, in 1887, she said,

> John Henry Douglas said we do not want the woman question raised, but we do want the woman question, and there is no doubt that in this we need more saving, real, personal salvation, being born of the Spirit, washed, sanctified, filled with the Holy Ghost, and walking with God; there is not any one subject that we need to leave before the world more than the privileges the Gospel brings to womanhood, and I feel the importance of our maintaining that principle of making no difference between man and woman. We scarcely realize this necessity until we go out into the world and see how women are held in bondage.[97]

Social Reform and Spirit-Led Women. The influence of Spirit-motivated, Quaker women in advancing social reform in the latter half of the 1800s is enormous. Quaker women, for example, were at the forefront of both the Women's Christian Temperance Union and the Women's Suffrage Movement. *The Friends' Review,* an influential Quaker journal, reported that reform for social purity must, in fact, be infused with Gospel influence.[98]

---

[95] Harris, 739.

[96] Spencer, 33.

[97] *Proceedings* 89-91 from the General Conference of Friends in Richmond, 1887, cited by Spencer, 34.

[98] *Friends' Review,* 41:570 cited by Spencer, 31.

This comment was made in response to an 1888 Women's Convention in Washington, D.C. attended by "the most distinguished women of the age . . . [including] Julia Ward Howe,[99] Susan B. Anthony, Elizabeth Cady Stanton, Frances A. Willard, Mary A. Livermore, and Lucy Stone Blackwell."[100]

"The Society of Friends has always held that Christians should obey the teaching of Christ literally,"[101] said highly respected Quaker, Mary W. Thomas.[102] Compelled by her Christian conviction, Mary ministered to prostitutes and female defendants oppressed by the judicial courts. She also stood courageously against the sexist laws of her state.[103]

Rhoda M. Coffin, wife of a prominent banker in Richmond, Indiana, was another force for social reform. Active in the bid for women's suffrage, she was honored by inclusion in the *History of Woman Suffrage*. Her unique contribution, however, was her founding of the Women's Prison and Girls' Reformatory in Indianapolis. This was the first state prison exclusively for women, and it was a place where reform founded on the belief in the value and dignity of every person–not punishment–was the order of the day.[104]

Hannah Whittal Smith (1832-1911) is, perhaps, the most widely known of the Quaker women among conservative Christians today. Her classic book *The Christian's Secret of a Happy Life*, first published in 1875, is still available.[105] She and her husband, Robert Pearsall Smith, were active in the Keswick "deeper life" movement in England. But Hannah, especially, was also involved

[99] Founder of Mother's Day and author/composer of The Battle Hymn of the Republic.

[100] *Christian Worker*, 18:163 cited by Spencer, 31.

[101] Mary W. Thomas, 245-246 cited by Spencer, 35.
[102]
    Hannah Whittal Smith, *The Christian's Secret of a Happy Life* (New York: Revell, 1888); Logan Pearsall Smith, ed., *Philadelphia Quaker: The Letters of Hannah Whittal Smith* (New York: Harcourt, Brace and Co., 1950), xiii. Mary W. Thomas was the sister of Hannah Whittal Smith.

[103] Helen Flexner, *A Quaker Childhood* (New Haven: Yale University Press, 1940), 108-109.

[104] Spencer, 36-37.

[105] Hannah Whittal Smith, *The Christian's Secret of a Happy Life* (New York: Revell, 1888).

in movements with special concerns for the welfare and equality of women.

Global Advance through the Temperance Movement

The Women's Crusade of the Winter of 1873-74. In late fall of 1873, in Ohio and New York, many women banned together protesting the sale of liquor in an all-out effort to halt the suffering of women and children brought on by drunken husbands. Beginning with the women in Fredonia, New York, the women, led by Mrs. Esther McNeil, met to pray. Then they marched to the local saloon where they knelt in prayer again.

In Hillsboro, Ohio, on December 24, 1873, seventy women led by Mrs. Eliza Thompson met in the Presbyterian church for prayer and then marched on the local saloons.

> Walking two by two, the smaller ones in the front and the taller coming after, they sang more or less confidently, "Give to the Winds Thy Fears," that heartening assurance of Divine protection now known to every WCTU member as the Crusade Hymn. Every day they visited the saloons and the drug stores where liquor was sold. They prayed on sawdust floors or, being denied entrance, knelt on snowy pavements before the doorways until almost all the sellers capitulated.[106]

These crusades met with much ridicule from scoffers. Nevertheless, in fifty days, the women halted the liquor traffic in "two hundred and fifty towns, increased by one hundred percent the attendance at church and decreased that at the criminal courts in like proportion."[107]

The founding meeting of the national organization, the National Woman's Christian Temperance Union (WCTU), con-

---

[106] Helen E. Tyler, *Where Prayer and Purpose Meet,* WCTU website, 1998.
[107] E. P. Gordon, *Women Torchbearers*, WCTU website.

vened in November, 1874, in Cleveland, Ohio. Mrs. Annie Turner Wittenmyer was elected president and Francis Willard, corresponding secretary. This was a Christian reform movement outside the jurisdiction of the church. It was a women's movement for women and for "the protection of the home." Its slogan was "For God and Home and Native Land." The women selected the watchwords *Agitate - Educate - Legislate* and the white ribbon to symbolize purity. The WCTU very quickly became the largest woman's organization in the United States, and later, through the work of Francis Willard, it became the largest woman's organization in the world. [108]

Francis Willard. Frances Willard (1839-98) became the WCTU's second president in 1879 and remained at that post until 1898.[109] She and Hannah Whittal Smith were close friends, and Hannah participated enthusiastically in the WCTU. In fact, in 1883, she became the first superintendent of the WCTU's Evangelistic Department.

As with the other women in the movement, Willard drew strength and direction from her relationship with God. She had grown up on Finney revivalism because her father studied for the ministry with Finney and Mahan at Oberlin College. At the age of twenty-seven, she experienced sanctification through faithfully attending Phoebe Palmer's meetings in Evanston, Illinois, in 1866. Her deep dependence on the Lord is obvious in her description of her divine call to become active in the suffrage movement.

> While alone on my knees one Sabbath, in the capital of the Crusade state [Columbus, Ohio], as I lifted my heart to

[108] WCTU Website: www.wctu.org

[109] Francis Willard, *Woman in the Pulpit* (Boston: D. Lothrop, 1888); Frances Willard, *Glimpses of Fifty Years: The Autobiography of an American Woman* (Chicago: H. J. Smith and Co., 1889), 419; Ray Strachey, *Francis Willard: Her Life and Work* (New York: Fleming H. Revell, 1913), 208; Anna A. Gordon, *The Beautiful Life of Frances E. Willard* (Chicago: Woman's Temperance Publishing Association, 1898); Nancy Hardesty, Lucille Sider Dayton, Donald W. Dayton, "Women in the Holiness Movement," *Women of Spirit*, ed. Rosemary Ruether and Eleanor McLaughlin (New York: Simon and Schuster, 1979), 235; Hardesty, 109-116.

God crying, "What wouldst thou have me to do?" there was borne in my mind, as I believe from loftier regions, this declaration, "You are to speak for woman's ballot as a weapon for protection for her home." Then for the first and only time in my life, there flashed through my brain a complete line of arguments and illustrations.[110]

Willard is probably best known for her work through the WCTU. It was her vision and administrative ability that made the organization the first large women's organization to be truly global. The "Round-the-World White Ribbon Missionaries," (as she called the WCTU representatives), were in fifty nations including such places as Asia, Australia, India, China, Japan, South Africa, Ceylon, Palestine, Canada, Europe, and South America.[111] Willard credits her vision and organizational ability to the Lord: "[Only] as I come close to God and through Christ's blood am made a new creature, am I ready for this work so blessed and so high."[112]

This tremendous work supporting family values not only protected women and children at home and work, but it also provided a vehicle for Bible study and evangelistic work among men on the jobsite. In addition, the WCTU proposed, supported, and helped establish the following:

- women's right to vote
- shelters for abused women and children
- the eight-hour work day
- equal pay for equal work
- founding of kindergartens
- assistance in founding the PTA
- federal aid for education

---

[110] Strachey, 209.

[111] Gordon, 149.

[112] Ruth A. Tucker and Walter Liefeld, *Daughters of the Church: Women in Ministry from the New Testament Times to the Present* (Grand Rapids: Zondervan, 1987), 273; See Gordon, Chapter IX, 147-203.

- stiffer penalties for sex crimes against girls and women
- uniform marriage and divorce laws
- prison reform and police matrons
- women police officers
- homes and education for wayward girls
- promotion of nutrition
- legal aid
- labor's right to organize
- passive demonstrations and world peace

In addition, the WCTU has worked against drug traffic, white slavery, child labor, and army brothels.[113]

All this was accomplished outside the bounds of the traditional, institutional church. As Willard said, this was the case, "not because they wish to be so," but because the church "is afraid of her own gentle, earnest -hearted daughters."[114]

Dr. Katharine C. Bushnell. Another remarkable Christian woman, one whose name was all but forgotten until very recently, was Katharine Bushnell (1855-1946). After a time as a Methodist Episcopal medical missionary in China, she had a medical practice in Denver. Then in 1885, Francis Willard persuaded Dr. Bushnell to become the National Evangelist of the WCTU's Department for the Advancement of Social Purity.[115] This meant giving up her medical practice, but she "had not studied medicine for its own sake, but as a help in Christian work." She sensed God calling her to this important new work, and from that time forward, she worked relentlessly for women.[116] One of her first efforts involved risking her life exposing the "white slave trade" of prostitutes and the horrific abuse

---

[113] WCTU website.

[114] Francis E. Willard, *Woman and Temperance* (Hartford: Park, 1883), 57-58.

[115] Dana Hardwick, *Oh Thou Woman that Bringest Good Tidings: The Life and Work of Katharine C. Bushnell* (St. Paul: Christians for Biblical Equality, 1995), 13-23.

[116] Cited by Harwick, 20; Bushnell, *Brief Sketch*, 5-6; Frances Willard, ed., *A Woman of the Century* (Buffalo: Moolton, 1893), 141. Glimpses of Fifty Years: The Autobiography of an American Woman

of girls and women in the lumber camps of Michigan and Wisconsin.[117] Her crusades against this cruelty to and degradation of women extended around the world to England, India, China, Hong Kong, and San Francisco.[118]

As Hardwick points out in her recent biography of Bushnell, her final crusade came through the power of the pen. While a doctor in China, she had begun to see how culturally-biased translations of the Bible intensified female bondage. Because she knew that the true Gospel heals and liberates, she devoted the last forty years of her life in diligent language study, biblical translation, and writing.[119] Among her voluminous writings is the treasure chest for women's Bible study, *God's Word to Women.*

Hardwick notes that Bushnell "saw the task of educated women as twofold." She believed, "They must spread to all women in all places the full gospel message of the same freedom and equality as men have in Jesus Christ." And she believed, "Educated women must attack the 'false teachings as to the place of women in God's economy' and break . . . the 'tyranny'" of biased, erroneous biblical translation and commentaries."[120]

Spirit-Led Women Fight for Freedom to Vote

Another friend and colleague of Hannah Whittal Smith was Susan B. Anthony (1820-1906), a Quaker schoolteacher from Rochester, New York. Along with Elizabeth Cady Stanton, she founded the National Woman Suffrage Association (1870).[121] Anthony was also active in the Temperance Movement with Francis Willard and had been an ardent abolitionist. She is best

---

[117] Hardwick, 25-34.

[118] Hardwick, 35-80.

[119] Hardwick, 81-88.

[120] Hardwick, 103-105

[121] Doris Stevens, *Jailed for Freedom: American Women Win the Vote,* ed. Carol O'Hare (Troutdale, OR: NewSage Press, 1995), 14; Spencer, 39.

remembered, however, for her persistent, pioneering efforts that culminated in women in the United States gaining the right to vote in 1920. She writes:

I do pray, and that most earnestly and constantly, for some terrific shock to startle women of the nation into a self-respect which will compel them to see the absolute degradation of their present position; which will compel them to break their yoke of bondage and give them faith in themselves; which will make them proclaim their allegiance to women first. . . . The fact is, women are in chains, and their servitude is all the more debasing because they do not realize it. Oh to compel them to see and tell and to give them courage and the conscience to speak and act for their own freedom, though they face the scorn and contempt of all the world for doing it![122]

Hannah Whittal Smith, too, was convinced that suffrage was a Christian cause, and in describing a speech she made on suffrage, she said,

In my speech I said I had come to the advocacy of this reform by the way of the gospel, that Christ came to break every yoke and set free all that were bound, and that I wanted to follow in his steps and share in his work. I said the gospel did not arbitrarily upset the existing order of things, but it put a mine under all wrong and oppression that finally blew it up. And that therefore women were made free by the working out of the principles of Christ who had declared there is neither male nor female in him.[123]

Indeed, Hannah Whittal Smith was an advocate of equality

---

[122] Cited by Stevens, 6.."

[123] Hannah Whitall Smith, Letter to Daughter I:29. 1882, cited by Spewncer, 39.

for women in the public arena. She was also an advocate of biblical equality in marriage. To her daughter, she wrote:

> I am thoroughly roused on the subject for I have had so
> many cases of grievous oppression of men over their wives
> lately that my blood boils with indignation. And before
> thee is married I want to have thy position as an equal
> with thy husband settled on a legal basis. The moment one
> looks into the subject at all it seems utterly incomprehen-
> sible how we women could have endured it as patiently has
> we have. Literally and truly up to within a very few years
> women have been simply *slaves*. And some women say they
> like it! Ugh! Nothing but the vote will set us at liberty but
> that will, for then we shall be not only women, but *human*
> beings as well. Now we are nothing but women.[124]

It was, in fact, Quaker women who led the seventy year-long
suffrage movement giving American women the right to vote.
This struggle gained corporate identity at Seneca Falls, New
York on July 13, 1848, through the leadership efforts of four
Quaker women Lucretia Coffin Mott, Martha Coffin Wright,
Jane Hunt, Mary Ann McClintock, and a Quaker sympathizer,
Elizabeth Cady Stanton.[125] Formulated by these Quaker women,
the Declaration of Women's Rights was ratified by one hundred
delegates.

Some see this event as the birth of feminism, and perhaps
they are correct. Regardless, it should be noted that this movement was born in the hearts of Spirit-oriented, Bible-believing
women. These women faced persecution, incarceration, suffering, and defamation not unlike that of their seventeenth-century
Quaker forerunners.

---

[124] Smith, Letter: to Daughter I:29. 1882 cited by Spencer, 40.
[125] Bacon, 1, 114.

Consider the following statements from the Declaration of Women's Rights written by these Quaker women.

- "We hold these truths to be self-evident; that all men and women are created equal."
- "He [man] has compelled her to submit to laws, in the formation of which she had no voice. . . ."
- "He has made her, if married, in the eye of the law, civilly dead."
- "He has taken from her all right to property, even to the wages she earns."
- "He has devoured, in every way that he could, to destroy her confidence in her own powers, to lessen her self-respect and to make her willing to lead a dependent and abject life."[126]

Key Quaker women devoted their entire lives to win the long and very difficult fight for women's right to vote.[127] And like the early Quaker women before them, they often found themselves persecuted and jailed. Nevertheless, driven by a sense of what was right and motivated by the Spirit of God, they pressed on. Lucretia Mott (1793-1880) served as the "wise elder states-woman to the new women's rights movement," and Elizabeth Cady Stanton (1815-1902) wrote forceful articles and planned strategy. In 1852, when Susan B. Anthony joined the women's movement, she provided the organizational ability and legwork needed by the young movement, and she carried it forward until 1906.[128]

Anthony's successor was another Quaker, Alice Paul (1885-1977).[129] She was at the helm when Congress passed the

---

[126] Cited by Jane Eisner, "Women's Issues: 150 Years of Progress Should Encourage Us to Change Focus," *The Dallas Morning News*, July 21, 1998: 9A.

[127] Margaret Hope Bacon, "Lucretia Mott: Pioneer of Peace," *Quaker History* 82, no. 2 (Fall 1993): 63-79. See also Bacon, "Quaker Women and the early Suffrage Movement," 120-136.

[128] Bacon, 1, 116-17.

[129] Stevens, *Jailed for Freedom*, 187; Bacon, 1, 190, 198-201. See also Bacon, Ch. 12, "The Quaker Influence in the Final Struggle for Suffrage," 184-201.

women's suffrage bill in June, 1919. This was the first significant step toward political equality for women in America. The 19th Amendment to the Constitution became law on August 26, 1920, giving women the right to vote. With this achieved, Alice Paul earned three law degrees and then authored the Equal Rights Amendment. Interviewed by *Newsweek* on the occasion of her ninety-first birthday, Alice Paul made reference to her Quaker heritage and expressed deep concern that equality for women was still not a reality.[130] She said,

> Women are still voiceless. We have to wait until complete equality becomes a reality. I grew up in a Quaker family and the Quakers believe in the equality of the sexes. It is hard to grow up in such a family and never hear about anything else. When you put your hand to the plow, you can't put it down until you reach the end of the row.

Women in the Missionary Movement

Another significant movement of the late nineteenth century that opened new opportunities for meaningful ministry for women was the Missionary Movement. It has been said that this endeavor was "substantially larger than any of the other mass woman's movements in the nineteenth century."[131] Both married and single women went abroad as "sent ones," while at home, thousands of women banned together in support of their sisters' missionary endeavors.

Women's Missionary Societies. Throughout the 1860s and 1870s, women were cooperating successfully with one another in women's societies formed for the express purpose of advancing world missions. In 1834, a pre-Civil War attempt by women to

---

[130] Stevens, 187-88; *Newsweek*, March 23, 1970: 18.

[131] Patricia R. Hill, *The Word Their Household: The American Woman's Foreign Mission Movement and Cultural Transformation, 1870-1920* (Ann Arbor: Univeristy of Michigan Press, 1985), 3; Ruth A. Tucker and Walter Liefled, *Daughters of the Church: Women and Ministry from New Testament Times to the Present* (Grand Rapids: Zondervan, 1987), 291.

band together to support missionary activities had collapsed, but almost thirty years later, the climate was right. By 1861, Christian women had developed sufficient autonomy and strength to proceed, and the interdenominational Woman's Union Missionary Society of America emerged as the successful prototype for numerous others that sprang up, especially within Protestant denominations.[132]

There were several reasons for the success of the women's efforts. For example, American Protestantism in general at this time was missions oriented. Also, women were emerging in new leadership capacities within the larger society. Since middle and upper class women had only "one tenth of the work in the home that their grandmothers bore," they became "huge reserves of untapped volunteer labor to 'work for the life of the world.'"[133]

These women's societies accomplished several noteworthy achievements. They raised large sums of money even though they were prohibited from doing so in the context of the larger congregation. They "provided the first readable and widely available" missionary literature. They held missionary conventions, missionary exhibits, institutes, and summer schools for missions. They sent and supported single women missionaries and rendered critical support to wives of missionary husbands.[134]

> By 1882 the sixteen existing women's missionary societies had raised almost six million dollars and had sent out 694 single women missionaries. By 1900 the women's societies were supporting 389 wives, 856 single women missionaries, and 96 doctors. They were responsible for numerous

---

[132] Virginia Lieson Brereton and Christa Ressmeyer Klein, "American Women in Ministry: A History of Protestant Beginning Points," ed. Rosemary Ruether and Eleanor McLaughlin, *Women of Spirit* (New York: Simon and Schuster, 1979), 304-05.

[133] Brereton and Klein, 307; Louise Armstrong Cattan, *Lamps Are for Lighting: The Story of Helen Barrett Montgomery and Lucy Waterbury Peabody* (Grand Rapids: Eerdmans, 1972), 57-58.

[134] Brereton and Klein, 308.

orphanages, hospitals, schools and dispensaries around the world.[135]

Special Challenges for Women. Missionary women of this era, too often excluded from the annals of missions, were, nevertheless, outstanding pioneers and heroes of the faith. Mary Slessor pioneered in Nigeria for almost forty years. Amy Carmichael spent fifty fruitful years in India. Lottie Moon was a dynamic missionary in China. Both married and single women gave their lives to spread the Gospel around the world.[136]

The lot of married women in overseas missions was especially trying. They were not acknowledged as missionaries, but only as "assistant missionaries," merely the wives of missionaries.[137] This, of course, points to the unfortunate exporting of traditional, patriarchal ideas, propagating the erroneous notion that the Bible teaches the subordination of women.

In addition to the normal hardships of female subjugation, married women suffered additional stress from frequent pregnancies, dangerous childbirths, sickness, extreme poverty, isolation, and husbands who were, in some cases, more concerned about their missionary call than about their families. It was often the case that missionary men married up to three times, their wives having died of the extreme hardships on the field.[138]

Emotional breakdown was also too common. Such was the fate of Dorothy Carey, wife of famous missionary to India, William Carey.[139] Also Mary Livingstone, wife of famous missionary David Livingstone, returned to England alone with the children where, abandoned by her husband, she was homeless and friendless, "often living on the edge of poverty in cheap lodg-

---

[135] These sixteen boards are listed in Brereton and Klein, 305. Cited by Brereton and Klein, 306 from R. Pierce Beaver, *All Loves Excelling: American Protestant Women in World Missions* (Grand Rapids: Eerdmans, 1968), 107-108.

[136] Tucker and Liefeld, 292. See Ruth A. Tucker, *From Jerusalem to Irian Jaya: A Biographical History of Christian Missions* (Grand Rapids: Zondervan, 1983).

[137] Tucker and Liefeld, 293, Beaver, 53.

[138] Ticker and Liefeld, 293-299.

[139] Tucker and Liefled, 293-294; Mary Drewery, *William Carey: A Biography* (Grand Rapids: Zondervan, 1979), 81.

ings."[140] Then too, in China, Priscilla Studd, wife of C. T. Studd, lost her health and returned to England, and her husband, leaving her ill, ministered in Africa, for twenty years.[141]

Ann Hassletine Judson, wife of Adoniram Judson, in some respects was an exception to this pattern. She went with her husband, not because he went, but because she had "a full conviction of its being a [personal] call."[142] Although she, like other married women, was severely hampered by sickness and the problems associated with frequent pregnancies on the field, she found writing to be an effective tool of ministry. In reporting the conditions of women in Burma, for example, she stirred her readers: "The wife receives the appellation of *my servant*, or *my dog*, and is allowed to partake of what her lordly husband is pleased to give at the *conclusion* of his repast."[143] She challenged her readers thus:

> Shall we, my beloved friends, suffer minds like these to lie dormant, to wither in ignorance and delusion, to grope their way to eternal ruin, without an effort on our part, to raise, to refine, to elevate, and point to that Savior who has died equally for them as for us? . . . let us make a united effort, let us call on all, old and young, in the circle of our acquaintance, to join us in attempting to meliorate the situation, to instruct, to enlighten and save females in the Eastern world."[144]

Reaching Women, the Priority. Many women began to recognize that the single most important missionary endeavor was to

---

[140] Tucker and Liefeld, 294; George Seaver, *David Livingstone, His Life and Letters* (New York: Harper, 1957), 276; Oliver Ransford, *David Livingstone: The Dark Interior* (New York: St. Martin's 1978, 118.

[141] Tucker and Liefeld, 294; *Norman Grubb, Once Caught, No Escape: Norman Grubb's Life Story* (Fort Washington, PS: Christian Literature Crusade, 49).

[142] Tucker and Liefeld, 295; Quoted by Courtney Anderson *To the Golden Shore: The Life of Adonirma Judson* (Grand Rapids: Zondervan, 1972), 84

[143] *American Baptist Magazine*, 4 (Jan. 19223): 20, cited by Tucker and Liefeld, 296.

[144] *American Baptist Magazine*, 4 (Jan. 1923): 20 cited in Joan Jacobs Brumberg, *Mission for Life: The Story of the Family of Adoniram Judson* (New York: Macmillan, 1980), 87 and in Tucker and Liefeld, 296.

reach the mothers. It was said that "a man's church will last for one generation," but "mothers are the conservators of religion, bringing up their children in their own faith."[145] In this endeavor, the need for single women missionaries became obvious, and by 1894, thirty-three women's foreign mission boards had sponsored about one thousand women as teachers, doctors, evangelists, and relief workers.[146] This development, however, brought censor in 1888 from the Baptist leaders who warned women "to recognize the leadership of men . . . so as not to discredit the natural and predestined headship of man in Missions."[147] But as Lottie Moon said, "What women want who come to China is free opportunity to do the largest possible work . . . . What women have a right to demand is perfect equality."[148] As Tucker and Liefeld correctly note, "The vast majority of women missionaries were motivated by a deep sense of commitment to God far more than by any desire to attain personal recognition or power."[149]

Women in the Healing Movement

Another significant expression of the Holy Spirit in the nineteenth century was the Divine Healing Movement.[150] Pioneers of this movement included women leaders such as Mother Anna Lee, Ellen G. White, and Mrs. Elizabeth Mix. Leaders of later years included such women as Carrie Judd Montgomery (1858-

---

[145] Hill, *The World Their Household*, 47, 49

[146] Tucker and Liefled, 301; Rosemary Keller, "Lay Women in Protestant Tradition," ed. Rosemary Ruether and Rosemary Keller, *Women and Religion in America: The Nineteenth Century, A Documentary History*, 3 vols. (New York: Harper and Row, 1981), 1:242-43.

[147] Cited by Jane Hunter, *The Gospel of Gentility: American Women missionaries in Turn-of-the-Century China* (New Haven: Yale Univeristy Press, 1984), 13-14.

[148] Cited by Tucker and Liefeld, 303.

[149] Cited by Tucker and Liefeld, 303.

[150] The chief source for this section is Paul G. Chappell who is the leading authority on Healing Movements. See Paul Chappell, "The Divine Healing Movement in America," Ph.D. dissertation, Drew University, 1983; Paul Chappell, "Healing Movements," Dictionary of Pentecostal and Charismatic Movements, ed. Stanley M. Burgess and Gary B. McGee (Grand Rapids: Zondervan, 1988), 353.

1946)[151] and Maria Woodworth-Etter (1844-1924).[152] The prominence of these and other women indicates the effectiveness of their ministries, ministries that were powerfully anointed by the Holy Spirit.

Women in the Early Days of the Healing Movement. The Shakers were people of the Spirit, who, in addition to their unique spiritual dancing and rule of celibacy, prayed for the sick and saw abundant healings. The leader of this interesting group was Mother Anna Lee (1736-81). In addition to prayer, the Shakers eventually advocated personal hygiene and natural preventive medicine.[153]

In the 1840s, the Adventists also prayed for the sick based on biblical precedents. Led by Ellen Gould White (1827-1915), the Adventists experienced divine healing and advocated healthful living. In 1866, she established a clinic in West Battle Creek, Michigan, staffed only by Christian doctors, and treated the sick with a combination of diet, medicine, and faith. In 1910, she founded Loma Linda University to train doctors in this approach to health and healing. [154]

In mid-century, an articulate and well-educated woman named Mrs. Elizabeth Mix from Wolcottville, Connecticut, was healed of tuberculosis through the ministry of Ethan O. Allen. She became the first African-American healing evangelist. Her unique contribution to the Healing Revival was her admonition to the sick that, having received the prayer of faith, they were to act upon that faith regardless of feeling. In 1879/80, through Mrs. Mix's anointed ministry, Carrie Judd Montgomery, an in-

[151] Carrie Judd Montgomery, *Triumps of Faith*, vol. 65, no. 9, Sept. 1946: 105; W. E. Warner, "Carrie Judd Montgomery," *Dictionary of Pentecostal and Charismatic Movements*, 627-628.

[152] Maria Woodworth Etter, *Signs and Wonders* (1916; reprint, Tulsa: Harrison House, 1980).

[153] Chappell, 354, E. L. Blumhofer, "Shakers," *Dictionary of Pentecostal Charismatic Movements*, 782.

[154] Chappell, 355.

valid at the time, received complete healing and became a minister of healing herself. [155]

Faith Homes and Women. Faith homes were an important part of the nineteenth century Healing Movement. The concept probably began in Germany with Johann Christoph Blumhardt. He was a Lutheran minister who began seeing miraculous healings in his ministry in 1843. When, on the basis of Mark 16:18, he prayed for a dying girl named Katarina Dittus and she was immediately healed, a revival broke out. In 1852, he was forced to withdraw from the Lutheran Church but opened a successful healing center. He would minister to the sick by first building faith through the Word of God and then, on the basis of faith and the principles of Scripture, he would pray the prayer of faith.

Another inspiration for faith homes came from Dorothea Trudel in Switzerland. When, in the midst a medical crisis in her village, Dorothea prayed on the basis of James 5:14-15 for her neighbors, they were miraculously healed. To accommodate the crowds of sick people who swarmed to the village for prayer, Trudel opened several faith homes. So successful was this woman that she was charged with "practicing the healing art without a license"–the first of many others to be similarly charged, even in the twentieth century. She was acquitted and her popularity increased dramatically. To accommodate those seeking healing, she began corresponding with them through letters, a pattern still followed by many ministers today.

By 1887, the practice of divine healing and the concept of the faith home had become so popular, especially in America, that more than thirty such centers were in operation. The practice of divine healing and the concept of faith homes merged with the

---

[155] Chappell, 358; W.E. Warner, "Carrie Judd Montgomery" *Dictionary*, 626.

Holiness Movement so that many of the healing homes were operated by Holiness women.[156]

Ministers of Divine Healing. The single, most important figure in the Healing Movement was Dr. Charles Cullis, a Boston physician. He was able to persuade leading Holiness figures, including Hannah Whittal Smith, that full salvation included healing. Cullis, had, in fact, received his sanctification experience in 1862 through Phoebe Palmer's ministry. This event marked the beginning of a vast benevolent ministry that would characterize Cullis for the remainder of his life. It was through reading the *Life of Dorothea Trudel* in 1869 that he accepted that diving healing is a permanent aspect of biblical Christianity.

The years between 1881-85 were critical developmental years for the movement. By 1887, facilitated by Cullis' healing conventions, by various publications, and by the proliferation of faith homes, divine healing may have been the fastest growing belief among American Christians.

Dr. A. J. Gordon (1836-95), a Boston pastor of great intellectual and spiritual stature was an ardent Holiness advocate and supporter of divine healing.[157] His classic book *The Ministry of Healing* (1882) is still available. Also, Dr. Gordon and his Clarendon Street Church were on the forefront of important social action including world missions, temperance, and women's rights. His 1894 book *The Ministry of Women* remains an important statement of support for women.[158] In 1889, he founded the Boston Missionary Training School, now Gordon College.

A. B. Simpson (1843-1919), a Presbyterian pastor and Holiness leader, founded the Christian and Missionary Alliance in

---

[156] Chappell, 355f.; R. M. Riss, "Faith Homes," *Dictionary*, 300-01.

[158] Ernest B. Gordon, *Adoniram Judson Gordon: A Biography* (New York: Revell, 1896).

[157] A. J. Gordon, "The Ministry of Women," *Missionary Review of the World* (Dec. 1894): 910-912; Dayton, "Evangelical Roots," 12.

1887.[159] Having been miraculously healed in 1881 through the ministry of Charles Cullis, Simpson became a strong advocate of divine healing. But Simpson was also a woman's advocate and facilitated the ministry of Spirit-led women.

Simpson expressed astounding insights related to the woman question. For example, concerning the nature of God, he rejected the idea that God is male. He said that God is neither male nor female, but that God exhibits characteristics that we understand as masculine and feminine. For example, in one of his books, Simpson discusses "The Motherhood of God." He writes, "The heart of Christ is not only the heart of man, but has in it all the tenderness and gentleness of women." In one place, he speaks metaphorically of the Holy Spirit as "our heavenly Mother," noting that the "Comforter assumes our nurture, training, teaching, and the whole direction of our life."[160]

Simpson facilitated women in both the educational and ministerial arenas. He established the coeducational Missionary Training College now called Nyack College in Nyack, New York. Several of the strong, Spirit-led women of God who worked with Simpson became leaders in the early days of the Pentecostal Revival at the turn of the century.

Carrie Judd Montgomery (1848-1946), a colleague of Simpson, had been active in the healing movement since her healing in 1879 through Elizabeth Mix' ministry. In 1880, Carrie Judd's book *The Prayer of Faith* was well-received internationally. She was the first woman to itinerate across America and she established Faith Rest Cottage, a healing home. In 1890, Judd married George Montgomery, and after moving to the outskirts of Oakland, California, they opened the Home of Peace, the first faith healing home on the West Coast. She experienced the

---

[159] A. B. Simpson, *Echoes of the New Creation* (Brooklyn, NY: Christian Alliance, 1903), 10.
[160] A. B. Simpson, *When the Comforter Came* (New York: Christian publications, 1911), 11.

Baptism of the Spirit in 1906 through a visit to Azusa Street and in 1914 was a charter member of the Assemblies of God.[161]

Maria Woodworth-Etter (1844-1924) began itinerant evangelistic meetings in 1882.[162] During her ministry that spanned forty years, she preached to crowds of 25,000. These meetings were characterized by great signs and wonders, by cripples being healed, the deaf hearing, the blind receiving their sight, healings, prophecies, singing in the Spirit, speaking in tongues, dancing, and people going into trances and falling under the power of God. She became close friends with Carrie Judd Montgomery and Aimee Semple McPherson. She participated in the great Pentecostal Revival, and Paul Chappell reports that in 1912,

> she conducted a five-month campaign for F. F. Bosworth in Dallas where miracles of healing seemed almost common and the list of influential Pentecostals who flocked to Dallas was like a "Who's Who" of early Pentecostalism.[163]

In the Healing Revival of the later nineteenth century, women were in leadership along with, in cooperation with, and independent of men. From the independent faith healing homes to the great healing meetings, the women of God were visible. The Holy Spirit anointing on their lives was the one outstanding feature that made room for them.

Conclusion

The convergence of Methodist-Holiness ideas and Quaker practices went a long way in furthering the cause of equality for women in the nineteenth century. Simply put, this was a work of the Holy Spirit even though it was expressed in a variety of ways and means in a complex society. The evidence clearly indi-

---

[161] *Triumphs of Faith, A Monthly Journal* ed. by Carrie Judd Montgomery, Sept. 1946: vol. 65, no.9.

[162] W. E. Warner, "Maria Woodworth Etter," *Dictionary*, 900-01.

[163] Chappell, "Healing Movements," 365.

cates that the men and women in the forefront of the various movements were motivated by the Spirit to forge reform.

The direction of the activity of the Spirit was toward equality, elevation, and liberation of women. This activity was obvious both inside institutional Christianity and outside the parameters of the institution in the Church at large. In the case of institutional Christianity, the extent to which women were elevated was limited by traditional notions of male headship and the idea of separate gender spheres. Outside the institution, in newly formed efforts such as the Woman's Christian Temperance Union, women were able to create new opportunities for themselves.

In some cases, men were willing to function side-by-side with women. Seth Cook Rees, founder of the Pilgrim Holiness Church, speaking in 1897, said it well:

> Nothing but jealousy, prejudice, bigotry, and a stingy love for bossing in men have prevented women's public recognition by the church. No church that is acquainted with the Holy Ghost will object to the public ministry of women.[164]

Rees represents a host of significant men and women, who, by the 1890s, were advocating either inclusion of or equality for women in the Church, in the home, and in society at large. The Holiness Revival, the Missionary Movement, the Healing Movement, the Women's Christian Temperance Union, the Suffrage Movement—these were all movements motivated by the Spirit of God and all served in one way or another to move women toward equality. It was a new day for women, and it was in such a milieu that the twentieth century Pentecostal Revival occurred.

---

[164] Seth Cook Rees, *The Ideal Pentecostal Church* (Cincinnati: M. W. Knapp, 1897), 14.

12

IT ALL CAME TOGETHER,
AT LEAST MOMENTARILY

December 31, 1901, marks the beginning of a revival movement that has, in this century, swept the globe. Since then, this tremendous, twentieth century outpouring has periodically ebbed in strength, but it has continued in resurgent tidal waves even to the present time. Now numbering 540 million adherents, and growing at the phenomenal rate of 24 million per year, this one hundred year old Pentecostal/Charismatic/Renewal Movement is the second largest group in Christendom, being outnumbered only by the centuries-old Roman Catholic Church.

The status of womanhood in this revival movement has fluctuated, but during the first decade of this revival, the early Pentecostal Revival, a unique blend of theological forces converged producing a rare time of equality for women. Generally, American women had been prepared by their social advancements and religious activities of the previous fifty years. But specifically, the elements for equality in the revival were embodied in the leaders of the revival: Charles Fox Parham (1873-1929) and Sarah Thistlethwaite Parham (1877-1937), and Lilian Thistlethwaite (1873-1939). Thus, it was not an isolated event that catapulted women from the silent pew to the public platform. A combination of factors converged to produce a Spirit-motivated, egalitarian climate

---

[1] Vinson Synan, "Policy Decisions on Tongues as an Indicator of Future Church Growth," A Paper presented at the Evangelical Theological Society Meeting, Orlando, FL, Nov. 20, 1998.

in both ministry and marriage, especially during the early years of the revival.[2]

The Birth of the Pentecostal Revival

The twentieth century Pentecostal Revival began in the 1900 New Years' Eve Watchnight at Bethel Bible College, in Topeka, Kansas. Bethel was a missionary training school opened by Charles and Sarah Parham in October, 1900, in a mansion rented from the American Bible Society on the outskirts of town.[3] The purpose of the school was to fit men and women to go to the ends of the earth to preach "'this Gospel of the kingdom' Matt. 24:14 as a witness to all the world before the end of the age."[4] Prayer was the central focus of the school and a serious effort was made to acquire both "head knowledge" and "heart-felt experience" of Scriptural principles. To do this, the forty students spent prolonged periods in prayer and study before gathering in plenary sessions to share their findings on the topic under study.[5]

The final topic under scrutiny was the baptism of the Holy Spirit. "Dad" Parham assigned the forty students the task of searching the Scripture for the answer to the question:[6] What is the Bible evidence whereby a person may know that he or she has been baptized in the Holy Spirit? On December 31, 1900, after three days of personal study, the students shared their unanimous conclusion: The Bible evidence for being baptized in the Holy Spirit is speaking in tongues.[7]

That evening at the Watchnight Service, Agnes Ozmun (1870-1937), a Holiness preacher and student at the school, was the first

---

[2] Telephone interview with Pauline Parham (1909-), daughter-in-law of Charles and Sarah Parham, 16 Oct. 1993.

[3] The material about the Parhams is based on primary resources and the manuscript for the unpublished book *The Pioneer of Pentecost: Charles Fox Parham,* Pauline Parham with Eddie and Susan Hyatt written in 1989-1991. The best primary source, published material is Sarah Parham, *The Life of Charles Fox Parham* (Joplin, Tri-State, 1930).

[4] S. Parham, 51.

[5] The major topics covered were: repentance, conversion, consecration, sanctification, healing, and the soon coming of the Lord, and the baptism of the Holy Spirit.

[6] Parham, 51.

[7] Parham, 52.

to receive the experience accompanied by speaking in tongues.[8] For three days and nights they continued in prayer, praise, and worship.[9] This event marked the first time that the doctrine of speaking in tongues as the initial evidence of the baptism of the Holy Spirit had been articulated, believed, and acted upon.

The Thistlethwaite-Parham Factor

For about the next five years, the pioneers of Pentecost were Parham disciples either directly or indirectly.[10] The Parhams, Charles and Sarah, together with Sarah's sister, Lilian, typified an important segment of devout believers in the American religious scene of the 1890s. They benefited, however, from a unique blend of elements from the Holiness, Wesleyan-Methodist, Quaker, and Missionary, and Healing Movements. These characteristics, I would suggest, qualified them to be pivotal figures in the Pentecostal Revival and as advocates of biblical equality.

Sarah "Nellie" Thistlethwaite Parham. "Mother" Parham (1877-1937), born and raised a Quaker in Tonganoxie, a Kansas Quaker community, was a well-schooled young lady with all the graces of her affluent home and training. In a Quaker wedding ceremony in 1896, she married Charles Fox Parham, a young Holiness evangel-

---

[8] Naomi Gibson, "Mother Was the First," *Pentecostal Evangel*, 9 May 1976, 6-7.

[9] "So significant was the outpouring at Bethel that any narrative of modern Pentecost should begin with Parham and the events at Bethel." Klaude Kendrick, *The Promise Fulfilled* (Springfield: Gospel Publishing House, 1966), 18.

"With the possible exception of the Church of God and the girls' home in India operated by Pandita Ramabai, every Pentecostal unit in existence today can be traced back to this obscure beginning in the state of Kansas." J. Roswell Flower, "Historical Review of the Pentecostal Movement," *A/G Heritage* (Fall 1985): 10.

William J. Seymour, the leader of the Azusa Street Revival (1906-1909) also esteems Parham and these events as the beginning: "This work began about five years ago last January, when a company of people under the leadership of Charles F. Parham who were studying God's word, tarried for Pentecost in Topeka, Kansas. After searching through the country elsewhere, they had been unable to find any Christian that had the true Pentecostal power. So they laid aside all commentaries and notes and waited on the Lord, studying His word, and what they did not understand they got down before the bench and asked God to wrought out in their hearts by the Holy Ghost." William J. Seymour, "Pentecost Has Come," *Apostolic Faith Magazine*, Sept. 1906, n.p.

J. Roswell Flower remarks, "It made the Pentecostal Movement of the Twentieth Century." J. Roswell Flower, "Birth of the Pentecostal Movement," *Pentecostal Evangel*, 26 Nov. 1950, 3.

Holiness Pentecostal scholar, Vinson Synan, concurs: "It was precisely this settlement, that tongues were the only initial evidence of the reception of the Holy Spirit, that gave Pentecost its greatest impetus." V. Synan, *The Holiness-Pentecostal Movement in the United States* (Grand Rapids: Eerdmans, 1971), 122.

[10] *Selected Sermons of the Late Charles F. Parham and Sarah E. Parham, Co-Founders of the Original Apostolic Faith Movement*, Robert L. Parham, compiler (Baxter Springs: Robert Parham, 1941).

ist who shared her intense devotion to the Lord.[11] Both Sarah and her sister, Lilian Thistlethwaite (1873-1939), who remained unmarried throughout life were preachers and teachers.

Charles Fox Parham. Charles Parham (1873-1929) was a young man of mid-west pioneer stock. He studied for the Methodist ministry, was the youngest person licensed by the Winfield [Kansas] District, and successfully pastored the prestigious Eudora Methodist Church, Eudora, Kansas (1893-1895).[12] While being groomed for a bright future to rise through the ranks of Methodism, his adherence to Holiness doctrine, his support of prohibition, and especially his dislike of "popery" and church politics, led to his leaving the denomination. In addition, he had been influenced toward a more Quaker-like perspective as a result of many hours reading Friends' literature and discussing the Bible with David Baker, a birthright Friend born in England and grandfather of his future wife. Consequently in 1895, he found himself among the 100,000-strong ranks of the "come-outers" of Methodism.[13] The following year, 1896, he and his wife and sister-in-law opened Bethel Healing Home in Topeka where they ministered to the sick, helped the needy and homeless, and published a biweekly periodical called *The Apostolic Faith Magazine*.[14]

Aspects of the Parhams' Theology. Two primary factors shaped the Parhams' theology: prayerful reading of the Bible and experiences with the Holy Spirit that empowered them to live an overcoming life of faith. In addition, the strong Quaker influence and intentional interaction with theological trends of the day helped

---

[11] P. Parham with Hyatt, 22.

[12] He attended Southwest Kansas Conference College, Winfield, Kansas in 1889-90, 1891-92, and 1892-93. He was licensed in March, 1893 before his twentieth birthday. Hyatt, 15-19; S. Parham, 4-9 and various pages following.

[13] P. Parham with Hyatt, 18; Synan, *Lectures*. Tulsa: Oral Roberts University, Spring, 1991.

[14] This reflects Parham's theme (Jude 3) which exhorts believers "to earnestly contend for the faith which was once delivered to the saints."

shape their views.[15] They believed in an old-fashioned conversion experience and a subsequent sanctification experience. They taught divine healing as being in the atonement, not because they had read about it in religious books, but because they had experienced God's healing power through faith in the Gospel. Maintaining an end-time perspective, they anticipated global revival followed by the soon return of the Lord. In view of this, they believed that the purpose of a modern Pentecost was the same as that of the original Pentecost (Acts 2:4): empowerment for missions.[16] Ecclesiastically, although the Parhams did not reject denominationalism, they did avoid institutionalism.[17] Ministry was essentially the expression of personal experience with God in the Word and in the Holy Spirit. "The power that was to accompany Pentecost was not foolish, ridiculous, insane, fleshly performances, but the power to witness."[18]

The Parhams' Approach to Understanding the Bible. Clearly, Charles and Sarah Parham and Lilian Thistlethwaite held the Bible in highest esteem as the inspired Word of God. They depended on the Holy Spirit to help them understand accurately what they read. It would be helpful to understand how much importance they placed on four factors that are often considered critical in helping us determine what the Bible says to us: the Holy Spirit, the Written Word, human reason, and church tradition.

1. **The Holy Spirit.** The Parhams' authorities for interpretation arose from a quest for dynamic Christian experience parallel to that of first century Christianity, "to contend for the faith

---

[15] In 1900, for example, Charles Parham embarked on an extended study tour of the significant Holiness centers including John Alexander Dowie's center in Chicago, God's Bible School in Cincinnati, Stephen Merritt's in New York City, A. B. Simpson's in Nyack, New York, A. J. Gordon's in Boston, and Frank Sandford's Holy Ghost and Us Bible School near Durham, Maine. Hyatt, 30-41.

[16] "No Fanaticism," *Houston Post,* 27 Aug. 1906, 1. "They believed in 'Bible time Christianity' up-to-date and working in the twentieth century in obedience to Christ's commission."

[17] They maintained that the formation of another denomination on the basis of a Pentecostal distinctive would hinder, not facilitate, God's purpose of world evangelization. They did advocate an outpouring of the Holy Spirit that would infiltrate existing denominations.

[18] *Apostolic Faith,* Aug. 1926, 1.

once delivered to the saints" (Jude 3). Because they embraced the present-day activity of the Holy Spirit, they could appeal to the Spirit to inform and confirm their reading of Scripture. In this, they affirmed the primacy of the "inner witness" identified by John Wesley, the "inner light" identified by George Fox, and the obvious activity of the Spirit in the Holiness Movement. A. J. Gordon also affirms the vital role of Spirit experience in the process of interpretation, saying, "The final exegesis is not always to be found in the lexicon and grammar [because the] Spirit is also in the Church, the body of regenerate and sanctified believers."[19]

2. **The Bible.** The Parhams maintained a highly conservative view of Scripture, the Bible being the inspired Word of God authoritative for life, doctrine and ministry.[20] The whole purpose of Bible study was to discover the will of God and then to act on that knowledge. Biblical content was understood according to a Creation-Fall-Redemption motif.[21]

3. **Reason.** The Parhams were not anti-intellectual. The Thistlethwaite sisters were products of a gracious home that valued education and were themselves graduates of a private boarding school in Kansas City. Parham, himself a diligent reader from his childhood, had studied at a Methodist college. They were, however, opposed to liberal trends in Biblical criticism that dominated higher education in their day.

4. **Tradition.** For the Parhams, what the Bible said held unquestionable precedence over what the church fathers or traditional institutional theology had to say. As "come-outers," they did not reject Wesleyan-Holiness tradition, but they did reject modern, liberal Methodism. They also stood firmly opposed to

[19] A. J. Gordon, "The Ministry of Women," *Missionary Review of the World* (Dec. 1894): 910-912.

[20] F. L. Arrington, "Historical Perspectives on Pentecostal and Charismatic Hermeneutics," *Dictionary of Pentecostal and Charismatic Movements*, eds. Gary McGee and Stanley Burgess (Grand Rapids: Zondervan, 1988), 378.

Claude Welch, *Protestant Thought in the Nineteenth Century, 1799-1870* (New Haven: Yale Univ. Press, 1972), 28.

Roman Catholicism and the idea of apostolic succession advocated by Catholicism.[22]

Ed Aultman, an elderly resident of Melrose, Kansas, and member of the first Pentecostal congregation, says,

> Brother C. F. Parham came preaching the way of salvation and life, to all those who would believe and receive the full Gospel as recorded in the Holy Writ. But he found us a stiff necked people. We were so bound up in creed and tradition of men, that we just 'sot back' in the harness and our long deaf ears refused to hear the Bible. My! yes, dignified we were; not ready to endure sound doctrine. (II Timothy 4:3,4) But praise be to Christ our Lord, who gives victory; Bro. Parham was determined to preach nothing (no creeds or tradition) but Jesus and Him crucified. (I Corinthians, 2:2) Preaching Jesus, His teaching, his salvation and life and power to heal. Brother Parham surely preached God's Holy Word straight from the shoulder; in chunks, big, pure and hard enough to knock the scales from our eyes. Tradition, formalism, sectarianism, and all other isms began to peel off and we became hungry to hear God's truths. People began to pray in earnest for full salvation; and God came in mighty power to save, to cleanse, to heal; and all praised God for the "Old Time Religion' once more returned to bless and fill us with joy unspeakable and full of glory (1 Peter, 1:8).[23]

In studying the Parhams, it is possible to determine the principles that guided them in their interpretation of the Bible. Four principles, in particular, stand out.

1. **The Principle of Individual Prayer.** Communion with the Holy Spirit in prayer within the context of a consecrated life was

---

[22] Hans Kung, ed., *Ecumenical Theology: Concilium, Theology in the Age of Renewal*, vol. 34 (New York: Paulist, 1968).

[23] S. Parham, 100.

their primary consideration. "Prayer was the central focus of the school [Bethel Bible College, Topeka] and a serious effort was made to acquire both 'head knowledge' and 'heart-felt experience' of Scriptural principles."[24] This is the approach out of which came the articulation of the doctrine of Spirit baptism that launched the Pentecostal Revival in 1901.

2. **The Principle of Group Evaluation.** An interpretation of a passage was not considered valid simply because a consecrated, prayer-soaked individual arrived at an opinion while in prayerful study of Scripture. Interpretations were evaluated in group discussions and were accepted only when "It seemed good to the Holy Spirit and to us" (Acts 15:28).

3. **The Principle of Spirit Confirmation.** The Parhams anticipated God's confirmation of correct interpretation by experiences corresponding to Biblical manifestations. This experience came by the inner witness of the Spirit as defined, for example, by Wesley and Fox, and by a relevant outward manifestation. Because they realized not all spiritual experiences originated with the Holy Spirit, experiences were subject to testing, and fanaticism was forbidden.[25]

4. **The Principle of Biblical Harmony.** Proof-texting, the hurling back and forth of biblical verses taken out of context, had been disavowed as vain during the abolitionist debate. Henceforth, it was required that interpretations of isolated passages harmonize with the whole Bible. In other world, interpretations were not to contradict Biblical principles.

The Parhams' Bible courses at Bethel Bible College were thematic in nature. That is, they focused on what individual Biblical writers such as Luke said particularly about salvation, the Holy

---

[24] S. Parham, 52.
[25] S. Parham, 87, 161-170.

Spirit, and end-time topics. Students spent prolonged periods in focused prayer and Bible study before gathering in plenary sessions to share their findings on the topic under study. When they met, they discussed their findings and worked toward a consensus. Parham would summarize their conclusions and compare them with the perspectives of other, knowledgeable people. William J. Seymour, one of the Parhams' most notable students, writes, "They laid aside all commentaries and notes and waited on the Lord, studying His word, and what they did not understand they got down before the bench and asked God to wrought out in their hearts by the Holy Ghost."[26]

The Fruit of Holy Spirit Revival

This, then, is what contributed to the remarkable egalitarian atmosphere of the early Pentecostal Revival. The inclusivism of the Methodist approach was overridden by the Quaker beliefs of equality in both marriage and ministry. Gender was not the determining factor in relationships or in ministry.

The Parhams' emphasis, then, on the manifest activity of the Holy Spirit and the inspired Word of God was important in women having a prominent place in all of the initial hot-spots of revival. These included the Kansas-Missouri-Oklahoma-South Texas region (1901ff.), Zion City (1901ff.) and Azusa Street (1906ff.). In addition to students and visitors who went forth as Pentecostal ministers from Bethel Bible College in 1901, a Mrs. Waldron who attended Parham meetings in 1901, took the message of Pentecost to Des Moines, Iowa, and to Dowie's Zion City, Illinois.[27] In so doing she laid the foundation for the Parhams' revival there in mid-1906, a revival which precipitated one of the

---

[26] William J. Seymour, "Pentecost Has Come," *Apostolic Faith Magazine*, Sept. 1906, n.p.

[27] Mrs. Waldron of Joplin, MO had received the baptism of the Holy Spirit in 1901 in Parham meetings in Lawrence, KN, within weeks of the outpouring at Bethel. The same year she moved to Zion City where she held meetings in her home. Some of the influential people of Zion had accepted here teachings, including John G. Lake. P. Parham with Hyatt, 123-124.

most important religious events of the twentieth century.[28] Not only did it mean the incorporation of the doctrine of divine healing as a permanent part of the twentieth century Pentecostal Movement[29] but it also thrust about five hundred[30] mature, consecrated men[31] and women ministers[32] into nations around the world with the Pentecostal message.

Martha Wing Robinson. One of these capable women to come out of the Parhams' Zion City Revival was Martha Wing Robinson (1874-1938).[33] Under John Alexander Dowie's ministry, she had been healed of a terminable illness in 1899, and in 1901 he had ordained her to the ministry, only after marrying, since Dowie was not an egalitarian but believed that women must be married to minister.[34] After receiving the baptism of the Spirit in Parham's meetings, Martha and her husband attended Parham's short-term Bible school in Zion City (1906-07).[35] They ministered to Pentecostal believers in Toronto (1907-1911) before Martha returned to Zion City to establish the Zion Faith Homes. The purpose of these homes was to help people know Jesus better, and they served as training centers for young ministers and retreat centers for weary evangelists and missionaries. Mrs. Robinson led

---

[28] Gordon P. Gardiner, "Out of Zion . . . Into All the World," *Bread of Life*, Oct. 1981, 3.

[29] Paul Chappell, The Divine Healing Movement in America" (Ph.D. diss., Drew Univ., 1983), 356; Gardiner, Oct. 1981-1986.

[30] Parham, "The Latter Rain," *Apostolic Faith*, Aug. 1926, 2.

[31] Some of these were: F. F. Bosworth, Cyrus B. Fockler, John G. Lake, William E. Moody, L. C. Hall, William J. Mitchell, Harry Bowley, Eli Noble Richey, Raymond T. Richey, and Charles E. Robinson.

[32] Gardiner, May-June 1985. Martha Wing Robinson, Gardiner, Oct. 1981. Emma Lang, Gardiner, Oct. 1981, 4. Marie Burgess Brown, Gardiner, Oct. 1981, 5. Jean Campbell Hall Mason, Gardiner, Oct. 1981, 6. Bernice C. Lee, Gardiner, Oct. 1981, 6; Bernice C. Lee, "A Night of Nights!" *Bread of Life*, Oct. 1981, 11-14. Mrs. Eugene Brooks, Gardiner, Dec. 1981, 7. Charlotte Smale, Gardiner, April 1982, 7. Iva Rust, Gardiner, April 1982, 7. Mrs. F. A. Graves, Gardiner, April 1982, 7. Lydia Markley Piper, Gardiner, April 1982, 7. Marie Burman, Gardiner, April 1982, 11. Mary Charlotte Reed, Gardiner, May 1982, 9. Anna C. Reiff, Gardiner, May 1982. Bertha Meyer Glauser, Gardiner, May 1982, 13. Rose Meyer Gardiner, Gardiner, May 1982. Maggie Boyer Vogler, Gardiner, June 1982, 5-14. Margaret Fielden Cantel, Gardiner, July 1982, 7. Eliza Gordon, Gardiner, Dec. 1982, 7-16. Dr. Lilian B. Yeomans, Gardiner, Jan. 1983, 5-15. Mother Emma Whittemore, Gardiner, April 1983, 5-15. Eleanor F. Gardiner, Gardiner, May 1983, 7-11. Wilhelmina Blekkink Polman, Gardiner, Dec. 198, 11-15; Jan. 1984, 5-11. Katherine Cook, Gardiner, Feb.-April 1984. Mother Daisy Katherine Robinson, Gardiner, June-July 1984. Edith Baugh, Gardiner, May-June 1985. Minnie Moore Chastagner, Edith L. Blumhofer, "Out of Zion . . . Into All the World," *Bread of Life*, Oct. 1986, 5-10.

[33] Gordon P. Gardiner, *Radiant Glory: The Life of Martha Wing Robinson* (Brooklyn: Bread of Life, 1962); S. Hyatt, *Women Who Led the Way*, 22-36.

[34] Gardiner, *Radiant Glory*, 100. Dr. Dowie championed the cause of women's ministries, but he insisted they marry.

[35] Gardiner, *Radiant Glory*, 110-123.

a life of prayer and Bible study out of which she ministered very personal and practical teaching to those who came to the Faith Homes that they might go forth victorious in their life and service.[36] One of her disciples was Hans R. Waldvogel (1893-1969), who became a leader among German Pentecostals in the United States as pastor of Ridgewood Pentecostal Church, Brooklyn, NY.[37] He was the father of Pentecostal scholar Edith Waldvogal Blumhofer.

Marie Burgess Brown and Dr. Lillian B. Yeomans. Two other outstanding women who were products of the Parhams' ministry in Zion City were Marie Burgess Brown (1880-1971) and Dr. Lilian B. Yeomans (1861-1942). Parham sent Marie, a graduate of Moody Bible Institute, to New York City in 1907 where she founded Glad Tidings Tabernacle, one of the greatest missionary churches on the East Coast.[38] Dr. Yeomans, a medical doctor by profession, had been healed of an addiction to prescription drugs through Dowie's ministry and was baptized in the Spirit through the Parhams. She spent her latter years teaching at Aimee Semple McPherson's LIFE Bible College in Los Angeles, and was still active in ministry at 80 years of age.[39]

Mary Arthur and Francene Dobson. During the four years prior to the Zion City Revival, the Parhams had led 25,000 converts into the Baptism of the Holy Spirit, particularly in the South Texas and in the tri-state region of Missouri, Kansas, and Oklahoma.[40] In El Dorado Springs, Missouri, in 1903, their ministry resulted in the miraculous healing of Mary Arthur of Galena, Kansas,[41] and the subsequent first area-wide Pentecostal revival of

[36] Gardiner, *Radiant Glory*, 215-253.

[37] Gardiner, *Radiant Glory*, 296.

[38] Gardiner, "Out of Zion . . . Into All the World," *Bread of Life*, Oct. 1981, 5; N. Benjamin Crandall, President of Zion Bible Institute, Barrington, RI, in interviews with author, 1991-92.

[39] Gardiner, "Out of Zion . . . Into All the World," *Bread of Life*, Jan. 1983, 5-15.

[40] Pauline Parham, interview with author, 1989.

[41] S. Parham, 88.

modern times[42] in Galena. As a result of these meetings, Mary Arthur and Francene Dobson founded the first mission begun as a direct result of Pentecostal preaching.[43]

Lucy Farrow. Out of the Parham revival in Houston in 1905-6 came thousands of Spirit-baptized men and women. Among these were William J. Seymour (1870-1922), of the Azusa Street Revival, and Lucy Farrow (dates unknown).[44] Rev. Farrow, who had been born in slavery in Virginia, was serving as a Holiness pastor in Houston when Parham arrived there in 1905. She worked closely with the Parhams serving as governess to the Parham children and ministering in the meetings[45] before going to Los Angeles to assist Seymour. Although Seymour is universally acclaimed as the leading figure of the Azusa Street Revival (April 1906 - 1909), no one experienced the Pentecostal baptism until Lucy Farrow arrived and began praying for people to receive it.[46] In August, 1906, she conducted a Pentecostal revival in Portsmouth, Virginia, during which 200 were saved and 150 were baptized in the Spirit. Also, she was one of the first Pentecostal missionaries to Liberia, West Africa.[47]

An Unnumbered Host of Women. The Azusa Street Revival thrust thousands of Pentecostal men and women into the mission fields of the world.[48] The initial directing board of Azusa, including Seymour, consisted of five men and seven women.[49] One of

---

[42] S. Parham, 87-100; Edith Blumhofer, "Mary Anna Arthur," *Pentecost in My Soul* (Springfield: GPH, 1989), 119-130. It embraced all social classes throughout the region, and in a three-month period, over 800 people were saved, 500 were sanctified, no less than 250 received the baptism of the Holy Spirit, and hundreds were healed. *The Joplin Herald, The Cincinnati Inquirer,* and the *Philadelphia Ledger* reported the revival as the greatest display of miracles since the days of the Apostles. These are available in the Parham Archives.

[43] Blumhofer, "Mary Anna Arthur," 121. Mary Arthur was ordained on December 11, 1910.

[44] C. M. Robeck, "Lucy F. Farrow," *Dictionary of Pentecostal and Charismatic Movements,* 302-303.

[45] Ethel Goss, *The Winds of God* (New York: Comet, 1958), 56.

[46] Mother Cotton, "Message of the 'Apostolic Faith,' 1," 1939.

[47] Robeck, *Dictionary,* 302-303.

[48] Chappell, 356. The Zion City Revival brought in many from Dowie's international network of churches. Its focus was upon founding new independent ministries and churches.

[49] Fred T. Corum, collector, *Like as of Fire: A Reprint of the Old Azusa Street Papers* (Wilmington, MA: Fred Corum, 1981), photo in Preface. Jennie Moore, Florence Louise Crawford, Sister Price, Rachel Sizelove, and Sister Lum, possibly Phoebe Sargent, and one other.

these, Florence Crawford (1872-1936), moved to Portland, Oregon where she founded the Apostolic Faith Mission in 1907.[50] Other women involved were Mabel Smith,[51] Mrs. Hall, and Mrs. Walter Oyler and her husband whom Charles Parham had dispatched to Los Angeles in response to Seymour's request for help. Another key woman was "Mother" Emma Cotton (1877-1952), an evangelist, church planter, pastor, and editor who ministered at Azusa beginning in 1906 and who later founded Azusa Temple in Los Angeles in the 1930s.[52]

Freda Lindsay and Pauline Parham. Although the revival institutionalized, "Dad" Parham continued holding evangelistic meetings across the nation until his death in 1929. In one December, 1924, meeting in John G. Lake's church in Portland, Oregon, nineteen-year-old Gordon Lindsay (1906-1973) surrendered his life to the Lord and immediately entered the ministry. Lindsay and his wife Freda (1914-) founded *The Voice of Healing* and the great missionary organization known as Christ for the Nations with its headquarters and main teaching institute in Dallas, Texas. When Gordon died in 1973, Freda succeeded Gordon as President of CFN, and under her prayerful leadership it has become one of the world's largest Pentecostal/Charismatic, Revival-oriented missionary organizations.[53]

Pauline Parham (1909-), whose mother was a faithful member of Parham's ministry even before Pauline was born, served as Charles Parham's secretary and became a daughter-in-law through marriage to Robert Parham. Over the years, Pauline served as a pastor, evangelist, Bible school teacher and director, and as Dean of Women at Oral Roberts University and Christ for the Nations Institute where she also served as a teacher for many years. Her

---

[50] L. F. Wilson, "Florence Louise Crawford," *Dictionary*, 229.

[51] Smith also helped Parham in the Zion City Revival. Her name appears frequently in early literature.

[52] Mother Cotton, "Message of the 'Apostolic Faith,' 1," 1939; C. M. Robeck, *Dictionary*, 227.

[53] Freda Lindsay, *My Diary Secrets* (Dallas: CFN, 4th ed. 1984); Arlene Samuels, "Freda Lindsay to Retire Next Year," *Charisma*, Nov. 1993, 74.

intimate relationship with Dad and Mother Parham and Aunt Lilie Thistlethwaite has enabled her to be a rich resource, not only as a witness of the early Pentecostal Revival, but also as a witness to the egalitarianism in ministry and marriage of the Parhams and the early revival.

In a wide variety of ways, the Parhams were responsible for Pentecostal egalitarianism until at least about 1910. By that time, however, the Thistlethwaite-Parham element had been diluted as thousands of people embraced the Pentecostal message of speaking in tongues. Most of these people lacked the unique theological combination held by the Parhams that enabled them to live an egalitarian lifestyle as something quite normal. Instead, the new Pentecostal people and emerging leaders tended simply to attach the doctrine of tongues speaking to their theological baggage, thus squeezing out the egalitarian theology of the Spirit.

Other Examples of Significant Women in the Pentecostal Revival

Nevertheless, the practical and theological foundation established by the Parhams worked in conjunction with the other elements such as healing homes and holiness missionary ministries, both of which were already facilitating egalitarian leadership. Furthermore, in the important arena of Bible education and leadership training in the Pentecostal Revival, women led the way.[54] Primarily working alone but occasionally side by side with men, they functioned as founders, administrators, and teachers of the first and most influential Bible schools, and as equal partners with their husbands in training the men and women who later became the leaders in the emerging denominations. Elizabeth Duncan Baker (1849-1915) and her four sisters established a multifaceted

---

[54] S. Hyatt, *Women Who Led the Way: Discoveries About Women in Leadership in Early Pentecostal Bible Schools* (Tulsa: Hyatt Int'l Ministries, 1989).

ministry in Rochester, New York, a ministry which included the first permanent Pentecostal Bible school, Rochester Bible Training School (1907).[55] In 1912, Virginia E. Moss (1875-1919) opened Beulah Heights Bible and Missionary Training School in North Bergen, New Jersey.[56] Minnie Tingley Draper (1858-1921), a powerful evangelist with a significant healing ministry, established Bethel Bible Training School in 1916 in Newark, New Jersey.[57] Martha Wing Robinson (1874-1938) operated Faith Homes which were places of refreshing for tired ministers and missionaries as well as training centers for Pentecostal ministers.[58] Aimee Semple McPherson (1890-1944) who began her ministry in 1909, is the best-known woman preacher of the twentieth century and founder of the International Church of the Foursquare Gospel.[59] Christine Amelia Gibson (1879-1955), a Holiness preacher with Quaker influences, became pastor of the Church of the First Born in East Providence, Rhode Island in 1905, and in she 1924 opened Zion Bible Institute, now located in Barrington, RI.[60] Nora I. Chambers (1883-1953) was an evangelist, scholar, and the first teacher in the Church of God Bible Training School (now Lee College) in 1917.[61] In 1917, Robert (1872-1941) and Mary Craig were partners in founding Glad Tidings Bible Institute in San Francisco, now Bethany Bible College.[62] In 1920, Harold and Huldah Needham were partners in establishing Southern California Bible School in Los Angeles, now Southern California

[55] Elizabeth V. Baker, *Chronicles of a Faith Life* (reprint, New York: Garland, 1984); Hyatt, *Women Who Led the Way*, 2-13.

[56] Virginia E. Moss, *Following the Shepherd: Testimony of Mrs. Virginia E. moss* (North Bergen, NJ: Beulah Heights Assembly and Bible Training School, 1919); Hyatt, 14-17.

[57] C. J. Lucas, "In Memoriam," *Full Gospel Missionary Herald* (April 1921): n.p.; Hyatt, 18-21.

[58] Gardiner, *Radiant Glory*; Hyatt, 22-36.

[59] Edward T. James, ed., "McPherson, Aimee Semple," *Notable American Women 1607-1950, A Biographical Dictionary, II* (Cambridge: Belknap, 1971), 477-480; Hyatt, 37-43.

[60] Mary Campbell, *The Obedience of Faith: The Biography of Christian Gibson* (Barrington, RI: Zion Bible Institute, 1993); Hyatt, 44-55.

[61] "Youth Interviews Experiences," *The Lighted Pathway*, Oct. 1951: 14; Charles W. Conn, *Like a Mighty Army* (Cleveland, TN: Pathway, 1977), 148; Hyatt, 60-64.

[62] Everett A. Wilson, "Robert J. Craig's Glad Tidings and the Realization of a Vision for 100,000 Souls," *AG Heritage*, Summer 1988: 9-11; Hazel Buel Miller, "A Weekend at Glad Tidings Mission," *AG Heritage* (Summer 1988): 11; Hyatt, 67-71.

College.[63] In 1924, Ivan and Minnie Spencer opened Elim Bible Institute in Endwell, Upstate New York.[64]

Conclusion

In the early Pentecostal Revival, the determining factors in ministerial function and in the specific nature of the marriage relationship were the unique personality of each man and women and the manifest activity of the Holy Spirit in the life of the individual.[65] Authority was not determined by gender, but by the God-ordained expression of the Holy Spirit through the individual person. Especially among Parham disciples, in great part due to the strong Quaker influence, it was normal for men and women to relate as equals in both marriage and ministry.[66] It had all come together, at least momentarily.

[63] Hyatt, 72-73.

[64] Marion Meloon, *Ivan Spencer: Willow in the Wind* (South Plainfield: Logos, 1974); Hyatt, 74-84.

[65] Personal discussions with Pauline Parham, 1989-1993.

[66] This is based on primary resources and the manuscript for the book *Charles Fox Parham: Pioneer of Pentecost,* Pauline Parham with Eddie and Susan Hyatt, 1989-1991.

Retreat to Tradition

13

Enemies of Equality
Invade Pentecostalism

By 1908[1] the Pentecostal Revival had gained international momentum. With this expansion came social pressures and ideas that had not been part of the early Revival, and this eroded the egalitarian climate of the Revival. Specific elements that led to this change were institutionalism, professionalism, and the intrusion of Baptistic/Reformed theology. Then, with the Charismatic Renewal after 1958, the final vestige of Pentecostal egalitarianism succumbed to the traditional, hierarchical systems of Mainline Protestantism and Roman Catholicism. According to sociologist Max Weber, this trend is not unusual since egalitarian practices seldom extend beyond "the first stage of the formation of a religious community."[2]

The Impact of Institutionalism on Pentecostal Egalitarianism

As the events of the Pentecostal Revival unfolded, Pentecostalism fell prey to a social predator known as "institutionalism."[3] Whereas revival disrupts existing religious and social patterns, institutionalism tries to restore them. In this instance, the demands for organizational structure preempted the primacy of Spirit lead-

---

[1] By 1908, without any organized agenda, the revival had taken root in over fifty nations, and by 1914, its adherents were publishing literature in thirty languages. Douglas G. Nelson, "A Search for Pentecostal-Charismatic Roots," (Ph.D. diss., Univ. of Birmingham, 1981), synopsis.

[2] Cited by C. H. Barfoot and G. T. Sheppard, "Prophetic Vs. Priestly Religion: The Changing Role of Women Clergy in Classical Pentecostal Churches," *Review of Religious Research* 22 (September 1980)2-17. See also Max Weber, *From Max Weber: Essays in Sociology*, trans. H. H. Gerth and C. Wright Mills (London: Oxford Univ. press, 1991) 51-55, 264ff, 294ff.

[3] "Institutionalism," *Webster's 9th New Collegiate Dictionary. Webster's Dictionary.*

ership. As a result, human government supplanted divine order;
ministerial "offices" replaced charismatic "functions";[4] religious ritual replaced spiritual spontaneity. The doctrine of authoritarian
male headship replaced equality and the expression of that equality through the priesthood and prophethood of all believers.

Certain trends often indicate the advancement of institutionalism.[5] For example, attendance and financial support for the organization, generally speaking, become more important than the
free and open outworking of a deep, spiritual relationship with
God. Often a self-centered concern by the institution regarding its
own existence and progress overrides the mission for which it was
originally founded. Loyalty tends to be defined in terms of self-
sacrificing service for the preservation and growth of the institution. Finally, the promotion of distinctive doctrines becomes more
important than the quality of life experienced by church members.
One effect of these trends in the Pentecostal Movement was the
demise of equality for women.

The Onslaught of Institutionalism. In the Pentecostal Revival, the
onslaught of institutionalizing forces rallied as early as 1906 when
certain men associated with the Parhams in Texas insisted on a
more structured organization.[6] Parham contended that the
movement was not to organize new churches or to start new
movements which would elevate men or women to rulership. He
believed that God had commissioned them to preach "The Gospel
of the Kingdom" in all the world, but that He had not authorized
them to organize a church or to set the church in order. He urged

---

[4] Hans Kung, ed. *Ecumenical Theology* (New York: Paulist, 1968); Hans von Campenhausen, *Ecclesiastical Authority and Spiritual Power in the Churches of the First Three Centuries* (Stanford: Stanford Univ., 1969); James D. G. Dunn, *Jesus and Spirit* (Philadelphia: Westminster, 1975); Dunn, "Ministry and the Ministry," *Charismatic Experiences in History*, ed. Cecil Robeck, Jr. (Peabody: Hendrickson, 1985).

Findley B. Edge, "Experiential or Institutionalized Religion?" *A Reader in Christian Education*, ed. Eugene S. Gibbs (Grand Rapids: Baker, 1992), 210-212. Also see discussion in Chapter 4.

In an effort to organize a "real church," W. F. Carothers and Howard Goss organized an effort to destroy Parham's influence. In their framing of Parham, they were abetted by Zion City's new leader, Wilbur Voliva, an avowed enemy of Parham because Parham's 1906 revival in Zion had threatened his authority in that city. The Carothers-Goss group eventually dropped the name "Apostolic Faith" and adopted the name "Pentecostal." Eddie L. Hyatt and Susan Hyatt, *Charles Fox Parham: The Pioneer of Pentecost* (Tulsa: H.I.M., 1990.)

unity based on love produced by the Spirit and on the faithful performance of the various functions for which the Spirit had empowered individuals.[7] In this, an effective corporate expression would ensue.

The abatement of Parham's influence after 1907 and the subsequent encroachment of male-dominated institutionalism eroded the egalitarian quality of the revival by reinstating a male authority structure.[8] Holiness-Pentecostal denominations such as the Church of God (Cleveland, TN) which had been organized prior to the Pentecostal Revival, embraced the revival but retained their existing organizational forms and their policies regarding women.[9] New fellowships of Pentecostals having Baptistic roots,[10] such as those influenced by William Durham[11] began adopting patriarchal forms with which they had been familiar prior to the revival.[12] Groups founded by women such as Florence Crawford,[13] Aimee Semple McPherson,[14] the Duncan Sisters, and Christine Gibson,[15] originally adopted more egalitarian policies.

---

[7] Charles Parham, *Apostolic Faith Magazine*, Aug. 1926, n.p.

[8] Holiness-Pentecostal bodies which formed prior to the Pentecostal Revival include the Fire Baptized Holiness Church (founded in 1895), the Church of God (Cleveland, TN) (1896), the Pentecostal Holiness Church (1898), and the Church of God in Christ (1897).

[9] Charles W. Conn, *Like a Mighty Army Moves the Church of God*, 1886-1955 (Cleveland, TN: Church of God, 1955), 244. Conn writes, "Regarded as co-workers in the evangelization of the unconverted, women were permitted a restricted ministry which did not include ordination [in the Church of God (Cleveland, TN)]." Harold D. Hunter, "Making History: Voting Rights Extended to Women," *Reflections . . . Upon Church of God Heritage*, Spring 1993, 6-7. At its 1992 General Assembly, the Church of God extended voting rights to its female members. See also S. Hyatt, *Women Who Led the Way* (Tulsa: Hyatt Int'l Ministries, 1989).

[10] These include the Assemblies of God, Christian Church of North America, Elim Fellowship, Independent Assemblies of God, Open Bible Standard Churches, and Pentecostal Church of God (Anderson).

[11] Hyatt, *Parham: Pioneer of Pentecost*; Vinson Synan, "Lectures, No Title," *Charismatic Movement Today*, lecture, Tulsa, Spring 1991; M. M. Pinson, "The Finished Work of Calvary," *Pentecostal Evangel*, 5 April 1964, 7, 26-27; R. M. Riss, "William H. Durham," *Dictionary*, 255-256; Riss, "Finished Work Controversy," *Dictionary*, 306-309. The Finished Work controversy (1910) introduced Baptist views into the Pentecostal Revival. Chief proponent of this position was William Durham (1873-1912), Pastor of Chicago's North Avenue Mission, who was baptized in the Spirit in March 1907 at Azusa Street. In 1910 he launched an attack on the Holiness doctrine of sanctification as a second work of grace, arguing, instead, for the "finished work of Calvary" perspective whereby the benefits of the Cross, including sanctification, are to be appropriated over a lifetime rather than in at a point in time. Parham despaired of this teaching, finally praying, "Lord, if my position on sanctification is correct, take Brother Durham home, but if his position is correct, take me home." Shortly after this prayer, Durham died of pneumonia during the summer 1912. Parham lived until 1929.

[13] Apostolic Faith, Portland, Oregon.

[14] International Church of the Foursquare Gospel, Los Angeles, California.

[15] Elim Ministries, Rochester, New York.

Zion Bible College and Fellowship of Ministers, East Providence, Rhode Island.

An Example of Institutionalism. A classic example of the institutionalization of the Pentecostalism can be observed in the formation of the Assemblies of God.[16] The potential for tension regarding women's status in the Assemblies existed from the beginning because the constituents came from both Wesleyan/Holiness and Baptistic/Reformed backgrounds. The differences were neither confronted nor resolved in the founding process since the motivation for union was the need for cooperation around five major issues, none of which related to the preservation of the egalitarian features of the revival.[17]

The precedent of male rulership was firmly established from the outset when men holding Baptistic/Reformed theological persuasions dominated the founding convocation. The call for the gathering had been given by men only.[18] The first two chief executive officers were men,[19] and together with ten other men,[20] they were chosen to serve as a presbytery to administer the corporate legal affairs and to provide spiritual leadership. The new fellowship appointed two men to issue credentials[21] to "worthy ministers."[22]

The theological position of many of the founders was patriarchal. Some, for example, were men having a Baptistic affiliation prior to their Pentecostal experience[23] and this introduced a position strongly favoring traditional, patriarchal patterns. Others were men who demonstrated more propensity for political power

---

[16] C. M. Ward chides the Assemblies of God for being "overmanaged and underled." "We need to get back to what brought . . . [us] together: Voluntary cooperative fellowship." E. S. Caldwell, "The Assemblies of God Through the Eyes of C. M. Ward," *Charisma*, Aug. 1989, 47.

[17] E. N. Bell, ed. *Word and Witness*, 20 December 1913, 1. These were: 1) To attain greater theological unity; 2) To conserve results of the revival; 3) To coordinate foreign missions; 4) To charter new assemblies; 5) To develop a Bible training school.

[18]

[19] M. M. Pinson, E, N. Bell, Howard Goss, D. C. O. Opperman, and A. P. Collins.

[20] The first chairperson was E. N. Bell and the first secretary was J. Roswell Flower.

[21] Bell, Flower, A. P. Collins, R. L. Erickson, C. B. Fockler, H. A. Goss, D. W. Kerr, T. K. Leonard, D. C. O. Opperman, M. M. Pinson, John Sinclair, and J. W. Welch.

[22] Howard Goss and T. K. Leonard.

[23] William W. Menzies, *Anointed to Serve* (Springfield: GPH, 1971), 104-105.

E. N. Bell, M. M. Pinson, William Durham, and A. P. Collins.

than for Spirit-life.[24] Another contingent came from Zion City where John Alexander Dowie had operated under a policy of authoritarian male headship.[25] On the other hand, the original nucleus of the Assemblies also consisted of men and women who had been disciples of Parham,[26] of A. B. Simpson, and of the first permanent Pentecostal Bible schools in the Northeast which were founded and administered by Holiness women.[27] But for all intensive purposes, any voice for ongoing equality for women was silent.

Press reports of the founding convocation in Hot Springs, Arkansas in April, 1914,[28] indicate that women were present: "A few names of the better known men out of the 352 in the Church of God in Christ will indicate the influence the group had on the Assemblies of God: [but notice that two women were listed as men!] 'Mother' Mary Barnes . . . Agnes Ozman LaBerge. . . ."[29] Women seem not to have participated in leadership and decision-making, however. The new fellowship accepted the credentials of women already recognized by other groups; however, no provision was made to ordain women as pastors[30] and women were not permitted to voice opinions on issues under discussion.[31] In 1920, the General Council did grant women voting rights and ordination as evangelists and missionaries.[32] In 1935, it began ordaining women as pastors,[33] but as Edith Blumhofer points out, this occurred

---

[24] Howard Goss, a driving force in the organization, had a six-month lease on the Grand Opera House in Hot Springs, AR, the cite of the convocation. Although he had been a Parham disciple (1903-1906), he came under the influence of Bell, Durham, and others. Later, in 1916, he broke with the Assemblies and was a leader in founding the Oneness branch of Pentecostalism.

[25] Single women functioned in ministry but as team members, while full, independent pastoral ministry was permitted of a woman only in partnership with her husband. Gordon P. Gardiner, *Radiant Glory: The Life of Martha Wing Robinson* (Brooklyn: Bread of Life, 1962).

[26] J. Roswell Flower, "Historical Review of the Pentecostal Movement," *AG Heritage* (Fall 1985): 11; Gordon P. Gardiner, "Out of Zion . . . Into All the World," *Bread of Life*, Oct. 1981-86.

[27] See previous chapter and Hyatt, *Women Who Led the Way*.

[28] Carl Brumback, *Like a River* (Springfield: GPH, n.d), 4-5.

[29] Assemblies of God Public Relations Dept., *The Early History of the Assemblies of God*, Springfield: Assemblies of God International Headquarters, 1960), 6-8.

[30] Edith Blumhofer, "The Role of Women in Pentecostal Ministry," *AG Heritage* (Spring 1986): 11, 14.

[31] John Thomas Nichol, *Pentecostalism* (New York: Harper and Row, 1966), 140.

[32] This is the same year suffragettes gained political victory in the United States.

[33] Blumhofer, 11.

during the administration of General Superintendent Ernest S. Williams who had a theological commitment to male headship. He granted that "women may speak or expound truth under the guidance of elders, 'those that have the rule over them.'"[34]

The Assemblies of God has never had a woman serve as General Superintendent;[35] in fact, "none has ever been given administrative leadership in the denominational structure except in the area of women's ministries."[36] In clarification of the 1990 decennial report of the National Council of Churches that the Assemblies of God led the way in the eighties in affirming the ministry of women, Blumhofer notes that the statistics are misleading because they simply reflect a change in criteria for reporting.[37] In reality, the number of ordained women and of well-known women evangelists has declined.[38]

In 1990, the Assemblies of God commissioned a study to establish a policy on the issue of women's status. The "Position Paper on The Role of Women in Ministry as Described in Holy Scripture" does not make a commitment for or against male headship,[39] but affirms, in principle, the equality of women in ministry.[40] The paper concludes that none of the Biblical evidence suggests "that gender distinctives should not result in leadership limitations." Furthermore, it states that no convincing evidence supports the restriction of the ministry of women on the basis of a "sacred or immutable principle." It declares that "it is God who

[34] E. S. Williams, "May Women Preach?" Williams File, Assemblies of God Archives, Springfield, MO. cited by Blumhofer, 11.

[35] Assemblies of God, *Advance*, Feb. 1989, cover.

[36] Blumhofer, 14.

[37] Paul B. Tinlin and Edith L. Blumhofer, "Decade of Decline or Harvest? Dilemmas of the Assemblies of God," *The Christian Century*, 10-17 July 1991, 684-685. Previous statistics reflected only ordained women while the new statistics included ordained and licensed women. "By far the majority of credentialed women hold licenses rather than ordination certificates, and more than half of them are retired."

[38] Tinlin and Blumhofer, 685; Blumhofer, 14.

[39] The paper identifies accepted meanings of *kephale*, including "authority over," "source," and "origin," but does make a commitment to any one of them.

[40] "The Role of Women in Ministry as Described in Holy Scripture: "A Position Paper Adopted by the General Presbytery, August 1990," *Pentecostal Evangel*, 28 Oct. 1990, 12-15. Commission members were Gordon L. Anderson, Zenas J. Bicket (chairperson), Robert L. Brandt, Richard Dresselhaus, J. Harry Faught, William A. Griffin, Stanley M. Horton, Edgar R. Lee, Paul Lowenberg, Jesse Miranda, Robert D. Ross, Wesley W. Smith, Hardy W. Steinberg.

divinely calls and supernaturally anoints for ministry"; therefore, the Assemblies of God "must continue to be open to the full use of women's gifts in ministry and spiritual leadership."[41]

It is a helpful statement for it acknowledges what has been, can be, and should be. As the Assemblies of God and other Pentecostal denominations have become institutionalized, women have taken and been given a less active role in leadership. Women have either relinquished leadership roles in Spirit-oriented churches because of personal irresponsibility or have been severely restricted by the pressures of theological persuasions and cultural preferences. A statement of this nature, however potent, cannot legislate cultural prejudices and social preferences which ultimately determine the political trends in institutionalized Christianity. Only to the degree that people honor Jesus Christ as Lord and yield to His Holy Spirit can the ideals of biblical equality be fulfilled.

The Impact of Professionalism on Pentecostal Egalitarianism

As the Pentecostal Revival waned, the pressure from external cultural forces to conform to the greater social order exceeded the dynamism from within to maintain unique subcultural patterns of Pentecostalism.[42] Generations removed two, three, or four times from revival have little motivation to maintain revival distinctives such as egalitarianism. C. Peter Wagner warns against the loss of these Pentecostal distinctives because of the "the burning desire" for respectability.[43]

The cultural norm demanding an educated, professional clergy has pressured the Pentecostals to increase educational standards for the professional ministry that has developed with the institutionalizing of the movement. In fact, many of the early Pentecos-

---

[41] Stanley M. Horton, interview with author, 9 Nov. 1990. Although this is the official position of the AG, it met with considerable opposition.

[42] Donald W. Dayton, "Theological Roots of Feminism," photocopy, n.d., 7.

[43] C. Peter Wagner, "Characteristics of Pentecostal Church Growth," *Azusa Street and Beyond*, ed. L. Grant McClung (South Plainfield, NJ: Bridge, 1986), 131.

tals were educated men and women and not uneducated illiterates as is so often portrayed. Many early Pentecostal women were both charismatic and educated. Marie Burgess Brown, founder and Senior Pastor of Glad Tidings Tabernacle, New York City, was a graduate of Moody Bible Institute.[44] Also Susan Duncan (1854-1935) and Mary E. Duncan-Work, two of five Duncan sisters who founded Elim Ministries in Rochester, New York, were graduates of Genesee Wesleyan Seminary in Lima, New York.[45]

The dissipation of revival fervor and the subsequent move away from charismatic leadership, however, meant the decline of equality for women generally and the decline of women in leadership specifically. In the final analysis, increasing professionalism demanded increasingly higher standards of education and greater acceptance of social norms. Both factors favored the elevation of men to positions of authoritative leadership.[46]

The Impact of Baptistic and Reformed Perspectives on Pentecostal Egalitarianism

As Pentecostalism spread, it no longer drew participants only from the Wesleyan-Holiness-Quaker school of theology. Those of Baptistic and Reformed thought were also receiving the Baptism of the Spirit. This precipitated serious theological clashes, as in the battle over sanctification, as well as various, subtle changes.[47] One of the subtle changes was the gradual diminishing of the status of women. Whereas the original Pentecostals consisted mainly of either egalitarians or those with at least an inclusive view of biblical womanhood, those of a Baptistic/Reformed school were patriarchal and gender role oriented. Needless to say, as this

---

[44] Gordon P. Gardiner, "Out of Zion . . . Into All the World," *Bread of Life*, Oct. 1981, 5; Edith Blumhofer, "*Pentecost in My Soul*" (Springfield: GPH, 1989), 191-208; Benjamin Crandall, discussions with author, 1991-92.

[45] Elizabeth V. Baker and Co-Workers, *Chronicles of a Faith Life* (New York: Garland, 1984), 75, 100. Dayton, 7.

[47] For an overview of this controversy, see R. M. Riss, "Finished Work Controversy," *Dictionary*, 606-9.

view increased among Pentecostals, women's status corresponding decreased.

Baptistic/Reformed theology does not need to be discussed in detail at this point since it was dealt with in Chapter 7. It should be sufficient to recall three key points about Calvinism, in particular, that work against equality for women. The first was the preoccupation with authority, and delegated authority, in particular, which required a tight system of roles. These roles were gender-based, and women were designated as subordinates to men in the chain-of-command. The centrality of institutional government led to expressions such as "the law of man's headship" and "the law of [woman's] subordination."[48] The second questionable characteristic about Calvinism for egalitarians is its affinity with Augustinian theology which was prejudicial against women. The third was Calvin's position that the manifestations of the Holy Spirit had ceased with the deaths of the original twelve disciples. By this, the elevating and equalizing activity of the Holy Spirit was thwarted, and Calvin and his company relegated women to secondary, subservient status. It meant they would approach Scripture with a need to interpret what they read in a way that would reinforce these patriarchal ideas.

An Example of Baptistic/Reformed Interpretation. This tendency is prevalent today among Pentecostals, Charismatics and Revival people who tend to accept Baptistic/Reformed thinking without understanding its inherent problems. Articulating this standard position today is E. E. Ellis, a very gracious, Evangelical, Biblical scholar. In his book *Pauline Theology: Ministry and Society*, Dr. Ellis presents the Baptistic/Reformed justification for the subordination

---

48 J. M. Stevenson, *Woman's Place in Assemblies for Public Worship*, (New York: J. Sherwood, 1873) 50. This was reprinted in *The Presbyterian Quaterly and Princeton Review*, Vol. 2, Jan. 1873: 42-59.

of women.[49] His position is true to Calvin and definitely not egalitarian, but it would be helpful for egalitarian readers to understand his point of view.

He contends that the seeming contradictions in Paul's writings about womanhood are best understood in the light of the overlapping of the present age with the age to come. This produces a tension, for in our imperfect experience of the age to come, we sense that social and sexual distinctions are removed (Gal. 3:28). Yet, with this inner knowing, we must continue to live in this present "evil" world where the effects of the fall prevail. This is the context within which Ellis presents a somewhat restricted equality for women in ministry along with a required subordination in the home and, at times, in society.

For Ellis, the oft-called *difficult passages* (eg. 1 Cor. 14:34; 1 Tim. 2:12) refer to husbands and wives rather than to men and women in general. 1 Corinthians 14:34, which instructs women to remain silent in the churches, is postulated to be an admonition to the gifted wives of the prophets. These wives are instructed to refrain from publicly questioning or evaluating the messages of their husbands or of other prophets. Ellis interprets 1 Timothy 2:12 in a similar fashion: "I do not permit a wife to teach or have authority over a husband." These translations, of course, involve choices from a variety of meanings and are choices based on gender-biased presuppositions.

The starting point for Dr. Ellis' argument is Philippians 2:6-8, the passage in which Paul tells us that Christ, although He was equal with God, emptied Himself and took on the form of a servant. He brings to his interpretation of this passage the presupposition of male rulership/females subordination. This, and this

---

[49] E. Earle Ellis, *Pauline Theology: Ministry and Society* (Grand Rapids: Eerdmans, 1989); Workshop, Society for Pentecostal Studies Annual Conference, Assemblies of God Headquarters, Springfield, MO, Nov. 1992. Ellis' teaching is similar to that of Baptist/Pentecostal scholar, Dr. P. C. Nelson (1868-1942). See Kenneth E. Hagin, *The Woman Question* (Tulsa: Kenneth Hagin Ministries, 1975), "Acknowledgment" and Hyatt, *Women Who Led the Way*, 65-66. Dr. C. Nelson founded Southwestern Bible School in Enid, OK, in 1927. In 1941, he negotiated its merger with South Central Bible Institute in Ft. Worth, TX. The new school was Southwestern Bible College in Waxahachie, TX. Nelson was an astute Bible scholar who could read and write thirty-two languages.

alone, allows him to compare woman's "role" (note the presupposition of gender roles) in the creation to Christ's own servanthood in the Incarnation. That is, in the same way that Christ is equal with God while assuming the role of servant in the Incarnation, so woman, although one with man, is to assume the subordinate, servant role. Ellis contends, "Unity in Christ does not eliminate differences of rank in the church, in the world, or in the world to come."[50]

In assessing Ellis' position, we must ask a question. Is such a gender distinction present in the Philippians passage? Clearly, it is not. Paul's intent in this passage was that no Christian is ever to lord it over another believer. It is strange, then, that it should be used to assert male rulership and female subservience.

Ellis, nevertheless, uses his gender-biased interpretation of this passage as a springboard for the interpretation of other passages. Moving to Ephesians 5:21-6:9, for example, he prescribes the ruler-servant pattern to the husband-wife relationship. Proceeding then to 1 Corinthians 11:3-16, he extends the gender-defined pattern to ministerial activity. Thus, according to Ellis, all female ministry must be under the jurisdiction of male supervision, and a woman may never function as an overseer.

Ellis maintains that women are both equal and subordinate to men, with subordination taking precedence over equality. With all due respect to Dr. Ellis, his argument sounds like a legitimate, christologically-based syllogism, but it is a "cut-and-paste" argument based on a faulty premise imposed on Philippians 2. It faithfully serves the hierarchical presuppositions of Augustinian determinism.[51]

---

[50] Ellis, 85.
[51] See the discussion on Augustine's position in Chapter 5. Also see Richard and Joyce Boldry, *Chauvinism or Feminist? Paul's View of Women* (Grand Rapids: Baker, 1976), 2; Elizabeth Schussler Fiorenza, *Women: Invisible in Church and Theology* (Edinburgh: T. and T. Clark, 1985), 7.

Conclusion

As the Pentecostal Revival spread and diversified, equality waned and women tended to return to their socially acceptable place as subordinate partner. As the Holy Spirit's presence withdrew, the hierarchical social patterns of institutionalism, especially patriarchy, snuffed out the egalitarianism that had characterized the early revival period. The desire to be accepted by the larger society prompted a shift in values from the egalitarian, Spirit-empowered model to a model that determined human value and function on the basis on gender, education, economics, and social standing. Finally, a devastating blow to Pentecostal egalitarianism came in the theological arena, and this would intensify in the Charismatic Renewal.

14

Tradition and Heresy Grip
the Charismatic Renewal

The Charismatic Renewal (c.a. 1958-1987) was a revival of spiritual vitality within the traditional denominations.[1] It was an outpouring of the Holy Spirit. It was revival—a second great wave of revival in the twentieth century.[2]

Theologically the Charismatic Renewal was not disruptive except in those denominations that refused to relinquish the idea that the miraculous activity of the Spirit had ceased between the time the last of the twelve disciples had died and the emergence of the New Testament Canon.[3] In fact, it was called a *renewal* because the Spirit was infusing new life and hope into dead congregations in a remarkable way. Neither was it greatly disruptive of church authority structures, at least initially, since clergy and laity, men and women, participated together with keen interest and almost child-like enthusiasm. Nevertheless, with the emphasis on charismatic gifts, it was inevitable that tension would arise between charismatic and institutional authority. Even though the denominations were firmly established in male rulership, the question as to what constitutes legitimate authority emerged as the critical issue.[4]

---

[1] Vinson Synan, *In the Latter Days* (Ann Arbor, MI: Servant, 1984); Synan, *The Twentieth Century Pentecostal Explosion* (Altamonte Springs, FL: Creation House, 1987).

[2] For a discussion of the differences and similarities between the Pentecostal and Charismatic Movements, see Eddie L. Hyatt, *2000 Years of Charismatic Christianity* (Dallas: Hyatt Press, 1996), 1-10.

[3] The cessation theory, first proposed by Augustine, says that the extraordinary manifestations and charismata ceased between the death of the last of the twelve disciples and the development of the New Testament canon.

[4] This struggle is borne out by the fact that since 1960 over 3000 new charismatic denominations have been formed world-wide. See David B. Barrett, "Global Statistics," *Dictionary*, 811.

This struggle was not unlike that encountered by Luther and Calvin, and therefore, the solutions formulated by the Reformers were already in place for their Charismatic descendants. The major difference between the Reformation and the Charismatic Renewal, in dealing with authority, was the charismatic factor. Whereas Luther and Calvin had struggled with church order apart from much interest in the Holy Spirit, in the Charismatic Renewal, the Holy Spirit was at the forefront. People were experiencing dynamic relationship with God through His Spirit and were seeing His active Presence in their midst. But because the renewal was generally respectful of the local leadership and practices, authority structures remained in place. Therefore, women baptized in the Holy Spirit and stirred by the Holy Spirit to take initiative found themselves bound by male dominated church tradition and scriptural interpretation. Where they dared to transcend those lines, they were quickly corrected by teaching on authoritarian male headship and were coached—-and sometimes threatened—to take their proper place as submissive wives. They could minister as long as it was under the *covering* of a husband or otherwise designated male. To challenge this was to risk being labeled *rebellious* and everyone knew that "rebellion was as the sin of witchcraft." Indeed, it was a strange time for women!

In this move, unlike in the move of the Spirit at the turn of the century, women found themselves without the aid of Methodist/Holiness/Quaker theology and egalitarian ministers such as the Parhams. In addition, by this time, most Pentecostal women who were living an egalitarian lifestyle had not developed a theology and therefore could not to help the newly "Spirit-filled" women take their place.

The Influence of the Catholic Charismatic Renewal

The Roman Catholic Charismatic Renewal welcomed the spiritual awakening among both its clergy and laity. Charismatic leadership functioned under the leadership of institutional leadership.[5] This meant that women enjoyed a degree of freedom in ministry based on their spiritual giftings, but again, ultimate authority lay in the ordained, male hierarchy of the Mother Church. Furthermore, the service of women in the Roman church was not a new phenomenon since women have ministered in sisterhoods since medieval times, but always under the ultimate authority of men.[6] Thus, the renewal increased the number of Roman Catholic lay women ministering without requiring a change in church policy.[7] Moreover, the proliferation of Catholic Charismatic covenant communities[8] reinforced male rulership since authoritarian headship of the man was enforced within a strict, hierarchical format.[9]

The Influence of the Protestant Charismatic Renewal

The Renewal in the Protestant churches also upheld the doctrine of authoritarian male headship. By ascribing church authority to the local priest, pastor, or overseer, and by assigning domestic rulership to the husband or other appropriate man,[10] any threat to the traditional social structures was minimized and male dominance was preserved. Women functioned in ministry according to their spiritual giftings, but the principle of male rule was enforced with fresh vigor.

---

[5] Leon Joseph Cardinal Suenens, *A New Pentecost* (New York: Seabury Press, 1975); Edward D. O'Connor, *The Pentecostal Movement in the Catholic Church* (Notre Dame: Ave Maria Press, 1971), 166-167.

[6] Mary Ewens, "Removing the Veil," *Women of Spirit*, ed. R. Reuther and E. McLaughlin (New York: Simon and Schuster, 1979), 255-78.

[7] The elevation of women in general in society has prompted a segment of Catholic women to press for institutional authority as priests. See Elizabeth Gossman, "Women as Priests?" and Jan Peters, "Is There Room for Women in the Functions of the Church?" *Apostolic Succession: Rethinking a Barrier to Unity*, Hans Kung, ed. *Ecumenical Theology: Concilium, Theology in the Age of Renewal* (New York: Paulist, 1968), 115-140.

[8] O'Connor, 104-107; F. A. Sullivan, "Catholic Charismatic Renewal: Organization of Covenant Communities," *Dictionary*, 123-125.

[9] Sullivan, "Catholic Charismatic Renewal," 124; See also P. D. Hocken, "Charismatic Communities," *Dictionary*, 127-130.

[10] Larry Christenson, *The Christian Family*, (Minneapolis: Bethany Fellowship, 1970), 17-18.

The Discipleship-Shepherding Movement. The rise of enthusiastic Charismatics who felt no allegiance to any denomination became the concern of a group of Pentecostal/Charismatic ministers who had little or no allegiance to existing denominations. This group of men, commonly known as *The Ft. Lauderdale Five* because their headquarters was located in Ft. Lauderdale, Florida, included Derek Prince (1915-), Bob Mumford (1930-), Charles Simpson (1937-), Don Basham (1926-), and Ern Baxter (1914-). They formed Christian Growth Ministries (CGM), published an influential magazine called *New Wine* (1969-1986),[11] distributed tapes and books, conducted teaching seminars nationwide, and ministered extensively for Full Gospel Business Men's Fellowship International. Their influence grew rapidly.

The CGM leaders took it upon themselves to "shepherd" or "disciple" the throng of enthusiastic, Charismatic "renegades." Maintaining a basic conservative-evangelical perspective, they were careful to uphold the Bible as the ultimate authority for life and practice. In reality, however, their interpretation of Scripture was the final authority. They successfully extended their authority by means of delegated authority through an extensive pyramid network which they solidified by teaching the necessity of covenant loyalty "that evidenced devotion to God by submission to some man."[12]

CGM promoted theocratic "divine order" or "Apostolic government"[13] in which "the congregation recognized God's divine order of administration and respected the final decision of the recognized authority of the church."[14] God "tolerates" various types of church government, but His "ideal is to administer the affairs of the church through Holy Spirit-chosen-and-anointed men of God

---

[11] J. Buckingham, "New Wine Ceases Publication," *Ministries Today*, Nov.-Dec. 1986, 24.

[12] H. D. Hunter, "Shepherding Movement," *Dictionary*, 784-785; Derek Prince, "Forum: God's Government," *New Wine*, May 1974, 28-31.

[13] Derek Prince, 4, 28; Ken Sumrall, "The Kingdom of God: Church Government--Let's Be Practical," *New Wine*, June 1974, 9.

[14] Sumrall, 10.

(Ephesians 4:8-16 and 1 Corinthians 12:28)."[15] Ken Sumrall of Liberty Fellowship Pensacola, Florida wrote, "I do not believe the New Testament teaches equality of authority."[16] Further, he said, "Because of the authority involved, we have set only men in as elders. Paul qualifies the overseer as 'the husband of one wife' and not 'the wife of one husband.'" The "Shepherd" was not only to feed the "sheep" in his charge, they alleged, but he was also to rule them since the words "rule" and "feed" come from the same Greek word, *poimaino*, meaning "the governing power exercised by the shepherd."[17] This, of course, was a manipulation in translation and a perversion of meaning, but many were led astray by their "authoritative" teaching.

Accompanying the emphasis on government was the idea that role distinctions and authority were gender-based.[18] Dismissing Galatians 3:28, Sumrall said that it "obviously refers to our position and not to authority."[19] He continued, "God has a place for sisters as helps, intercessors, teachers of women, and even preaching in public so long as they do not usurp authority over the man." Women were permitted to minister

> spiritual gifts when under proper covering of authority as they minister, ministry in the company of their husbands to whom they are properly subject, and the teaching of younger women by older women."[20]

Women were not to teach since it allegedly put them in a position of authority over men. Illustrating the gentle but firm tone of this teaching is the following statement from *New Wine* Magazine:

---

[15] Sumrall, 9.
[16] Sumrall, 11.
[17] James Beall, "What a Sheep Can Expect from His Shepherd," *New Wine*, May 1974, 10.
[18] N.a., "Women in Ministry," *New Wine*, Oct. 1974, 18-19.
[19] Sumrall, 11; "Women in Ministry," 19.
[20] Hunter, *Dictionary*, 784.

Let us be grateful for the precious ministries they [women] are called to perform under the covering of their husbands and pastors, the men to whom God has entrusted all matters of spiritual government and oversight.[21]

Both married and single women were required to submit to a designated male *head* or *covering*. For the married woman, the *covering* was her husband. The authoritative headship of the man was thought to be essential in God's economy to the point that a married woman was forbidden to control her own household even if her husband were an unbeliever, for by submitting to her husband, she was thought to be submitting to God.[22] Single women were to be under the male headship of a pastor, an elder of house churches, or the male leadership of a Christian community.[23] The extent of the deception involved in this heresy is expressed in the writings of one young lady as she describes her submission to her *covering*. She wrote,

Dick is responsible for me to God. He is responsible for keeping me on the right track in my relationship with the Lord and for leading me into the kingdom, whatever pain and change that involves.[24]

Government and authority were so important in this movement that fatherhood was considered an "office"[25] in "the chain of authority" which "originates in the Godhead and extends to the home."[26] A close ally of this teaching was Larry Christenson (1928-), a Charismatic Lutheran who promoted this teaching in his best seller, *The Christian Family* (1970).[27] His theme was God's order for the family, and essentially he taught the priesthood and

21 "Women in Ministry," 21.
22 "Women in Ministry," 18-19.
23 "Women in Ministry," 21.
24 Nancy Clark, "The Single Woman," *New Wine*, Dec. 1975, 17.
25 Derek Prince, "Fatherhood," *New Wine*, April 1974, 6.
26 Prince, 7. See Bilezekian, "Subordination in the Godhead: A Re-emerging Heresy."
27 Larry Christenson, *The Christian Family* (Minneapolis: Bethany Fellowship, 1970).

authoritative headship of the man and the subordinate role of the woman.[28]

In 1975, other Pentecostal/Charismatic leaders confronted CGM about their teaching.[29] Finally in 1976, CGM "accepted responsibility for the excesses of those influenced by them."[30] They did not renounce the doctrine of authoritarian male headship but published material advising safeguards to help avoid extremes. In 1977, 1986, and 1987, they collaborated to oversee one of the largest contingents to major Pentecostal/Charismatic conferences in Kansas City and New Orleans. Numerous affiliated Covenant churches remain and form a protodenomination.[31]

Of greater significance is the fact that they left an indelible mark on millions in the Charismatic Movement. When the leaders disbanded CGM, the people they had been influencing did not disappear. Neither did their teaching simply dissipate. Rather, it was dispersed throughout the Pentecostal/Charismatic Movement, taking on a more dangerous state than before because in having no focal point, it avoids direct confrontation. Furthermore, few Pentecostal/Charismatics understand the need to question this heresy still so widely accepted.

During this period, women's fellowships emerged. Although this was helpful in giving women platforms for Charismatic fellowship, they unfortunately taught authoritarian male headship and female submission with a passion, some even requiring that one male minister attend each meeting to serve as the appropriate *covering*. A striking parallel occurred during the liberation of the slaves in America in the 1830s. Initially, the slaves were required to attend the services of their slave masters, but later they were granted the right to conduct their own religious services, but with

---

[28] Christenson, 17.
[29] Hunter, *Dictionary*, 784.
[30] Hunter, 784.
[31] Hunter, 785.

one stipulation: a white person must be present.[32] Both of these conditions reflect the hierarchical authoritarianism of Augustinian/Aquinas theology at its peak upholding authoritarian headship; in one case, racist; in the other, sexist. Thus, Christian women who fought valiantly for racial equality for others and won, now more than then, face inequality themselves in the Church, in particular, in Charismatic churches.

Other Developments. The idea of hierarchy (including both matriarchy and patriarchy) has its grip on the vast majority of Spirit-oriented people today. In most cases, they do not even understand why they believe as they do or where the teachings they follow arose. In fact, hierarchical church structure, so-called *divine order,* and either hierarchical or patriarchal interpretations of *headship* derive their life from medieval Roman Catholicism that is rooted in Augustine and Aquinas, or in Calvinism that also draws from the well of Augustine.

In most cases, women, liberated by the Blood of Jesus Christ and empowered by His Holy Spirit, are held captives by false teaching on authoritarian male headship. In other cases, men and women submit to the same erroneous teaching of headship/submission and are, therefore, held captive to hierarchical church structures. In a few cases, gifted women are falling prey to pre-Reformation hierarchical teaching and have developed matriarchal structures.

Indeed, some Charismatics are building on the Shepherding/Discipleship heresy of headship/submission, but they have added a dimension that is more dangerous still. This is the case because they look to institutional Church history prior to the Reformation for justification for what they practice. In 1976, for example, a group of Charismatic leaders, John Meares (1920-), Robert McAlister, and Earl Paulk (1927), all of whom had roots

---

[32] Vinson Synan, "Lectures, No Title," *The Holiness-Pentecostal Movement.*

in classical Pentecostalism, decided to adopt the Episcopal (Catholic) form of government.[33] McAlister arranged to have himself consecrated as a bishop and attempted to have an Anglican bishop perform the ceremony, believing that this would validate it through a doctrine of apostolic succession. When the Anglican bishop declined, however, McAlister had his associates perform the ceremony (1982). Later, Meares and Paulk were also consecrated as bishops in the same manner and all began wearing clerical collars and traditional regalia.

For several years prior to this, McAlister and Meares had participated in discussions known as the *Roman Catholic-Pentecostal Dialogues.*[34] According to Dr. Jerry Sandidge, himself a participant in the Dialogues, Meares and McAlister, over the years, moved toward the Catholic side of the Dialogue and often "would find themselves in greater agreement with the Roman Catholic delegation than with the Pentecostal side of a given subject." Not only did their views of church government change, but also their views drifted to the Roman Catholic position of the sacraments of baptism and Communion. In addition, they adopted the Catholic position of post-millenialism in their view of the end-time events.[35] This shift has not hindered their allowing women to advance through the hierarchical ranks of their episcopal government, but the question remains as to the biblical integrity of this form of hierarchy among God's people, whether it be partriarchy or matriarchy.

Whether or not these leaders realized it, the church structure they were adopting had, in fact, been copied from the civil government of the Roman Empire beginning with Ignatius (A.D. 67-c.a. 107). This was the beginning of hierarchy in the Church. It has since been imposed on interpretation of Scripture, including

---

[33] See *Dictionary*, 598-9; 683; 463.

[34] See J. L. Sandidge, "Dialogue, Roman Catholic and Classical Pentecostal," *Dictionary*, 240-4.

[35] Jerry Sandidge, "Roman Catholic/Pentecostal Dialogue: A Study in Developing Ecumenism" (Ph.D. diss., Katholieke Universiteit the Leunen, 1985), 296-8.

the doctrine of *headship*. One theologian exclaims, "What a price the church paid when it let go of Jesus' egalitarianism and adopted the hierarchical patterns of the heathen!"

Conclusion

The need is great to establish a Biblical theology and hermeneutic that harmonizes with the activity of the Spirit as observed in Scripture, in the personal life of the believer, and in times of revival throughout the past 2000 years. Theologies rooted in Augustine and Aquinas have no place in Pentecostal, Charismatic, Revival, and Renewal Movements. Furthermore, the doctrine of authoritative male headship, which draws its life from the teachings of these men, is the pivotal Biblical doctrine used to control and repress women. These teachings work against the teachings of Jesus, the activity of the Holy Spirit, and the Scriptures, accurately interpreted.

The Word and the Spirit agree, so what does the Bible really say about women and about headship? Is what James Dunn says about Paul true? He notes that Paul "consistently avoids using words which in Judaism denoted leadership of worship or of synagogue or of priestly office."[36] Is it possible, that Paul, like Jesus, promoted an egalitarian view? If so, it would be wise to examine biblical words that we are told are laden with authority, especially in relation to biblical womanhood.

---

[36] James D. G. Dunn, *Jesus and the Spirit* (Philadelphia: Westminster, 1975), 285.

Agreement of Spirit and Scripture

15

What Does Genesis
Really Say about Women?

What the Bible says will be in harmony with the witness and activity of the Holy Spirit. The Word and the Spirit agree. But how we understand the Bible often has to do with what we have been taught and the presuppositions that we bring to our reading of the Bible. These we tend to guard with passion! However, as the Holy Spirit, the Source of Truth (Jn. 15:26;16:12), leads us into all truth, we may need to look again at what we have been taught about biblical womanhood.

Made in God's Image
(Gen. 1:26-29; 2:18-24)

Genesis 1:26-29. Genesis 1:26-29 tells us that God made humanity as man and woman in His image. An eminent theologian and Bible scholar, W. Ward Gasque, writes, "It isn't simply man who is in the image of God—man as male—but man as male and female."[1]

We must not make the mistake of making God in our image! Since God is Spirit, He does not have gender, so the image of God has nothing to do with masculine or feminine. But God, in some mysterious way, made us—both male and female—in His Image.

Then God gave them both—male and female—responsibility. He told them both that they were to have dominion over His

---

[1] W. Ward Basque, "The Role of Women in the Church, in Society, and in the Home," A paper distributed by Christians for Biblical Equality.

233

creation. He did not delegate primary authority to man and secondary authority or subservient status to woman. According to this passage, God gave both male and female equal authority over and responsibility for His creation. And no where in this passage is there any indication that He gave one authority over the other.[2]

Genesis 2:18-25. The second record of creation, found in Genesis 2:18-25, reinforces the first creation story of Genesis 1. It further establishes two important biblical principles: 1) sameness of substance, and 2) oneness and unity.

Principle 1: The man and woman are made of the same substance. The woman is "bone of his bone and flesh of his flesh." This is an important Biblical truth that stands in opposition to the pagan idea that woman is made of a substance inferior to that of the man.

Principle 2: The man and the woman are one. Verse 24 says that because of this male/female unit that God has ordained, a man is to leave his parents and together with a woman, establish a new social unit. They are to identify with one another and be one. So verse 22 indicates that they came from one and verse 24 indicates that they are to return to being one.

This oneness reiterates the mandate expressed in Genesis 1:28 that they are both to have dominion over creation. It reinforces the notion that this dominion is not over one another. It is to be equally expressed through both individually since there is no indication of a breakdown of this mandate into a higher male authority and a lesser female authority.

Some have read into this passage that, since the male was created first that this establishes a patriarchal "order of creation." If, however, "order of creation," establishes male dominance, then it follows that the animals should have authority over man since

---

[2] Katherine Bushnell, *God's Word to Women: One Hundred Bible Studies on Woman's Place in the Divine Economy* (1923, 1930 edition published by Ray Munson, N. Collins, NY, n.d.), par. 25; Phyllis Trible, *God and the Rhetoric of Sexuality* (Grand Rapids: Eerdmans, 1975), 131, 13-14; Mary Evans, *Woman in the Bible: An Overview of All the Critical Passages on Women's Roles* (Downer's Grove: InterVaristy, 1983), 12.

they were created prior to man. In fact, nothing in the passage suggests that God provided for or intended male dominance of or authority over woman. Instead, it is obvious in both Genesis 1 or 2 that God has set up an interdependence of equal partnership. He mandated mutuality, not hierarchy.

Woman: Adam's Rib and Helper
(Gen. 2:18, 20)

Much has been made of the idea that woman is created merely to be man's "helper" or "helpmeet." But as we shall see, the word translated "helper" carries no sense of subjugation, subordination, servitude, or secondary status. Thus, the biblical use of this concept does not mandate patriarchy or male supremacy as we have traditionally been told.

Genesis 2:18, 20 expressed the idea that Adam was alone, that he could find no one of his kind with whom to communicate. With this awareness, Adam fell asleep and God took from this original, a portion and hand-crafted a woman. She would be a helper like him.

The idea that God fashioned this helper from one of Adam's ribs is absurd. Yet this is the traditional translation. The Hebrew word translated "rib" occurs forty-two times in the Old Testament, and the only time it is translated "rib" is in this one reference to Eve (Gen. 2:21). Normally, it was translated "side" or "sides." The Septuagint translators affirm this meaning. Another Hebrew word is, in fact, the legitimate word for "rib" (Dan. 7:5).[3]

The "rib" translation of the Hebrew word meaning "side(s)" is rooted in the tradition of the rabbis. The story that prevailed— just one of several fables about the event—to influence the translation of Genesis 2:21 comes from Rabbi Joshua. He says,

God deliberated from what member He would create

---

[3] Bushnell, par. 38, 39.

woman, and He reasoned with Himself thus: I must not create her from Adam's head, for she would be a proud person,
and hold her head high. If I create her from the eye, then
she will wish to pry into all things; if from the ear, she will
wish to hear all things; if from the mouth, she will talk
much; if from the heart, she will envy people; if from the
hand, she will desire to take all things; if from the feet, she
will be a gadabout. Therefore I will create her from the
member which is hid, that is, the rib, which is not even seen
when man is naked.[4]

The correct translation, "side(s)," suggests an entirely different
nuance to the creation of woman. God took a side of Adam and
created Eve. The result was "flesh of his flesh and bone of his
bone." The result was corresponding to him with whom He could
communicate and propagate God's human creation.

It is also important to correct another myth propagated by
tradition through mistranslation of this passage. We have been led
to believe that the word translated "helper" or "helpmeet" means
"servant" or "servanthood." The Hebrew word in question is *'ezer*
(ay'-zer) which is derived from the root *'ezer (aw-zar')* meaning "to
surround, protect, aid, help, succor."[5] This would indicate, then,
that woman is man's protector who surrounds him and nurtures
him. This is the opposite of what we are normally taught.

The word *'ezer* contains another surprise. It is used fourteen
times in the Old Testament to refer to God. It is used only twice
to refer to Eve. We would not think of God as inferior or subordinate![6]

Genesis 2:18, in the Hebrew, reads *'ezer neged.* This expression
means "a helper corresponding to." The King James Version

---

[4] Cited by Bushnell, pat. 43.

[5] *Strong's Exhaustive Concordance*, Hebrew Dictionary, 87.

[6] Mickelsen, Alvera and Susan Whitby Thimsen, *God Created Woman to Be a What?!* (St. Paul, MN: Step Back in Time, 1996).

translates it as "a helper meet for him." *Meet* is an old English word meaning "suitable," and as the context indicates, the purpose of the expression, "a suitable helper," is to contrast humanity from non-human forms of life and to reinforce the fact of sameness of substance. There is clear indication of interdependence in this passage, but there is no suggestion of hierarchical separation of male and female spheres of responsibility, authority, or social roles.

Recently a nationally acclaimed Word of Faith minister, Creflo Dollar, said that he has been learning to submit to his wife according to Eph. 5:21. By his own confession, he has begun to realize that she is anointed as his partner and "helper" and that it is to his benefit to obey the Word. No doubt his uniquely Pentecostal/Charismatic appreciation for "the anointing" has been instrumental in enabling him to see this truth. Without having to investigate word origins and cultural concerns, he was able to see truth "by the Spirit." As a result, he appears to be advocating mutuality and equality in marriage.[7]

He shall rule?
(Gen. 3:16)

Genesis 3:16 has been used to teach that, as a result of the fall, woman has been under a curse and that a major tenet of that curse is female subordination to men. First of all, this is listed with the curses that are coming as a result of the fall. It is not a prescription of what ought to be but a description of what will be because of human sin. As Christians, we are delivered from the curse of sin and it results (Gal. 3:5; Rom. 8:2). This passage should, therefore, never be used as an expression of God's desire for relations between the sexes. It should also be noted that the pattern of ruling had not existed prior to this time.

---

[7] Creflo Dollar, "The Anointing Series," 1998.

In addition, Genesis 3 does not teach that God cursed woman, but the notion arose during the period between the end of the Old Testament and the beginning of the New Testament when the Jews were attempting to reconcile the teaching of their Scriptures with Greek paganism. In this process, the biblical story of Eve became mingled with the classical myth about Pandora, a beautiful but deceitful woman sent to earth by the gods to bring misery upon the human race. The first reference to Eve as evil (like Pandora) and as the source of evil occurs in the Apocryphal book known as *Ecclesiasticus* in about B.C. 250. It says, "From woman a beginning of sin; and because of her all die" (25:24). Unfortunately, many of the church fathers quoted the Apocrypha as authoritative, and this book in particular is still accepted as inspired and authoritative by the Roman Catholic, Greek Orthodox, and Russian Orthodox Churches.[8] So it was that the pagan idea of Eve and of womanhood has gripped the Judeo-Christian tradition and perverted our understanding of the Genesis story.

Consequently, the normally unquestioned, traditional translation of Genesis 2:16 is:

> To the woman He [God] said: "I will greatly multiply your sorrow and your conception; in pain you shall bring forth children; Your desire shall be for your husband, And he shall rule over you."

And the traditional interpretation of this translation is that God sentenced woman to suffering, subjugation, and subordination to men. Is this, in fact, what the passage said in the Hebrew? And is the traditional interpretation accurate? What did God really say?

Gen. 3:16a I will greatly multiply your sorrow and your conception; in pain you shall bring forth children.

---

[8] Bushnell, par. 86, 87, 88; Craig A. Evans, *Noncanonical Writings and New Testament Interpretation* (Peabody: Hendrickson, 1992), 13.

Katharine Bushnell believes that this is an inaccurate rendering of this passage. She may well be right! Her evidence provides a persuasive case reconciling this passage with the Spirit of Jesus Christ.

It is possible to translate "I will greatly multiply your sorrow" with "A snare hath increased thy sorrow." Bushnell notes that a still more accurate rendering could be "A lyer-in-wait (the subtil serpent) hath increased thy sorrow." The case for Bushnell's' rendering is bound up in the placement of the Hebrew interlinear vowels. These were not present in the original manuscripts and were inserted, based on tradition and at the discretion of scribes between A.D. 600-800. The original text was composed simply of HRBARB. At the discretion of the scribes, this would have become "HaRBeh AaRBeh" meaning "multiplying I will multiply." The same could have been written "HiRBah AoReB" meaning "a lying-in-wait [snare] hath made great." The patriarchal mindset of the scribes would prompt them to select vowels that would support the "multiplying I will multiply" rendering. But the possibility of "a lying-in-wait [snare] hath made great...." being the correct meaning of the verse receives support from the fact that it flows more logically with the prophetic word in verse 15. It also occurs fourteen times in Joshua and Judges.[9]

Pursuing the meaning of this verse further, we must look at the English word *conception*. It is the translators' traditional rendering of the Hebrew word HRN, a word that does not mean "conception." As Bushnell points out, HRJWN is the correct Hebrew spelling of *conception*. It is unlikely, therefore, that it was ever intended to mean "conception." The Septuagint and many ancient authorities say that HRN means "thy sighing."

The correct rendering of the sentence, "I will greatly multiply your sorrow and your conception," would then be, "A snare hath

---

[9] Bushnell, par. 117.

increased thy sorrow and sighing."[10] Satan had laid a snare that would result in much sorrow for the woman. Since the Messiah would be born of woman, Satan would henceforth challenge every birth, and so, "in pain she would bring forth children."

Gen. 3:16b Your desire shall be for your husband and he shall rule over you.

As Dr. Bushnell correctly explains, this translation "has been made the keystone of an arch of doctrine subordinating woman to man, without which keystone the arch itself falls to pieces" (par. 139). She then shatters our preconceived notions about this verse by challenging the perverted traditional translation with truth. Bushnell leaves no stone unturned in her exposition, but we can only summarize her key points to enable us to see what the Hebrew really meant and what God really said!

The search for truth must begin with the Hebrew word *teshuqa*. This is the word traditionally translated "desire" and sometimes "lust" or "lustful appetite." The true meaning of this Hebrew word, however, is "turning" with no implication whatsoever of "desire" or "lust." Therefore, what this portion of the passage is saying is this: Eve is turning away from God toward her husband, and God is warning her that this turning will result in her coming under the domination of her husband (par. 136). Prof. H. G. Mitchell of Boston University notes that "the very tenderness of the woman for the husband would [eventually] enable him to make and keep her his inferior."[11]

The evolution of the translation of *teshuqa* from "turning" to "lustful desire" is both interesting and important. All of the best ancient versions of the Old Testament render *teshuqa* with the idea of "turning."[12] The most reliable of these is the Septuagint, the

---

[10] Bushnell, par. 121.

[11] Bushnell, pars. 136-140. H. G. Mitchell, *The Word Before Adam* cited by K. Bushnell, Par. 137.

[12] These include: Syriac Peshitto (A.D. 100-200), Samaritan Version, Old Latin version (A.D. 200), Coptic (A.D. 300), Bohairic Coptic (A.D. 350), Aethiopic version (A.D. 500), Arabic (uncertain date) cited by Bushnell, par. 139.

scholarly Greek translation of the Old Testament made in Alexandria, Egypt, in 285 B.C. As Bushnell correctly notes, "More was known about Hebrew then than at any time since."[13] The Septuagint was, in fact, the text probably used by the Lord Jesus.

A distortion of the meaning of this passage arose through the influence of the Babylonian Talmud which is a compilation of the traditions of the Jews. The teaching that God cursed Eve, and through her, all women, comes, not from the original Hebrew version of Genesis 3:16, but from the Talmud, which, in fact, teaches ten curses of womanhood.[14] The fifth curse is, "Thy desire shall be unto thy husband." A note by Bushnell says that this statement is "followed by language too coarse for reproduction, leaving no doubt of the rabbinical interpretation of 'desire.'" Bushnell's informed summation is this:

> The teaching of the Babylonian Talmud, in the "ten curses of Eve," and in parts of it unfit for quotation, has since 1528 been allowed to settle the meaning of an obscure word in Genesis 3:16, as "desire"—and that against all the testimony of the most ancient versions of Scripture. . . The teaching of the seventh and eighth curses has also been allowed to cast a shadow forward into the New Testament, and to pervert the meaning of St. Paul's words about veiling in worship, in the 11th chapter of 1st Corinthians.[15]

It is important to understand, then, how *teshuqa* in Genesis 3:16 came to be translated "desire" in the English translations. This distortion was introduced by Jerome through his Latin translation of the Bible known as the Latin Vulgate (A.D. 382). Bushnell notes that his study of Hebrew was under the tutelage of Jewish rabbis in Palestine who were influenced by the Babylonian

---

[13] Bushnell, Par. 130.

[14] Dr. Hershon, *Genesis with a Talmudic Commentary* (London, Bagster, n.d.) cited by Bushnell, par. 105-06.

[15] Curse seven is that "she is wrapped up like a mourner;" and eight, that she "dares not appear in public with her head uncovered." Cited by Bushnell, par. 106. Curse ten is that she "is confined to the house...." This is too reminiscent of some teaching today that the woman must stay at home!

Talmud.[16] Nevertheless, the first two English translations of the Bible, Wycliffe's version (1380) and the Douay Bible (1609) were not translations of the Hebrew Scriptures but of Jerome's Latin Vulgate.

Then, in 1528, an Italian Dominican monk named Pagnino translated the Hebrew Bible into English. Unfortunately, he, like Jerome, followed the linguistic tendencies of the rabbis. As might be expected, therefore, he ignored the legitimate meaning of *teshuqa* altogether and rendered it "lust." From that point on, every English translation of the Bible up to and including Geneva, Authorized and Revised Versions, followed Pagnino's lead. Thus the older English Bibles read, "Thy lust shall pertayne to thy husband."[17] This was modified in later versions to read, "Thy desire shall be to thy husband." Bushnell correctly charges, "Pagnino's word has been retained against the overwhelming authority of the ancient versions."[18]

There is, therefore, no justification for rendering *teshuqa* as "desire.'" As Bushnell's research makes abundantly clear, only "rabbinic perversion and addition to the Scriptures" related to the mythical ten curses on Eve "seems to be at the bottom of this extraordinary reading."[19]

With all of this in mind, then, a valid rendering of Genesis 3:16 is:

> *A snare has increased your sorrow and sighing. In sorrow you shall bear sons/children. You will turn toward your husband and he will rule over you.*

Even if this rendering is accepted, it still appears that these statements constitute God's sentence upon woman, His pronouncement of judgment on her, His cursing of Eve and all

---

[16] Bushnell, Par. 135, 140.
[17] Bushnell, Par. 143.
[18] Bushnell, Par. 143, 145
[19] Bushnell, Par. 140.

women from that time forth. But God spoke no curse on Eve. He did speak a curse on the serpent (Gen. 3:14-15) and on Adam (Gen. 3:17-19). He did, however, describe to Eve what the cause-and-effect on her would be. If, in fact, God did curse both man and woman, Christian men and women must remember that Jesus Christ has delivered both from any such penalty and redeemed both from any such judgment.

One final, very important observation must be made. Because a snare was set for the woman by Satan, she would find herself bearing children in sorrow, and because she was turning away from God toward her husband, he would become her ruler. "In sorrow you shall bear sons/children," and "He will rule over you" are predictions of what God knew would happen to the woman. They are not rules God is laying down, but future events He is describing. It was not a statement of God's original intent, desire, will, or plan, but a warning of the fruit of human-centered behavior.

Conclusion

In creation, God did not set up a male dominated hierarchy. Likewise, in the fall, God did not punish Eve with a sentence of subservience and subjugation to Adam. These ideas crept through a process of mingling with pagan cultures. These heathen ideas corrupted the transmission of the original intent of the Sacred Scriptures. But Jesus came and showed us a better way—God's way.

16

What Did Paul Really Say
About Women?

Genesis shows us that God intended an egalitarian model for human relationships. This model was disrupted in the fall by the probability that the woman would tend to turn her attention away from God to man. Consequently, for fallen humanity, the social norm would tend to be patriarchy.

When Jesus came, He taught an egalitarian model. By doing so, He restated God's original egalitarian model. On the Day of Pentecost, the Holy Spirit fell equally on men and women. He did not communicate with woman through man. He related equally to both. Thus, in the New Creation, God affirmed the egalitarian model of the original Creation.

We can, therefore, confidently expect that the model to be found in the Epistles will also be egalitarian. Research presented in Chapter 3 already indicates this is true. Nevertheless, certain passages that have been interpreted traditionally to enforce hierarchy, must be re-examined. What did Paul really say about women?

Headship in the Epistles
(1 Cor. 11:2-16; Eph. 5:21-33)

The Meaning of *Kephale*. The central New Testament doctrine allegedly mandating subordination of women is the Pauline doctrine of *headship*. The doctrine springs from the Greek word *kephale* which has been translated by the English word *head*. Because today *kephale* does not mean "head" in the modern sense of "authority over" or "leadership," we easily misinterpret the *kephale* passages (1 Cor. 11:2-16; Eph. 4:15, 23; 5:21-33; Col. 1:18; 2:10, 18) making them say something Paul never intended.

Nevertheless, hierarchs continue to maintain that *kephale* means "head" in the sense of "authority over." In terms of gender, they maintain a patriarchal order based on the premise that men are destined by God to rule as authoritative leaders over women.[1] In terms of church government, they hold to a chain-of-command authority structure which they describe as "divine order," usually involving apostolic succession in an institutional framework.

In recent years, many of these traditionalists, acknowledging the blatant misogyny in tradition, have moved to what they call a complementarian position. *Complementarians*, as their title suggests, maintain that women complement men, that women are of the same substance as men, but that women are destined by God to serve in a secondary and subordinate capacity to men. God certainly means for men and women to function as complementary parts on a team. The problem with the complementarian view, however, is the premise that this partnership is defined on the basis of gender with the man playing the leading role based solely on his one trait of maleness. The woman, likewise, is expected to play a subordinate role in this complementary model based solely on her one trait of femaleness. The idea remains that the man is the more prominent player on this team. But the complementarian view ignores the fact that God's complementarian plan is not based on gender, but on gifts, talents, abilities, and calling that He—not patriarchal culture—has determined. These He has not defined in terms of gender.

Biblical egalitarians promote the idea that God has gifted each person naturally and supernaturally for His purposes and that this is not gender defined or gender-role restricted. They, therefore,

---

[1] Vocal representatives of this position are Roman Catholics, Southern Baptists, Mormons, Vineyard Churches, International Communion of Charismatic Churches, Council for Christian Manhood and Womanhood, and many others.

promote the idea of mutuality, equal responsibility and authority, and complementarian partnership based on ability and giftings, not gender. This has motivated egalitarian scholars to do intensive biblical, cultural, linguistic, and historical research to clarify the passages that have traditionally been used to inhibit the egalitarian pattern promoted elsewhere in the Old and New Testaments. What they have uncovered reinforces the egalitarian teaching of Genesis, Jesus, and the Holy Spirit.

One area of intensive egalitarian study by these scholars has been the Greek word *kephale*. The best research shows clearly that *kephale*, in fact, carries no chain-of-command meaning or hierarchical intent. Instead, intensive research clearly indicates that *kephale* means "source of life" (in creation), a meaning entirely void of the idea of authority.[2] Read in the cultural and literary contexts in which Paul wrote, *kephale* clearly refers to the fact that woman came out of Adam in creation. He says that man was the source of woman in Creation and now woman is the source of man in procreation, and Christ is the Source of Life for both men and women.

A study by Alvera and the late Berkeley Mickelsen is an example of such research. They reported their finding in "The 'Head' of the Epistles" (*Christianity Today,* Feb. 20, 1981). They provide strong evidence that, in biblical Greek, *kephale* cannot mean "superior to" or "one having authority."[3] They garner support for their position from Liddell, Scott, Jones, and McKenzie (*A Greek-English Lexicon,* 9th ed., Clarendon Press, 1940) which renders the meaning as "source" with no implication of hierarchy or authority. Furthermore, they point out that the Greek scholar, Walter Bauer, does not provide support for his personal, hierarchical interpretation of Paul's use of *kephale* (*A Greek-English Lexicon of the New Tes-*

---

[2] Promoting this perspective are growing numbers of scholars, other informed individuals, and biblical feminists. Groups providing a platform for this include Christians for Biblical Equality, Institute for Contemporary Christianity, London, as well as Wesleyan-Holiness Women spearheaded by Dr. Suzie Stanley.

[3] Berkeley and Alvera Mickelsen, "The 'Head' of the Epistles," *Christianity Today* (20 February 1981): 20.

nent and Early Christian Literature, Wm. Arndt and F. W. Gin-
grich, eds., U. of Chicago Press, 1957/1979).

Perhaps the Mickelsen's most valuable contribution to the discussion is their study of *kephale* in the Septuagint. This scholarly
couple studied how the Hebrew/Greek scholars who translated the
Hebrew Scriptures (i.e. Old Testament) dealt with the Hebrew
word *ro'sh*, the Hebrew word meaning "head." They discovered
that *ro'sh* occurs 180 times in the Hebrew text, but these learned
translators used *kephale* to translate *ro'sh* only six times. Where the
Hebrew text conveyed the meaning "ruler, commander, leader,"
however, they used the Greek word *archon*. The translators, in
fact, avoided the use of *kephale* when the passage included the idea
of "authority over" because they understood that *kephale* did not
commonly carry this meaning."[4] The apostle Paul, also an astute
scholar, was also aware of this. If he had wanted to convey the
sense of "one having authority over or leadership of," he would
have used *archon* or other authority-laden words rather than
kephale.

The Mickelsens discovered that the Septuagint translators used
fourteen different Greek words to convey the various meanings of
the Hebrew word *ro'sh* (head).[5] These include the following:

1. *archon* (ruler, commander, leader)   109 times
2. *archegos* (captain, leader, chief, prince)   10 times
3. *arche* (authority, magistrate, officer)   9 times
4. *hegeomai* (to be a leader, rule, have dominion) 9 times
5. *protos* (first, foremost)   6 times
6. *patriarches* (father or chief of a race, patriarch) 3 times
7. *chilliarches* (commander)   3 times
8. *archiphules* (chief of a tribe)   2 times
9. *archipatriotes* (head of a family)   1 time

---

[4] Berkeley and Alvera Mickelsen, "What Does Kephale Mean in the New Testament?" *Women, Authority & the Bible*, ed. Alvera Mickelsen (Downers Grove: IVPress, 1986), 97-110.

[5] *Ibid.*, 103-104.

10. *archo* (verb; ruler, be ruler of)	1 time
11. *megas, megale, mega* (great, mighty, important)	1 time
12. *proegeomai* (take the lead, go first, lead the way)	1 time
13. *prototokos* (firstborn or first in rank)	1 time
14. *kephale* (where *head* can mean top or crown)	8 times
kephale (in head-tail metaphor)	4 times
kephale (manuscripts have variant readings)	6 times
ro'sh (not translated)	6 times

Eminent biblical scholar, David M. Scholer, has produced the definitive essay on *kephale*. This appears in *Women, Abuse and the Bible* (Grand Rapids: Baker, 1996). After thoroughly weighing all of the data now available, Scholer concludes that *kephale* "does not support the traditionalist or complementarian view of male headship and female submission." He states, "This data supports a new understanding in Christ by which men and women are viewed in a mutually supportive, submissive relationship."[6]

In her day, Katharine Bushnell (1855-1946),[7] did a remarkable job of building an egalitarian case despite the fact that she did not have the incredible wealth of biblical scholarship available today. She expresses the idea that Christ as "Head" is a reference to Psalm 118:22, "The stone which the builders refused is become the head stone of the corner." Its role was not to rule, but to give support to the entire building. In this metaphor, she points out that Christ supports His church and binds its members together into one cohesive unit (Eph. 4:15, 16; Col. 2:19). [8]

Discoveries about *kephale* have helped to harmonize Paul's teaching with Jesus' teaching on equality. As Catherine Kroeger observes, the egalitarian renderings of *kephale* agree with the

---

[6] David Scholer, "The Evangelical Debate over Biblical 'Headship,'" *Women, Abuse, and the Bible*, eds. Catherine Clark Kroeger and James R. Beck (Grand Rapids: Eerdmans, 1996), 44.

[7] See Dana Hardwick, *Oh Thou Woman that Bringest Good Tiding: The Life and Work of Katharine C. Bushnell* (St. Paul: CBE, 1995).

[8] Katherine C. Bushnell, "Lesson 37: Headship in the New Testament," *God's Word to Women* (North Collins, NY: Ray B. Munson, 1923), paragraphs 282-291.

overall tone of equality and mutuality expressed in over fifty New Testament passages.[9] She is, therefore, in agreement with views expressed by scholars such as the Mickelsens, Scholer, and Bushnell.

Marriage in the Greco-Roman World of Paul. Research into the nature of domestic life among people to whom Paul addressed his letters also sheds light on his use of *kephale*. For example, the Greeks believed that the gods created woman as a form of punishment for man and that she was inferior to man in substance and intellect. "Some women were made from the sow, some from the bitch, others from the high-stepping mare or the unstable waves of the sea."[10]

This depreciation of womanhood went hand-in-hand with the exaltation of manhood and promoted, among other evils, homosexuality. Plato, for example, held that "the truly noble soul was masculine and would seek another male as the object of its love. Lesser spirits might be content to bestow their affection within the women's court."[11] Additional evidence surfaces in a debate conducted slightly later than the New Testament. In it, the judge decided in favor of homosexuality because of the alleged moral inferiority of women. He announced: "Therefore let the obligation to marry be universal, but let the love of boys be reserved only for the wise, because perfect virtue flourishes least of all among women."[12]

When Paul wrote 1 Corinthians 11:11-12, he was communicating with people incultured with these beliefs. If we do not understand this, we cannot appreciate the fact that what he was actually

[9] Catherine Kroeger, "God's Purpose in the Midst of Human Sin," ed. C. Kroeger and J. Beck, *Women, Abuse and the Bible* (Grand Rapids: Baker, 1996), 203. For examples, see: Mk. 9:50; Jn. 13:14, 34, 35; 15:12, 17; Rom. 12:5, 10, 16; 13:8; 14:13, 19; 15:5, 7, 14; 16:16; 1 Cor. 7:5; 11:33; 12:25; 16:20; 2 Cor. 13:12; Gal. 5:13, 15, 26; 6:2; Eph. 4:2, 25, 32; 5:21; Phil. 2:3; Col. 3:9, 13; 1 Thess. 3:12; 4:9, 18; 5:11, 15; 2 Thess. 1:3; Heb. 10:24; James 4:11; 5:9, 16; 1 Peter 1:22; 4:9; 5:5, 14; 1 Jn. 1:7; 3:11, 23; 4:7, 11, 12; 2 Jn. 5.

[10] Seminodes, *On Women*, 83-93, cited by Kroeger, 278.

[11] Plato, *Symposium*, 180, 192, cited by Kroeger, 278.

[12] Lucian, *Erotes*, 51, cited by Kroeger, 278

doing was affirming heterosexual marriage. By declaring man the *kephale* ("source") of woman—not the *archon* ("ruler")— was denouncing the ever-present pagan notion that woman was a lesser substance than man, and he was proclaiming that she was, in fact, "bone of his bone, flesh of his flesh." Woman was indeed a fit partner for the man. Paul thus confirms this equality and then speaks of a mutuality between man and woman when he continues, "Neither is the woman independent of the man nor the man of the woman in the Lord; for just as the woman is from man, so man is from the woman, and all things are of God" (Cor. 11:11-12).[13]

Paul's references to marriage in Ephesians 5 must also be placed in historical, cultural perspective. During the New Testament era, the most common form of marriage throughout the Roman Empire was *sine manu* marriage, that is, marriage *without hand* or commitment. Under Roman law the oldest living male progenitor, "the most conspicuous member and the one by which the whole body is identified," was held accountable for the extended family.[14] A man who may have become a Christian would, under this system be deprived of freedom to live as a Christian because, by law, he was obligated to the family patriarch.[15] A woman in this pagan style of marriage remained officially attached to her birth family patriarch. She was, therefore, not an official member of her husband's household, and her legal relationship to her husband was that of a daughter. She could be married to someone else at the whim of the patriarch.[16]

It is to this Greco-Roman mindset that Paul writes Ephesians 5, instructing the new believers in the drastically different nature of Christian marriage. Thus he writes, "Therefore shall a man leave his father and mother and cleave unto his wife."[17] This has to do

---

[13] Kroeger, 278.

[14] Kroeger, 279. One of his prerogatives was to establish and maintain the religion of the family. Hence, the root of the "priest of the home" doctrine.

[15] Kroeger, 279.

16 Kroeger, 280-281.

[17] Kroeger, 281.

God's intention of intimacy and oneness between Christian band and wife. It was never intended to teach or promote an authoritative male headship and female subordination. Paul's comparison of the marriage relationship with our relationship with Christ is intended to show, not His lordship, but the sanctity of Christian marriage. (It is important to remember his 1 Corinthians 7 discussion on marrige in which he explicitly teaches mutuality.) The idea of Jesus' lordship is not inherent in the context of this passage, and good Bible interpretation does not impose a meaning not present in the text.

Ephesians 4:15-16; 1:22-23 and 5:22-23. The writer of Ephesians uses the term *kephale* in two key passages. In Eph. 4:15, Christ is referred to as "head" of a physical body. This is a metaphor providing a picture both of how we as believers are to be interdependent with others and dependent on Christ as the Source of Life.

In Ephesians 1:22-23, Paul says Christ is head of the church. Had Paul wanted to convey the idea of Christ's Lordship by means of the idea of Headship, he would have used a term such as *archon*, not *kephale*.[18] The use of *kephale* in this passage indicates Paul's desire to show Christ as the Source and Supplier of God's Life to His body, the Church.

In Ephesians 5:23, Paul again uses *kephale*, this time saying, "The husband is the head of the wife as Christ is the Head of the church." Since the Greek word *kephale* does not imply "authority over," the English word *head* cannot imply "authority over." Had Paul wanted to convey the idea of the husband being an authoritative person in the life of his wife, he could have used the term *archon*. But again, Paul chooses the word *kephale* because he wants to communicate the nature of Christian marriage with the husband and wife being one. Just as in becoming a believer in Christ,

---

[18] Mickelsen, 105; Kroeger, 273. Christ unquestionably does have authority over the church and over all the world, but that authority is established in other passages of Scripture, such as Matthew 28:18; Matthew 9:6; John 5:26-27.

she was born into a new social unit known as the Body of
in the same way, as a Christian woman, she has the opport
to form a new social unit with her spouse. This interpretatio
validated, not only by Paul's choice of *kephale*, but also by the co.
rect meaning of another word that he uses in the discussion, *hupotasso* translated "submission" (v. 22). (This will be discussed later
in this chapter.)

Colossians 1:18-23 and 2:10, 19. Colossians, an epistle that
scholars observe as being almost a duplicate of the Ephesian letter,
also uses the word *kephale*. With this in mind, one might antici-
pate a similar use of the word *kephale*. Indeed, this is the case. In
1:18, *kephale* refers to Christ being the First and, therefore, the
Source of the Church. "He is the Source of the body of believers,
the Church." In 2:10, we are told we are "complete in Him, who
is the Source of all principality and power." In 2:19, we are
warned not to be diverted from those things that would break our
connection with Our Source or that would, in any way, hinder the
flow of Life. Thus, to interpret "head" as "lord" in Colossians is to
impose a meaning that does not occur in the context. Had Paul
wanted to convey the idea of Christ's Lordship, he would have
used *archon* or another of the Greek words conveying rule or
authority. In Colossians, therefore, as in Ephesians, *kephale* means
"source."[19]

1 Corinthians 11:3 "But I want you to know that the *kephale* of
every man is Christ; the *kephale* of woman, man; and the *kephale* of
Christ, God" (Author's translation).

Traditionally, this verse has been interpreted in such a way as
to reinforce the subordination of women. Again, Paul's intended
meaning revolves around the meaning of *kephale*. So is this pas-

---

[19] See Gilbert Bilezikian, *A Hermeneutic of Mutuality*. videocassette (Tulsa: 1st International Conference of Christians for
Biblical Equality, 1990; Gilbert Bilezikian, *Subordination in the Godhead: A Re-emerging Heresy*, audio cassette (Wheaton:
3rd International Conference of Christians for Biblical Equality, 1993).

... act, a hierarchical statement as we have traditionally been
...?

... we substitute the accurate meaning of *kephale* in this verse, it
...ould read as follows: "But I want you to know that the *source* of
every man is Christ; the *source* of woman, man; and the *source* of
Christ, God." (Author's translation).[20] This translation was also
proposed by, among other early theologians, Cyril of Alexandria
(A.D. 376?-444):

> The *kephale* of every man is Christ, because he was through
> him and brought forward to birth. . . . And the *kephale* of
> woman is man, because she was taken from his flesh and has
> him as her source. Likewise, the *kephale* of Christ is God, be-
> cause He is from Him according to nature.[21]

Another very important consideration in understanding Paul's
intention in this verse is the non-hierarchical structure of his
statement. Paul, who is adept in developing hierarchical patterns
of thought, is obviously not developing a hierarchical structure in
this case.[22] If it were a statement intended to show "authority
over" based on order of creation, it would have read: God is the
kephale of Christ is the *kephale* of man is the *kephale* of woman. Furthermore, if it were a statement intended to indicate a chain-of-
command, it should read: God is the *archon* of Christ is the *archon*
of man is the *archon* of woman. Any interpretation that indicates a
hierarchical order to this verse is the reader's imposition of his or
her own thinking.[23] It is not what Paul said.

---

[20] This is the position held by Kroeger as well. Kroeger (277) cites Cyril of Alexandria, "De Recte Fide ad Arcadiam et Marinam" in *Cyrilli Opera* 1.1.5 5(2).63 (ed. Pusey), vol. 7, pt. 1, 182. She also cites (276) Saint Basil, Athanasius and Eusebius to confirm this position (*De Ecclesiastica Theologia* 1.11.2-3).

[21] Cited by Kroeger, 269.

[22] See also Gordon D. Fee, *The First Epistle to the Corinthians* (Grand Rapids: Eerdmans, 1987), 492-498.

[23] Walter L. Liefeld, "Women Submission and Ministry in 1 Corinthians," *Women, Authority and the Bible*, ed. Alvera Mickelsen (Downers Grove: IVP, 1986), 134-154. Liefeld observes, "The order one finds in this passage has to do with the interrelationships between pairs (Christ/man, etc.), and second with arrangement and decorum (cf. 14:33,40), but not with some military-like structure."

Another problem regarding the hierarchical interpret that it requires a hierarchy in the Godhead.[24] This pattern v. the equality of the Persons of the Godhead because, in asse. that "God is somehow authoritative over Christ [it] erodes t. Savior's full divinity."[25] This falsehood is not new, however. Ac cording to Chrysostom, certain heretics in his day "seized upon the notion of headship and derived from it a concept of the Son as somehow less than the Father." They argued that "although the Son is of the same substance as the Father, he is under subjection." Chrysostom pointed out that if Paul had intended to demonstrate rulership and subordination, "he would have chosen slave and master rather than wife and husband." Chrysostom understood *kephale* in the sense of "perfect unity and primal cause and source."[26] Indeed, Paul intended this passage to show equality.[27]

Conclusion. It can be confidently said that Paul used *kephale* in Ephesians and Colossians to mean "source." It can also be said that he did not use *kephale* to mean "authority over" in 1 Corinthians. To impose meanings other than Paul's, from outside the context in which he wrote, is to read into his writings something that he did not intend and that the Scripture, accurately interpreted, does not mean.

Submission
(Eph. 5:18-22)

Entwined with the doctrine of authoritative male headship is the teaching on female submission. It is important, then, to correct the erroneous teaching that has arisen around the doctrine of submission. It too must be bought into harmony with biblical

---

[24] Bilezikian, *A Hermeneutic of Mutuality* (1990) and *Subordination in the Godhead: A Re-emerging Heresy* (1993).

[25] Gretchen Gaebelein Hull, *Equal to Serve* (Old Tappan, NJ: Fleming H. Revell, 1987), 194.

[26] John Chrysostom, *Commentary on the First Epistle to the Corinthians, Homily 26* (migne, PG 61.214,216), cited by Catherine Clark Kroeger, "Appendix III: The Classical Concept of *Head* as 'Source,'" *Equal to Serve* by Gretchen Gaebelein Hull (Old Tappan, NJ: Fleming H. Revell, 1987), 283.

[27] Kroeger, 283.

g in general.

he Meaning of *Hupotasso*. *Submit* is the English word commonly used to translate the Greek word *hupotasso* in the New Testament. This word has several nuances. The correct meaning in each case must be derived from the context.

1. *Hupotasso* can mean "to show responsible behavior toward others." In 1 Corinthians 14, Paul admonishes the prophets (v. 32) and the women (v. 35) to behave in a responsible manner with the welfare of the group in mind. In Rom. 13:1 and 1 Peter 2:13, believers are instructed to behave as responsible citizens.

2. *Hupotasso* can mean "to be brought into a sphere of influence." Luke records the story of Jesus at the age of 12 staying behind in the Jerusalem temple unbeknown to his parents. When they found him, he returned with them to Nazareth and was "subject to them" once again. Catherine Kroeger says, "This, I suggest, did not necessarily imply obedience, as later stories of his dealings with his mother and brothers indicate." She adds, "Rather, he reenters the sphere of his parents, and identifies, associates, and integrates himself with them and their world of everyday life, rather than with the learned doctors of Jerusalem."[28]

3. *Hupotasso* can mean "to add or unite one person or thing with another." The thrust of this meaning is the idea of unity. In the cultural "household code" integrated into Ephesians 5:22-33, a married woman is directed to identify herself with her husband (v. 33) even as believers identify with Christ, being members one of another. We have been taught to read this passage through hierarchical lenses with the only possible meaning of the text being that a married woman is to obey her husband as she also obeys the Lord. We are, in fact, to obey the Lord, but this is not the thrust of the passage. When considered in context, it is clear that

---

[28] C. Kroeger, "God's Purpose in the Midst of Human Sin," *Women Abuse and the Bible*, ed. C. Kroeger and J. Beck (Baker: Baker, 1996), 211. This same concept is clear in Rom. 8:20; 2 Cor. 9:13, and in non-biblical writings of the day.

the thrust and inherent directive of the text is that we are
identified fully with the Lord. This meaning becomes abunda
clear when we understand the cultural setting and the reason
the admonition.

The Household Code. As was noted previously in the discussion
of *kephale*, family life in the Greco-Roman word of the New Testament era was, from our point of view, dysfunctional. Paul,
therefore, found it necessary to advise his converts about family
relationships (Eph. 5). In doing so, he drew on something they
were familiar with called the "household code." This he used
merely as a jumping off point leading his readers to truth; he did
not use this cultural element as the final standard for Christian
relationships.

What Paul is really saying in Ephesians 5:18-33 is that he
wants the married woman to identify with and be committed to
her husband rather than to her birth family. This is the meaning
of submit (*hupotasso*). He asks the children and slaves to obey
(*hupakouo*). He asks the husband to love (*agape*) his wife, another
new idea, indeed, in that culture! And he also instructs the husband to submit (*hupotasso*) to his wife (v. 21). He asks husband
and wife to be committed to one another only (v. 31) in an atmosphere of mutual identification and unity (v. 21).

Unilateral obedience and subjugation of the wife to the husband is not a biblical doctrine. This idea of mutual identification
and unity occurs in various other passages. Consider, for example:
1 Corinthians 7:3-4; Galatians 5:13; Philippians 2:3; 1 Peter 3:7.
Indeed, the thrust of New Testament relationships and of Christian marriage revolves around mutuality and interdependence, not
patriarchy and authority over/subordination to others.

Again, in understanding Paul's words in Ephesians 5 regarding
hupotasso, it is critical to remember the low status of women and
the dysfunctional nature of marriage in the Greco-Roman world.
These are the issues underlying Paul's address. He would have

ı, not despised, used, and abused, but cherished and valued
qual with men. The issues here are identity and unity
ısband and wife as a cohesive unit of equal partners), sameness
ı substance, and equality in value. Accurately interpreted, the
passage does not promote authoritative male dominance and female subjugation.

Other Considerations. Beginning in Chapter 4 of Ephesians,
Paul is instructing the believers how to live or "walk." This embraces a wide range of topics, and in 5:15-18, he is telling them to
walk in wisdom and to be filled with the Spirit. The principal verb
in the passage is *be filled* (verse 18); that is, "Be filled with the
Spirit. . . ." This main verb is followed by five present participles
that describe how a person would behave when filled with the
Spirit: *addressing* (v. 19a), *singing* (v. 19b), *making* (v. 19b), *giving*
(v. 20), and *being subject* (v. 21). Verse 21, in fact, reads, "Being
subject to one another. . . ." This clearly speaks of gracious mutuality, and this is the context in which Paul places his discussion
of the household codes of that culture.

In the Greek text, verse 22, referring to the wife's relation with
her husband, does not contain the verb "submit" or "be subject
to." It reads, "wives to your own husbands." Translators have
taken the liberty to insert the words "submit to." Further, they
have inserted these as though they were a command. Upon these
two words that do not even appear in the Greek text, many
Christians have built a doctrine of female subordination and have
then proceeded to interpret the rest of Scripture on the basis of
this statement that does not exist. What, then, does the passage
say?

> *Be filled with the Spirit (v. 18) . . . submitting to one another (v.
> 21) . . . wives to your own husbands (v.22) (Author's translation).*

Verse 22 is, in fact, a continuation of the participle ("being
subject to one another") in verse 21, which, in turn, is an adver-

bial modifier of the main verb, which is the imperativ
mand in the passage: "Be filled with the Spirit. . . ." (v. 1c
22, because it does not contain a verb, is not a commar
cannot stand on its own. It serves only as a continuing tho.
connected to verse 21 which states that mutual submission (t.
"identification with or responsible behavior toward") is one of five
behaviors that indicate that people are, in fact, filled with the
Spirit. This is confirmed by the remainder of the passage that also
describes mutual submission.

Covering
(1 Cor. 11:3-16)

Since the Shepherding/Discipleship Movement of the 1970s in
the Charismatic Revival, [29] the notion that women need a *covering*
has flooded the church with the destructive force of a tidal wave.
This teaching is derived primarily from 1 Corinthians 11:3-16.
The term has been applied to the personal and domestic realms. It
has also been stretched to include the idea of church government
and order with believers being told that they must function under
"a covering." This idea has absolutely no scriptural basis, unless
one comes to the passage with an agenda and imposes a meaning
on the passage that does not exist in the passage. But what about
the idea of a woman needing "a covering"? Is this a valid teaching?

It is interesting to note how various groups in our day interpret
and dogmatically apply this passage. Mennonites, for example,
insist that it means that women must always wear a headcovering,
a bonnet, a specific style of cap. Holiness-Pentecostals, on the
other hand, insist that it means that women must not cut their
hair. Many modern Pentecostals and Charismatics have spiritualized it insisting that it is related to hierarchical authority. In this

---

[29] H. D. Hunter, "The Shepherding Movement," *Dictionary of Pentecostal and Charismatic Movements*, eds. Stanley M. Burgess and Gary B. McGee (Grand Rapids: Zondervan, 1988), 783-784.

...isist that it means that a woman must always be under ...ority of a man or organization that serves as a *covering*. Of ..., this is not what the verse says, and it is a splendid example ...*gesis* (i.e. imposing a meaning on a passage rather than exeget-..., or extracting the actual meaning of a word, verse, or passage.)

Translated literally, 1 Corinthians 11:10 reads, "Therefore the woman ought to have authority over her own head because of the angels [or messengers]." Both the King James Version (KJV) and the New International Version (NIV) read "a sign of authority" where the Greek should be translated "to have authority." The insertion of the words "a sign" is a grave error because it alters the meaning of the passage." The Living Bible rendering: "So a woman should wear a covering on her head as a sign that she is under man's authority," is totally in error.

Alvera and the late Berkeley Mickelsen, in their *Christianity Today* article (Oct. 5, 1979), provide wonderful insight regarding this verse and the various interpretations of it. They acknowledge that the passage, indeed, is "open to several interpretations." They caution, however, that most readers do not realize this or that they are reading "commentaries on what individual translators think Paul meant." They warn,

> All the one-man translations—Taylor, Phillips, Bratcher— added *man* or *husband* to this passage despite the fact that Paul says nothing about a man or a husband. (The same Greek word *aner* is used both for man and husband.) The unsophisticated reader is led to think that Paul wrote about a woman being under a man's or her husband's authority. If that was what Paul had in mind, he did not say it..[30]

Pentecostal Bible scholar, Gordon Fee, has examined the various possibilities resident in the Greek.[31] After careful analysis of

---

[30] Berkeley and Alvera Mickelsen, "Does Male Dominance Tarnish Our Translations?" *Christianity Today* (5 October 1979): 26.

[31] Gordon Fee, *Commentary on the First Epistle to the Corinthians* (Grand Rapids: Eerdmans, 1987), 518-22.

all available possibilities, he concludes that Paul "is a...
'freedom' of women over their own heads." He admits t...
mystery in the passage but believes that this arises beca...
passage (1 Cor. 11:10)—in fact, the entire Corinthian le...
addresses specific, local problems and was never intended fc...
generic interpretation apart from its local, cultural context i...
Corinth.[32]

One possible key to understanding the verse is to translate *tous angelous* as "the messengers" rather than as "the angels." This rendering could then fit a cultural context in which the Christian women were admonished to retain the custom of wearing a head covering so that traveling couriers would not proposition them as prostitutes. But as scholars agree, mystery shrouds this passage. But there is nothing in the text to indicate the interpretation given it by Mennonites, Holiness-Pentecostals, or contemporary Pentecostal/Charismatics.

The Issue of Authority
(1 Tim. 2:12)

Another important consideration involves the word *authority* in 1 Timothy 2:12 (context 11-15), which reads, "I do not permit women to teach or to have authority over a man; she must be silent." Two activities, teaching and having authority over a man, are apparent prohibitions according to this verse. In the broader context of the New Testament, however, it is clear that women did teach both men and women, so if this one verse is not a blatant contradiction of a New Testament principle, then it is indeed addressing a unique situation in Ephesus.

It is the second prohibition, therefore, that needs to be addressed: I do not permit a woman to have authority over a man. First, Jesus clearly stated that we are not to exercise authority over

---

[32] Fee, 521.

. That was the way of the gentiles. Second, Genesis
ɔve man authority over woman, nor woman over man.
e them both authority or dominion over creation. With
. thoughts in place, and the issues previously discussed in this
ɔpter fresh in our minds, let us look at the statement in point.

What is particularly interesting about "I do not permit a
woman to have authority over a man" is not obvious in the English translations. It is this: the Greek word *authentein*, translated
"authority" in this verse, is not the word normally used for
"authority" in the New Testament. This is, in fact, the only occurrence of the word *authentein* in the New Testament. It is good exegetical practice never to build a doctrine on one verse of Scripture.
A doctrine should not, therefore, be built on this statement.

Beyond this exegetical issue, however, is the actual study of the
key word *authentein*. Since it occurs only this one time in the Bible, we must go outside the Bible to learn its meaning. Leland
Edward Wilshire has done comprehensive research into the
meaning of this word, and he has observed that it always carried
connotations of violence and did not mean simply "to have
authority over." In the Greek of the New Testament era, *authentein* always carried the meaning of "murder" or "murderer."[33]

David Scholer agrees, saying that what Paul is denouncing by
the use of the word *authentein* is violent, inappropriate behavior.
He is persuaded that the text (1 Tim. 2) is not prescribing a
transcultural norm of male leadership and female subservience.
Rather, he concludes that the data supports the view that 1 Timothy 2 is opposing the negative behavior of certain women,
"probably the women mentioned in 1 Timothy 5:15 who follow
and represent the false teachers 1 and 2 Timothy are dedicated to
opposing."[34]

---

[33] Leland Edward Wilshire, "The TLG Computer and Further Reference to *authentein* in 1 Timothy 2:12," *New Testament Studies* 34 (1988): 120-34.

[34] Scholer, 50.

Richard and Catherine Kroeger concur. In their book
Not a Woman; Rethinking 1 Timothy 2:11-15 in the Light of
Evidence, they provide background information critical to a cc
understanding of *authentein.* Their studies reveal that 1 Timoth,
is confronting a problem in Ephesus wherein a fusion of Gnost.
cism and worship of the goddess, Artemis, was promoting the idea
that, in Creation, Eve had been the source *(kephale)* of Adam. Artemis was a fertility goddess whom, it was believed, could reproduce without male intervention. They suggest that a reasonable
translation of 1 Timothy 2:12 would be: "I do not allow a woman
to teach or to proclaim herself author of man."[35] A translation of
verses 12-13 might correctly read: "I do not permit a woman to
teach nor to represent herself as the originator of man but she is to
be in conformity [with the Scriptures] . . . For Adam was created
first, then Eve."

"Lord" Abraham
(1 Peter 3:6)

Even with all of this evidence in place, some loyalists of the
traditional position will remind us that Sarah *obeyed* Abraham and
called him *lord* (1 Pet. 3:6). In seeking the true meaning of this
verse, it is important to note that the Greek word that is translated "obeyed" is derived directly from the verb "to listen," and
for that reason, may just as accurately be translated "listened attentively to." We could, therefore, say, "Sarah listened attentively
to Abraham."

Even if we reject this possible translation and retain the idea
that "Sarah obeyed Abraham," there are other interesting things
to consider. In the Old Testament story to which this New Testament passage refers, Sarah, in fact, did cooperate with Abra-

---

[35] Richard Clark Kroeger and Catherine Clark Kroeger, *I Suffer Not a Woman: Rethinking 1 Timothy 2:11-15 in Light of Ancient Evidence* (Grand Rapids: Baker, 1992), 103.

...eme (Gen. 20:1-18). But consider verse 3: "But God Abimelech in a dream by night, and said to him, Behold, ...art but a dead man for the woman which thou hast taken; ...she is a man's wife.'" The interesting word here is *wife*. This is ...e only place in the Old Testament that the word *ba'al* is translated *wife*! The normal Hebrew word for *wife* is *ishshah*. In every other instance, the word *ba'al* is translated or means *lord, master, owner.* So God called Sarah, Abraham's *ba'al.* God called Sarah Abraham's lord, master, owner!

It is also interesting to note the structural context of 1 Peter 2 and 3. Of course, it was not written in verses and chapters. These were imposed by the translators. It *is* permissible, therefore, to suggest that the thought of respect *is* the real theme and it begins in verse 11 and particularly in verse 13, "Submit yourselves. . . ." A pattern is apparent in 3:1, <u>likewise</u>, wives . . . ; and 3:7, <u>likewise</u>, husbands. . . . This appears to be encouraging the same mutuality, identification with, and unity observed in other passages such as Ephesians 5:18-22.

However, continuing to explore the verse, we need to consider that Sarah called Abraham *kurion* (kurion) meaning "lord, master, or sir." But it should be remembered that this did not necessarily carry a hierarchical, chain-of-command connotation, for *kurion* was commonly used to show common courtesy or respect for another person. It was used as a salutation in letters; i.e., "My Lord."

Further insight can be derived from this passage. Catherine Kroeger, for example, tells us there is a lesson to be learned from Sarah's apparent compliance with Abraham's wishes: it made him less than "a blessing to all nations" (Gen. 12:10-20, 19; 20:2-18; 26:6-11). In addition, the idea of mutuality is apparent when God commanded Abraham to heed his wife's advice (Gen. 21:12).

bial modifier of the main verb, which is the imperative or command in the passage: "Be filled with the Spirit. . . ." (v. 18). Verse 22, because it does not contain a verb, is not a command and cannot stand on its own. It serves only as a continuing thought connected to verse 21 which states that mutual submission (i.e. "identification with or responsible behavior toward") is one of five behaviors that indicate that people are, in fact, filled with the Spirit. This is confirmed by the remainder of the passage that also describes mutual submission.

Covering
(1 Cor. 11:3-16)

Since the Shepherding/Discipleship Movement of the 1970s in the Charismatic Revival, [29] the notion that women need a *covering* has flooded the church with the destructive force of a tidal wave. This teaching is derived primarily from 1 Corinthians 11:3-16. The term has been applied to the personal and domestic realms. It has also been stretched to include the idea of church government and order with believers being told that they must function under "a covering." This idea has absolutely no scriptural basis, unless one comes to the passage with an agenda and imposes a meaning on the passage that does not exist in the passage. But what about the idea of a woman needing "a covering"? Is this a valid teaching?

It is interesting to note how various groups in our day interpret and dogmatically apply this passage. Mennonites, for example, insist that it means that women must always wear a headcovering, a bonnet, a specific style of cap. Holiness-Pentecostals, on the other hand, insist that it means that women must not cut their hair. Many modern Pentecostals and Charismatics have spiritualized it insisting that it is related to hierarchical authority. In this

---

[29] H. D. Hunter, "The Shepherding Movement," *Dictionary of Pentecostal and Charismatic Movements*, eds. Stanley M. Burgess and Gary B. McGee (Grand Rapids: Zondervan, 1988), 783-784.

case, they insist that it means that a woman must always be under the authority of a man or organization that serves as a *covering*. Of course, this is not what the verse says, and it is a splendid example of *isogesis* (i.e. imposing a meaning on a passage rather than exegeting or extracting the actual meaning of a word, verse, or passage.)

Translated literally, 1 Corinthians 11:10 reads, "Therefore the woman ought to have authority over her own head because of the angels [or messengers]." Both the King James Version (KJV) and the New International Version (NIV) read "a sign of authority" where the Greek should be translated "to have authority." The insertion of the words "a sign" is a grave error because it alters the meaning of the passage." The Living Bible rendering: "So a woman should wear a covering on her head as a sign that she is under man's authority," is totally in error.

Alvera and the late Berkeley Mickelsen, in their *Christianity Today* article (Oct. 5, 1979), provide wonderful insight regarding this verse and the various interpretations of it. They acknowledge that the passage, indeed, is "open to several interpretations." They caution, however, that most readers do not realize this or that they are reading "commentaries on what individual translators think Paul meant." They warn,

> All the one-man translations—Taylor, Phillips, Bratcher— added *man* or *husband* to this passage despite the fact that Paul says nothing about a man or a husband. (The same Greek word *aner* is used both for man and husband.) The unsophisticated reader is led to think that Paul wrote about a woman being under a man's or her husband's authority. If that was what Paul had in mind, he did not say it..[30]

Pentecostal Bible scholar, Gordon Fee, has examined the various possibilities resident in the Greek.[31] After careful analysis of

---

[30] Berkeley and Alvera Mickelsen, "Does Male Dominance Tarnish Our Translations?" *Christianity Today* (5 October 1979): 26.

[31] Gordon Fee, *Commentary on the First Epistle to the Corinthians* (Grand Rapids: Eerdmans, 1987), 518-22.

all available possibilities, he concludes that Paul "is affirming the 'freedom' of women over their own heads." He admits to lingering mystery in the passage but believes that this arises because the passage (1 Cor. 11:10)—in fact, the entire Corinthian letter—addresses specific, local problems and was never intended for a generic interpretation apart from its local, cultural context in Corinth.[32]

One possible key to understanding the verse is to translate *tous angelous* as "the messengers" rather than as "the angels." This rendering could then fit a cultural context in which the Christian women were admonished to retain the custom of wearing a head covering so that traveling couriers would not proposition them as prostitutes. But as scholars agree, mystery shrouds this passage. But there is nothing in the text to indicate the interpretation given it by Mennonites, Holiness-Pentecostals, or contemporary Pentecostal/Charismatics.

The Issue of Authority
(1 Tim. 2:12)

Another important consideration involves the word *authority* in 1 Timothy 2:12 (context 11-15), which reads, "I do not permit women to teach or to have authority over a man; she must be silent." Two activities, teaching and having authority over a man, are apparent prohibitions according to this verse. In the broader context of the New Testament, however, it is clear that women did teach both men and women, so if this one verse is not a blatant contradiction of a New Testament principle, then it is indeed addressing a unique situation in Ephesus.

It is the second prohibition, therefore, that needs to be addressed: I do not permit a woman to have authority over a man. First, Jesus clearly stated that we are not to exercise authority over

---

[32] Fee, 521.

one another. That was the way of the gentiles. Second, Genesis did not give man authority over woman, nor woman over man. He gave them both authority or dominion over creation. With these thoughts in place, and the issues previously discussed in this chapter fresh in our minds, let us look at the statement in point.

What is particularly interesting about "I do not permit a woman to have authority over a man" is not obvious in the English translations. It is this: the Greek word *authentein*, translated "authority" in this verse, is not the word normally used for "authority" in the New Testament. This is, in fact, the only occurrence of the word *authentein* in the New Testament. It is good exegetical practice never to build a doctrine on one verse of Scripture. A doctrine should not, therefore, be built on this statement.

Beyond this exegetical issue, however, is the actual study of the key word *authentein*. Since it occurs only this one time in the Bible, we must go outside the Bible to learn its meaning. Leland Edward Wilshire has done comprehensive research into the meaning of this word, and he has observed that it always carried connotations of violence and did not mean simply "to have authority over." In the Greek of the New Testament era, *authentein* always carried the meaning of "murder" or "murderer."[33]

David Scholer agrees, saying that what Paul is denouncing by the use of the word *authentein* is violent, inappropriate behavior. He is persuaded that the text (1 Tim. 2) is not prescribing a transcultural norm of male leadership and female subservience. Rather, he concludes that the data supports the view that 1 Timothy 2 is opposing the negative behavior of certain women, "probably the women mentioned in 1 Timothy 5:15 who follow and represent the false teachers 1 and 2 Timothy are dedicated to opposing."[34]

---

[33] Leland Edward Wilshire, "The TLG Computer and Further Reference to *authentein* in 1 Timothy 2:12," *New Testament Studies* 34 (1988): 120-34.

[34] Scholer, 50.

Richard and Catherine Kroeger concur. In their book, *I Suffer Not a Woman; Rethinking 1 Timothy 2:11-15 in the Light of Ancient Evidence,* they provide background information critical to a correct understanding of *authentein.* Their studies reveal that 1 Timothy 2 is confronting a problem in Ephesus wherein a fusion of Gnosticism and worship of the goddess, Artemis, was promoting the idea that, in Creation, Eve had been the source *(kephale)* of Adam. Artemis was a fertility goddess whom, it was believed, could reproduce without male intervention. They suggest that a reasonable translation of 1 Timothy 2:12 would be: "I do not allow a woman to teach or to proclaim herself author of man."[35] A translation of verses 12-13 might correctly read: "I do not permit a woman to teach nor to represent herself as the originator of man but she is to be in conformity [with the Scriptures] . . . For Adam was created first, then Eve."

"Lord" Abraham
(1 Peter 3:6)

Even with all of this evidence in place, some loyalists of the traditional position will remind us that Sarah *obeyed* Abraham and called him *lord* (1 Pet. 3:6). In seeking the true meaning of this verse, it is important to note that the Greek word that is translated "obeyed" is derived directly from the verb "to listen," and for that reason, may just as accurately be translated "listened attentively to." We could, therefore, say, "Sarah listened attentively to Abraham."

Even if we reject this possible translation and retain the idea that "Sarah obeyed Abraham," there are other interesting things to consider. In the Old Testament story to which this New Testament passage refers, Sarah, in fact, did cooperate with Abra-

---

[35] Richard Clark Kroeger and Catherine Clark Kroeger, *I Suffer Not a Woman: Rethinking 1 Timothy 2:11-15 in Light of Ancient Evidence* (Grand Rapids: Baker, 1992), 103.

ham's scheme (Gen. 20:1-18). But consider verse 3: "But God came to Abimelech in a dream by night, and said to him, 'Behold, thou art but a dead man for the woman which thou hast taken; for she is a man's wife.'" The interesting word here is *wife*. This is the only place in the Old Testament that the word *ba'al* is translated *wife*! The normal Hebrew word for *wife* is *ishshah*. In every other instance, the word *ba'al* is translated or means *lord, master, owner*. So God called Sarah, Abraham's *ba'al*. God called Sarah Abraham's lord, master, owner!

It is also interesting to note the structural context of 1 Peter 2 and 3. Of course, it was not written in verses and chapters. These were imposed by the translators. It is permissible, therefore, to suggest that the thought of respect is the real theme and it begins in verse 11 and particularly in verse 13, "Submit yourselves. . . ." A pattern is apparent in 3:1, <u>likewise</u>, wives . . . ; and 3:7, <u>likewise</u>, husbands. . . . This appears to be encouraging the same mutuality, identification with, and unity observed in other passages such as Ephesians 5:18-22.

However, continuing to explore the verse, we need to consider that Sarah called Abraham *kurion* (kurion) meaning "lord, master, or sir." But it should be remembered that this did not necessarily carry a hierarchical, chain-of-command connotation, for *kurion* was commonly used to show common courtesy or respect for another person. It was used as a salutation in letters; i.e., "My Lord."

Further insight can be derived from this passage. Catherine Kroeger, for example, tells us there is a lesson to be learned from Sarah's apparent compliance with Abraham's wishes: it made him less than "a blessing to all nations" (Gen. 12:10-20, 19; 20:2-18; 26:6-11). In addition, the idea of mutuality is apparent when God commanded Abraham to heed his wife's advice (Gen. 21:12).

Conclusion

In conclusion, it can be confidently stated that the evidence simply does not support the doctrine of authoritarian male headship and female subjugation. As a foremost authority on this issue, David M. Scholer writes,

> I am fully convinced that the Bible does not institute, undergird, or teach male headship and female submission, in either the traditionalist or complementarian forms of evangelical thought, which exclude women from equal participation in authority with men within the body of Christ, whether in ministry or marriage or any other dimension of life.[36]

When the Scriptural strongholds of female subjugation are read in context with historical accuracy, it is clear that these interpretations are inaccurate and self-serving. It is also clear that their intended meanings agree with Jesus' teaching in which men and women are regarded as equal in both substance and function. Accurately interpreted, these passages also confirm the equalizing activity of the Holy Spirit through the centuries.

---

[36] Scholer, 51.

17

How Does Culture Condition?

A friend who is eager to do what is biblically correct regarding women cautiously expressed his one remaining concern. Despite the sound research into individual problem texts clearing the way for a sound egalitarian position, he is still concerned about the general patriarchal overtone of Scripture.[1] This makes him wonder if, perhaps, the debate over "woman's place" will eventually come down to whether or not the Bible is the inerrant, inspired Word of God.

To address my friend's concern fairly requires that we understand not only the word/text studies of the previous chapters but also the dual nature of the Bible. As some have charged, the Bible does seem to be steeped in partriarchalism. How do we account for this, if it is true, while maintaining the position that the Bible teaches gender equality?

The answer lies in the fact that the Bible, like the Lord Jesus Himself, is both fully human and fully divine. In its human dimension, it reflects fallen culture—which is both highly patriarchal and hierarchical. It describes cultural conditions that, because of the fall, are patriarchal and hierarchical. Because of the hardness of human hearts, it even accommodates this in some instances.[2] But like the Lord Himself, it ultimately prescribes neither patriarchy nor hierarchy as the way acceptable to God for His redeemed. Although the biblical authors reflect their cultures, God's Word neither begins nor ends with human culture but with

---

[1] Example: Ex. 13:2,13,15/Lk. 2:22-23 indicate that the first-born male has priority status. This is apparently to say that the female is of less value than the male to God!

[2] Mt. 19:3-8.

God Himself, the *Alpha* and the *Omega*.

Culture is the milieu in which we live. Like the air we breathe or the water in which fish swim, it is ever-present. It is constantly shaping us and we are forever affecting it.

God is also ever-present. Unlike culture, however, God is not ultimately subject to human restrictions and social customs. He is Spirit and lives in a beyond and outside the confines of humanity.

Through the miracle of the Incarnation, however, God and human culture met. He came and lived among us in the Person of Jesus Christ, Who showed us God's will and ways. Then He sent His Holy Spirit to abide in us, to empower us from within, to carry on the work that Jesus had begun.

In the same way that Jesus was not called to reflect the values of the culture into which He was born, the Church is not called to reflect the values of fallen culture. Instead, as Jesus demonstrated the values of Heaven, the Church is called to follow in His ways and demonstrate God's values in a fallen world.

Nowhere does God call us to affirm the values of fallen culture, but rather to be instruments of cultural change. To do this, He empowers us with His indwelling Holy Spirit, and to help us more accurately understand the workings of His Spirit, He reveals Himself to us through the Living Word (Jesus Christ) and the Written Word (The Bible). Since God is the Master of communication, His self-revelation comes to us in terms that we can understand; therefore, it comes to us within our culture. God meets us where we are but does not leave us there. He takes us where He is in terms of attitude, and behavior. Then, as we change, we become instruments of change, infusing our culture with God's values.

Jesus, the Living Word

Jesus Christ was, at once, both the express image of God and a Jewish man. This is the miracle of the Incarnation. He was born of Jewish parents. He spoke their language. He ate their food. He conformed to their manner of dress. He wore His hair the way customary to the people among whom He lived. He was, in these ways, a person of culture.

Yet the important issue for this discussion is that in the Incarnation, "The Man Jesus has the authority of Lord."[3] And as Lord, He demonstrated and demanded a way of life that was very different from the culture in which He lived. He lived from a value base that transcended any earthly cultural value system. Consequently, by word and deed, precept and example, He constantly challenged the people to put aside cultural values and to adopt new forms of behavior consistent with God's values. He lived in a patriarchal society, but He was not patriarchal. He lived in an hierarchical society in which he could have climbed the proverbial corporate ladder of the Temple to become the High Priest. But He showed absolutely no interest in this. He already was the Great High Priest in terms that far exceeded the bounds of culture and he obviously saw no need to compromise with culture to gain social recognition. In fact, He did things that baffled and angered the religious leaders. He told illustrative stories with insights that transcended His earthly environment. He was constantly pointing to God's ways that are above the ways of any human culture.

Jesus was totally human and totally God, and He showed us that we are to reject the ways and means of fallen human culture to adopt God's values. These values are expressed in terms of principles that transcend human culture and yet can infuse culture and change it. One of these principles is biblical equality.

Scripture, the Written Word

The Bible also has a dual nature. It is "both divine revelation and human record, the divine message historically written, of two-

---

[3] G. W. Bromiley, *The New Bible Commentary*, 3rd. ed., eds. D. Guthrie and J. A. Motyer (Grand Rapids: Eerdmans, 1970), 11.

fold origin, yet one book."[4] The New Testament is both the Word of God and the words of people who lived in culture.[5] Thus, in the same way that Incarnation does not erode the authority of the God-Man, Jesus, the human aspect of the Written Word does not erode the authority of the written revelation. The New Testament retains its authority just as the Man Christ Jesus did.

In its human aspect, the New Testament is indeed "a historically-culturally conditioned document.[6] This is, perhaps, the point of greatest tension related to New Testament interpretation and application.

The Scriptures, in their original manuscripts, are the Written Word, inspired, inerrant, and authoritative. Like Jesus, they came forth in a cultural setting. They were authored by people who wrote from various cultural perspectives as they were moved upon by the Holy Spirit. So, like Jesus, in certain respects, they resemble the cultures in which they were written. They used language that people understood to teach precepts that God wanted to impart—concepts that transcend the culture in which they were written.[7] They used illustrations and analogies that people understood to teach principles that they did not previously understand. Jesus, for example, compared people to sheep because the people of His day understood sheep. We do not! We have to learn about sheep and shepherding in Jesus' day before we can fully appreciate what Jesus was saying when he used illustrations about sheep and shepherding. To impose our uniformed view, as we so often do, is to make Scripture mean something God never intended it to mean. Because Scripture is subject to culture in this way, it is important to separate those elements that are culturally contingent from the principles of God that are transcultural.

---

[4] Bromiley, 11.

[5] G. E. Ladd, *The New Testament and Criticism* (Grand Rapids: Eerdmans, 1967), 215.

[6] Scholer, 7. In his discussion, Scholer suggests eight guidelines for distinguishing items which may be culturally relative from those which may have transcultural normativity for the Church (19-20).

[7] E. F. Harrison, *Introduction to the New Testament* (Grand Rapids: Eerdmans, 1964), 53.

Does this cultural relevance diminish its status as an authoritative, inspired document? On the contrary, it strengthens it. It tells us that it is not myth or legend detached from the real world. Rather, it conveys the fact that the New Testament is an authentic witness in touch with real people in real life in a genuine historical setting.[8] It assures that The Book does not come to us from the realm of myth, but that it stands as a reliable, historical witness to the self-revelation of God to humanity.

The Authoritative Word of God

The Bible is the authoritative text for the Church regarding both men and women. It is abundantly clear, however, that, to hear God accurately in the text, we must not be afraid to acknowledge the cultural contingency of Scripture. We must be willing to separate culturally conditioned aspects of the text from the principles that transcend culture. It is not the purpose of this book to delineate this issue fully but simply to point out that this is a vital component of the correct interpretation and application of Scripture.

We have to deal with the reality that cultures in which the various parts of the Bible were written were highly patriarchal and charged with negative presuppositions about women. For this reason, we have a responsibility to distinguish between what in Scripture is, in fact, culturally dependent, on the one hand, and what transcends culture, on the other. David Scholer, in his article, "Issues in Biblical Interpretation," offers several helpful directives.[9] For example, he notes that it is important to distinguish between the central core of the Gospel, that is, the resurrection of Jesus, and a social custom such as the admonition to greet one another with a holy kiss. The further away something is from the

---

[8] David Scholer, "The Evangelical Debate over Biblical 'Headship,'" *Women, Abuse, and the Bible*, eds. Catherine Clark Kroeger and James R. Beck (Grand Rapids: Eerdmans, 1996), 44.

[9] David M. Scholer, "Issues in Biblical Interpretation," *The Evangelical Quarterly* 88:1 (1988):19-20.

central core, the more likely it is to be a cultural contingent rather than spiritually mandated issue.

Scholer also points to the need to compare the cultural setting of the New Testament with that of the era of the reader since "significant differences may uncover culturally limited applications." One example of this occurs in 1 Cor. 14:34-35 where the women are addressed in a certain manner due to that culture's refusal to educate women. This is not appropriate in our day when women are afforded equal educational opportunities. Another appropriate example is the admonition for women to wear a headcovering. It apparently was beneficial in the culture of Corinth for women to wear a hat or veil of some sort over their heads in public in order to differentiate themselves from prostitutes. But that is not true in our culture.

Conclusion

The New Testament, correctly interpreted, is authoritative regarding men and women and how we are to relate to one another. We must not, however, confine our interpretations of the teachings of Jesus, Luke, Paul or any other New Testament writer to our own limited and culturally influenced understanding. Paul himself calls upon us to "rightly divide" the Scriptures. In this process, cultural contingency is a factor we must be willing to take into account.

Free at Last!

18

Informed and Free

The love of God displaces pride, prejudice, prestige, and political power struggles. It also displaces the fear that is rooted in ignorance. Therefore, that love and truth may prevail regarding biblical equality, this chapter provides helpful insights about feminism.

What is Feminism?

Feminism is a convenient term that has come to describe various ideologies of womanhood that seek to establish equality for women. The word *feminism* is derived from the French word *feminisme*. It originally meant "the development of female characteristics in a male person." In the 1890s, however, it began to be used in English to refer to "the advocacy of women's rights on the grounds of equality of the sexes."[1] Initially it referred to female political activity in Europe and America, but through the influence of liberal theology, it has been applied to a theology of womanhood.

The message of feminist theology is essentially a cry for human equality. This cry presupposes the existence of a patriarchal paradigm in the church which it denounces as restrictive, prejudicial, and intolerable. It advocates the recognition of women as "fully human" and made in the image of God, and thereby prescribes a shift from a gender-based, hierarchical social structure to an egalitarian system characterized by interdependent partnership be-

---

[1] Richard J. Evans, "The Concept of Feminism," Ruth-Ellen B. Jones and Mary Jo Maynes, eds. *German Women in the Eighteenth and Nineteenth Centuries* (Bloomington: Indiana Univ. Press, 1986), 247-248.

tween the two sexes in all spheres of life. Theologian Clark Pin-nock says,

> Feminism is an advocacy of the rights of women based on a theory of the equality of the sexes. It is a belief in social role interchangeability, especially in regard to leadership roles in church and society. Feminism holds that it is bad that males dominate leadership roles in church and society, and biblical feminists deny that the Bible justifies such a situation. Biblical feminists want to prove that the Bible, fairly read, does not teach the subordination of women to men or a hierarchy of authority that places men over women.[2]

Using this broad definition, I would say that two very different responses prompt a feminist theology. The first is a positive response; the second, a negative reaction. As a response, a feminist perspective springs from an individual's desire to be a good steward of ability and talent. This may be an act of discipleship to the Lord Jesus Christ in response to the stirring of the Holy Spirit resident in a born-again woman, or it may be a humanistic desire to maximize personal potential. Token approval and blatant resistance to this positive initiative tend to produce a reaction, even bitterness.

These are reasonable replies given that the misogynous features of traditional theology are no longer acceptable. The mistaken response of the outsider to all of this is that the singular basic cry for equality yields a single, cohesive theology called *feminism*. Not true. Feminist theology is multifarious with the cry for equality being heralded by at least three different schools of thought. These may be described as secular, religious, and biblical.

The definitive factor in this difference is the position held on biblical authority.[3] Secular feminists do not believe equality is

---

[2] Clark Pinnock, "Biblical Authority and the Issues in Question," *Women, Authority, and the Bible*, 51.

[3] "Feminist Theology," eds. Sinclair B. Ferguson and David F. Wright, *New Dictionary of Theology* (Downers Grove: IVP, 1988), 255.

possible within biblical Christianity. Religious feminists believe equality is impossible within a traditional biblical hermeneutic, and biblical feminists believe equality is possible *only* within the context of the Bible correctly understood and acted upon.

These schools of thought have more differences than similarities. They reflect their sources and features common to the historical-cultural context in which they emerged and evolved. They also echo various worldviews, experiences, and hermeneutic principles resulting in diverse perspectives on various theological topics such as christology, pneumatology, soteriology, and ethics.

Secular Feminism

Secular feminism is a *rejectionist* or *post-Christian* model of feminism. It rejects the Bible and the Judaeo-Christian tradition as not being authoritative because it perceives these as thoroughly patriarchal. In fact, Christianity becomes the major force in the oppression of women.[4] Because of this rejection, secular feminism easily embraces, in whole or in part, witchcraft, pagan religions, pantheistic religions, goddess worship, and Greek mystery religions popular in New Testament times.[5] It includes a wide spectrum of non-Christian convictions common to women's liberation, modern witchcraft, and New Age cults. Perhaps the best articulation of this position was a comment by a young feminist-witch on a television documentary aired recently in New England. She said, "You can be a feminist and not be a witch, but you cannot be a witch and not be a feminist."

The witchcraft of which this woman spoke is neo-paganism, a variety that emerged in Europe in the nineteenth century. It represents the resurgence of a widespread fertility cult of pre-

---

[4] Donald W. Dayton, "Evangelical Roots of Feminism," Photocopy, n.d., 1.
[5] Ferguson and Wright, 255.

Christian paganism.[6] This tradition merged with the fertility-cult anthropology of Margaret Murray in the 1940s and 1950s. In addition, *The White Goddess* (1948) by Robert Graves promoted the idea of a worldwide cult of the earth and moon goddess. Also Gerald Gardner, who claims to have been initiated into ancient witchcraft in 1939, has invented a religion on the basis of Murray and occultist Aleister Crowley. His movement has become a global religious movement.

Witchcraft is attractive to womanhood because it confronts impoverishment and repression with the promise of empower-ment, however questionable and tenuous. Its tenets and traits in-clude: [7]

- a reverence for nature expressed in worship of a fertility goddess and sometimes a god.

- a restrained hedonism that advocates indulgence in sensual pleasures as long as such indulgence hurts no one.

- the practice of group magic aimed usually at healing or other positive ends.

- colorful rituals.

- release from a sense of guilt and sexual inhibitions.

- a sense of the feminine principle in the godhead, a principle almost entirely forgotten by masculine symbolism of the great monotheistic religions.

Secular feminism flourishes in the post-Christian American cul-ture. Organizations, such as the National Organization of Women (NOW), founded in 1966 with Betty Friedan as the first presi-dent, tend to facilitate the secular feminist model. Friedan's 1963 book *The Feminist Mystique* was the most important catalyst for secular women's liberation in the early 1960s. It is interesting that

---

[6] Jeffrey Burton Russell, "Witchcraft," Mircea Eliade, ed. *The Encyclopedia of Religion*, vol. 15 (New York: MacMillan, 1987), 421.

[7] Russell, 422.

NOW's pro-abortion agenda facilitates pre-birth murder. Is it possible that, in certain respects, this practice parallels infant sacrifice and the eating of the aborted fetus in witchcraft and pagan goddess worship?[8] Perhaps the common factor is disregard for human life—and could it be that represents *the disregarded in life* expressing *disregard for life?* Could this be *the controlled in life* expressing ultimate *control in life?*

Women in the field of secular feminism constitute a field that is highly resistant to evangelism. And for the most part, Christians are not prepared to reach these women. Perhaps because we lack self-understanding in terms of the biblical and theological issues presented in this book, we are not prepared to handle their charges. And we lack awareness of the deep bitterness in these women who see Christianity not unlike a bird cage for women for which men are the door keepers in charge of the keys. These women, like people everywhere, seek truth and need a vital, saving relationship with God who created them, but they are by no means willing to put aside their personhood to become victims of patriarchal religion.

Religious Feminism

Religious feminism refers to a model of feminism that subscribes to the tenets of liberal Christianity. Other terms applicable to this model are *reformist* or *liberation feminism*.[9] This model rejects Scripture on the basis that it is patriarchal, but it remains committed to the message of human liberation which it perceives as the central message of the Bible. Perhaps Virginia Mollenkott expresses the position of religious feminism well when she writes,

---

[8] For a succinct and readable study of the ancient goddess worship that made inroads into Gnostic Christianity in the Greco-Roman world, see Catherine Clark Kroeger, "The Challenge of the Re-Imaging God Conference," *Priscilla Papers* (Spring 1994): 7-11.

[9] Ferguson and Wright, 255.

I am beginning to wonder whether indeed Christianity is patriarchal to its very core. If so, count me out. Some of us
may be forced to leave Christianity in order to participate in
Jesus' discipleship of equals.[10]

Religious feminism has European ancestry with roots in the
Enlightenment.[11] Desiderius Erasmus (c. 1469-1536) was a
Christian humanist who stressed women's right to education, including Bible reading.[12] As it developed within a European milieu,
two main branches developed. One appears in political philosophies; the other, in liberal Christian tradition.

Political feminism arising from the enlightenment eventually
found expression in the birth of Communism, Nazism, and Italian
Fascism.[13]

Lenin knew that without the ardent support of women, the
communist revolution would have a brief career if any career
at all. And to win their support full recognition of their
"right" to full participation in the Communist regime was
immediately given.[14]

In Italy (1920), Germany (1930), Japan (1935), Spain (1936),
anti-Communist, anti-democratic revolutions "all confronted the
necessity of winning the approval of women . . . to provide the
sanction essential to success on the home front and aggression
abroad.[15] Professor Maria Castellani explained her allegiance to
Italian Fascism in *Italian Women, Past and Present*. She said,

Fascism recognizes women as a part of the life force of the
country, laying down a division of duties between the two

---

[10] Virginia Mollenkott, *Christian Century* (7 March 1984): 252.
[11] Rosemary Radford Reuther, "The Task of Feminist Theology," *Doing Theology in Today's World*, eds. J. D. Woodbridge and T. E. McComiskey (Grand Rapids: Zondervan, 1991), 372.
[12] J. R. Hassey, "Christian Feminism," Daniel G. Reid, ed., *Dictionary of Christianity in America* (Downers Grove: IVP,
1990), 435.
[13] Mary R. Beard, *Woman as a Force in History* (New York: MacMillan, 1946), 1-19.
[14] Beard, 2.
[15] Beard, 5.

sexes, without putting obstacles in the way of those women who by their intellectual gifts can reach the highest positions.[16]

This model has infiltrated mainstream America particularly through political philosophies taught in colleges and universities holding a post-Christian philosophy.

Religious Feminism arising from the Enlightenment follows the liberal view developed in the Protestant theological tradition of Europe. It therefore maintains a liberal view of Scripture, a bias which skews interpretation and attitudes in biblical research and theological development. Leading religious feminists, Elisabeth Schussler Fiorenza and Rosemary Radford Ruether, agree that it is hopeless to try to make the Bible teach feminism.[17] They contend that "unless the Bible is edited along feminist lines, it cannot be made to support feminism."[18]

Resembling other branches of liberal theology, it finds its true starting point outside of Scripture. According to Reuther,

> I regard this tradition [i.e. egalitarian] as rooted in the prophetic understanding of Hebrew faith, which experiences God as located, not on the side of the wealthy and powerful of society, but on the side of the poor and victimized. The message was renewed by the Jesus movement within the first-century Judaism with its good news to the poor and its criticism of the oppressive power of the ruling social and clerical classes.[19]

Thus, feminist theology retains the message of liberation which it perceives as central to the Bible. It then focuses on the female "victims" of the "oppressor," that is, male-dominated religion.

---

[16] Quoted by Beard, 5.

[17] Elisabeth Schüssler Fiorenza, *In Memory of Her: A Feminist Theological Reconstruction of Christian Origins* (New York: Crossroad, 1983); Rosemary Radford Ruether, *Sexism and God-Talk* (Boston: Beacon Press, 1983).

[18] Stanley N. Gundry, "Biblical Authority: Response to Pinnock, Nicole and Johnson," *Women, Authority, and the Bible*, 61.

[19] Reuther, "The Task of Feminist Theology," 370-371

Consequently, the first task of feminist theology is to unmask sexist bias in traditional theology.

The First Task of Feminist Theology. In *In Memory of Her,* Fiorenza's starting point is "the modern experience of feminism itself. One starts from a commitment to feminism and proceeds from there to put the Bible in order."[20] Her approach is reconstructionism, a method also used by Jewett and Mollenkott.[21]

In *Sexism and God-Talk*, a systematic theology, Rosemary Radford Ruether insists that the Bible is the product of a sexist church.[22] Feminist experience is the guiding principle in approaching the Bible. She maintains that the Bible and Christian theology are hopelessly and irrevocably patriarchal; therefore, "Christianity cannot be a religion that affirms women's full humanity."[23] Because of this, she and other religious feminists such as Mary Daly, encourage men and women to leave the Christian churches and "seek out or create alternative spiritualities, perhaps from ancient nature religions conducive to real gender equality and mutuality."[24]

The Second Task of Feminist Theology. The second task of religious feminism is to write women back into history.[25] Indeed, a feminist orientation is not a prerequisite in recognizing that the influence of women has been minimized and in some cases erased, while the influence of men has been maximized in reporting history.[26] In some cases the work of women has been attributed to men for no apparent reason except the sexist bias of the historian. Nevertheless, this phenomenon is characteristic of history in gen-

---

[20] Quoted by Pinnock, "Biblical Authority and the issues in Question," *Women, Authority, and the Bible*, 52.

[21] Pinnock, 54.

[22] Pinnock, 54.

[23] Reuther, 370.

[24] Reuther, 370; Mary Daly, *Pure Lust: Elemental Feminist Philosophy* (Boston: Beacon, 1984). Mary Daly, *Beyond God the Father* (1973); Starhawk, *The Spiral Dance* (1973).

[25] See Bernice A. Carroll, ed. *Liberating Women's History: Theoretical and Critical Essays* (Urbana: Univ. of Illinois Press, 1976).

[26] The author, as a Pentecostal/Charismatic research historian, has been instrumental in documenting the leadership of women in the twentieth century revival. See, for example, S. Hyatt, *Women Who Led the Way: Discoveries About Women Early Pentecostal Bible Schools,* (Tulsa: Hyatt Int'l Ministries, 1989): Ruth Tucker, "Colorizing Church History," *Christianity Today* (20 July 1992): 20-23.

eral and should not be used to denounce Christianity, which has, in spite of female suppression, still given more status to women than other religions. Eminent Evangelical scholar, Roger Nicole, notes,

> The standing of women among Jewish people was more favorable than in some other contemporary nations, and the intimations of the Old Testament rise well above the practice of the Jews. The rabbinic outlook, developed after the close of the canon, does not do justice to the ennobling elements presented in the Hebrew Scriptures. Furthermore, the New Testament, particularly the teaching of Jesus—lifts womanhood to new heights. The practice of the Apostle Paul, often viewed as chauvinistic, does in fact militate strongly in favor of the aspirations of women. Only by misunderstanding Scripture can the Bible be interpreted as inimical to the appropriate feminist case."[27]

The Third Task of Feminist Theology. The third task of religious feminism is to state a feminist theology. This begins with a "hermeneutic of suspicion" which presumes that the Bible was written, translated, canonized, and interpreted by men only.[28] This male orientation demands a radical reconstruction of the text so that women "enter again the center stage that they occupied in early Christian history."[29]

This feminist "hermeneutic of suspicion" leads to a new definition of many theological terms. According to Reuther, for example, the patriarchal understanding of sin involves issues relating to domination and subordination.[30] The feminist understanding, on the other hand, perceives sin as sexism, patriarchy, and anything

---

[27] Roger Nicole, "Biblical Authority and Feminist Aspirations," ed. Alvera Mickelson, *Women, Authority and the Bible*, 43.

[28] Ferguson and Wright, 255.

[29] Ferguson and Wright, 256.

[30] Reuther, 373.

else that devalues people, especially women. Redemption, then, means "building new human relationships, personally and systematically, based on mutual cohumanity."[31]

Figuratively speaking, religious feminism appears to be adrift on a troubled sea. This is obvious in the developments in the theologies of feminist theologians such as Fiorenza, Reuther, and Mollenkott. Having rejected the authority of Scripture, they have lifted their theological anchor and are drifting on prevailing tides. This is especially evident in the recent embracing of Sophia as the goddess of the religious feminists. Reuther notes,

> Our experience of Christ as the presence of God reveals the nature of God as the power of co-humanity. Christ is our revealed paradigm of the Logos-Sophia, or Word and Wisdom of God. God's Word-and-Wisdom is beyond male and female and at the same time is personified in both women and men.[32]

Hence, enters Sophia worship. In November, 1994, the World Council of Churches, in conjunction with the WCC's Decade of Churches in Solidarity, sponsored Sophia worship.[33] Heralded as *The Second Reformation* by many of its 2,000 women, the ceremony was a "re-imaging" event designed to introduce a new, female god and a new road to salvation. Participants rejected the incarnation and atonement of Jesus Christ as patriarchal constructs, and blamed the church for the oppression of women. Purported as having been "with God in Creation," Sophia was esteemed as the "embodiment of wisdom" (Prov. 1-9) and "the tree of life to those who lay hold of her." The attendees "blessed, thanked, and praised Sophia as a deity," and leaders replaced the Lord's Supper with "the banquet table of Creation, in which they said, "Sophia,

---

[31] Reuther, 373.
[32] Reuther, 373.
[33] Susan Cyre, "Fallout Escalates Over 'Goddess' Sophia Worship," *Christianity Today* (4 April 1994): 74.

we celebrate the nourishment of your milk and honey." Members of Christian churches joined in this prayer.

> Our maker, Sophia, we are women in your image, with the hot blood of our wombs we give form to new life . . . with nectar between our thighs we invite a lover . . . with our warm body fluids we remind the world of its pleasures and sensations.[34]

Goddess worship is nothing new, even among our Jewish ancestors in the faith. When the Israelites came out of Egypt, they brought with them a corrupt religious form that syncretized the worship of Almighty God with pagan female deities portrayed in sexual human form referred to in Scripture as *Asherahs* (eg. Deut. 12:3-4; Judges 3:7; 1 Kings 14:15,23; 18:4; 21:7).[35] From time to time, the practice was banned, and especially during the Exile in Babylon, the Jews forsook the worship of a female deity. Nevertheless, in post-exilic Judaism, some began to exalt a feminine concept known as Wisdom (*Sophia* in Greek) or Life (*Zoe* in Greek). They adopted traits of pagan goddesses such as Isis and the Great Mother of the Gods. Catherine Kroeger explains the resulting syncretism:

> The introduction of this Judaized paganism into Christianity thus embraced a very ancient tradition with its roots in the ecclecticism of Egypt, Iran, India, Asia Minor and Syria. Full-blown Gnosticism drew on the figures of great goddesses (Sophia in particular) and the rituals associated with them. Groups who purported to be Christian incorporated the rites of the Great Phrygian Mother of the Gods into their cultic worship, venerated Sophia as mother goddess, and utilized body fluids in their rituals. Both semen

---

[34] Quoted by Cyre, 74.

[35] J. Glen Taylor, "Was Yahweh Worshipped as the Sun?" *Biblical Archaeology Review* 20, no. 3 (May/June 1994): 52ff referred to by Catherine Clark Kroeger, "The Challenge of the Re-Imaging God Conference," *Priscilla Papers* 8, no. 2 (Spring 1994): 7-8.

and menstrual blood were offered to the divine Powers. Some of the communities were said to have engaged in a variety of sexual activities as part of their worship, while Epiphanius describes the forced abortion of Phibionite women and of the ritual meal they made of the fetus. The feast was called 'the perfect Passah". Irenaeus, Epiphanius and other early Christian writers roundly condemned not only the theology of these deviants but also the abhorrent practices which they incorporated into their worship services."[36]

As Kroeger notes, the Church is again confronted with the merger of pagan female deities through the current worship of the Sophia concept by professing Christians. This trend, it seems to me, would be unnecessary were the Church espousing truth, especially in relation to the true nature of God as presented throughout Scripture, the truth regarding Jesus egalitarian treatment of women, and the experiential baptism of the Holy Spirit.

Biblical Feminism

Some theologians have coined the term *biblical feminism* for what some call *loyalist* or *evangelical feminism*. This model has arisen among Protestant, Evangelical scholars who trace their roots to Conservative Reformation theology. It holds tenaciously to the inspiration and inerrancy of Scripture, and it sees in the biblical data the message of equality and mutual submission.

One of the first comprehensive volumes providing a platform for debate on this issue among Conservative Evangelicals was *Women, Authority, and the Bible*, edited by Alvera Mickelson and published by IVPress in 1986. It contains edited-for-print versions of the papers and responses presented at the Evangelical Colloquium on Women and the Bible which was held October 9-11, 1984, in Oak Brook, Illinois. Thirty-six evangelical leaders at-

---

[36] Kroeger, "The Challenge of the Re-Imaging God Conference," 8.

tended the three-day colloquium in hopes of furthering dialogue on the biblical and hermeneutical issues surrounding women in ministry. Catherine Clark Kroeger, David M. Scholer, and Stanley N. Gundry were the conference conveners.

Since that time, several Conservative Evangelical scholars have formed a coalition called Christians for Biblical Equality. Founded in 1986 with Dr. Catherine Clark Kroeger as president, it maintains a Board of Reference including such well-known scholars as: Millard Erickson, Gordon D. Fee, Roger Nichole, Lewis Smedes, and Ruth Tucker. According to its material,

> Christians for Biblical Equality is an organization of Christians who believe that the Bible, properly interpreted, teaches the fundamental equality of men and women of all racial and ethnic groups, all economic classes, and all age groups, based on the teaching of scripture as reflected in Galatians 3:28: There is neither Jew nor Greek, there is neither slave nor free, there is neither male nor female; for you are all one in Christ Jesus.[37]

C.B.E. "equips believers to serve as Christ's agents of reconciliation by affirming the Biblical truth of equality and promoting communities of wholeness."

Recently, I hosted a C.B.E. book table at an annual meeting of a conservative scholars' society. This society provides a platform where scholars can freely debate various sides of theological issues. It is not surprising, then, that some delegates would display open hostility to biblical equality. Although most of the delegates are polite when they visit the C.B.E. booth, one man asked my husband, "What are you doing here? This is about women!" Eddie, an advocate of biblical equality, laughed and said, "Women helped bring sin into the world, and I think they should be doing

---

[37] *Christians for Biblical Equality* brochure. See also Fact Sheet: *Men, Women, and Biblical Equality.*

more to help get it out." The man smiled and walked away with something to think about!

As this same conference was ending, another man came to the booth. It was as though he came with a mission to drive a knife through my heart and to let me know how wrong I was. Despite his belligerence, I chose to share quietly and graciously with him the reason for my position. I explained that, in addition to the historical and biblical data to which I have access, I have had an ongoing, vital relationship with the Holy Spirit since I was baptized in the Spirit many years ago. This one fact seemed to overwhelm him, so much so that his whole demeanor darkened. He literally took a step backwards, waved his hands in the air, and said, "Oh, then, there's no sense talking to you!" And he walked away, not smiling!

Because the Holy Spirit is an indispensable part of my life and beliefs, my position is not based on exegetical dissection of the Word alone. It is, indeed, based on sound exegetical practice, but it is also based on academically sound knowledge of the activity of the Holy Spirit in history and on my personal experience of walking with the Lord Jesus Christ in the power of the Holy Spirit, now, for almost thirty years.

Conclusion

As Spirit-oriented believers, we are members of a rapidly growing global community. With this comes the wonderful privilege of living together in the manifest presence of Our Creator. But with it also comes the awesome responsibility of flowing together as a River in the manifest power of the Spirit of God. This experience should be as thoroughly inviting to women as it is to men; it should never resemble a male-controlled bird cage for women. Kroeger asks the right question, one that all Spirit-oriented believers have a responsibility to answer: "How can we lead our sisters to Jesus the Friend of Women, who offered living

water to a marginalized woman and told her about the true worship of the God who is Spirit?"

Feminism is not the real problem; feminism is present because
we have failed to reach women with the genuine Good News of
Jesus Christ. Yes, secular feminism is pervasive in contemporary
culture and is leading many women astray. And religious feminism, like its liberal parent, has drifted into secular humanism,
paganism, and occultic mysticism. It, too, is destroying would-be
women of God.

The message of biblical equality confronts every believer individually and the church corporately. It is not a luxury for a few
radical believers. If we are to see Revival flow unhindered in our
day, we must remove the boundaries set up by our faulty theology
that restricts the Holy Spirit in women and confines them to culturally determined roles and subjugation to men.

The principle of Spirit-empowered, biblical equality should ignite Spirit-oriented women who have, until now, been lukewarm.
It should catapult them forever far from the comfort zones of religiously imposed roles. Indeed, it calls for a halt to the vast waste
of human and spiritual potential in women. Arise, Daughter of
Zion! Awake from your slumber!

19

FREE OF PREJUDICE, PRIDE, PRIVILEGE AND POLITICS

Why is it difficult for some to accept biblical equality? Perhaps it is because it means change, and human nature resists change. Change threatens us. It takes us outside our comfort zones and puts new expectations and demands on us. But when we became Christians, whether we realized it or not, we made a commitment to change and to grow—and to keep on growing into the likeness of our Lord Jesus Christ.

Roots of Resistance

Nevertheless, resistance does arise to this truth. This causes Dr. Walter Liefeld to suggest, "It would make one think that there is something else at issue here other than a theological question."[1] Timothy Weber is, no doubt, correct when he says it is a matter of power and control. He writes,

> Although the role of women in the church is usually debated in theological and Biblical terms, the argument frequently has little to do with the Bible or theology. It is about power and control, and until we are willing to face up to that, no one will make much headway in the raging debate concerning women's roles in the church.[2]

---

[1] Quoted by M. Gay Hubbard, Ph.D. and Joseph Hubbard, Ph.D., "Psychological Resistance to Egalitarianism," Journal of Biblical Equality 2, 1990, p. 26.

[2] Timothy Weber, "Evangelical Egalitarianism: Where are we now?" *Journal of Biblical Equality* 1:82.

Drs. Gay and Joseph Hubbard have studied the intensely emotional resistance demonstrated against biblical equality. They have published their findings in a paper entitled "Psychological Resistance to Egalitarianism."[3] The thesis of their paper is that such resistance is "an emotionally-motivated defense of a social belief system rather than a theological rejection of unsound doctrine." According to the Hubbards, "Highly Resistant Males" exhibit four major characteristics: prejudice, power, pride, and privilege.

1. Prejudice. Resistance to female equality on the part of some men appears to be related to the internalized stereotype that has become part of self-identity. The stereotype arises from the teaching that men are superior to women and therefore have a responsibility to rule over them. This is ingrained in the psyche at an early age and becomes an integral part of the "masculine belief system." It is so deeply internalized as a part of personal male identity that they come "to believe that they cannot alter what they think about women without altering who they are as men." In fact, for Highly Resistant Males, "to think more positively about women is by definition to think more negatively about themselves." Furthermore, because the discounting and humiliation of women has traditionally been a normal part of society and the church, most men are not aware of the social reinforcement that rewards them for prejudicial attitudes and behaviors. In fact, when they begin to acknowledge their prejudice, many face both a crisis of identity and a crisis of faith.

2. Power. Resistance to female equality is also bound up in a man's perception of power and the threat of losing that power. For Highly Resistant Males, all relationships are win/lose propositions, and "winning is the power to control relationships and to diminish or destroy the power of others, particularly women." Any equalizing of power is seen as a loss of power for Highly Re-

---

[3] Hubbard and Hubbard, 26-52.

sistant Males, and for these men, the power to control women is a necessary part of their ability to control their own lives." Being powerful means being in control, and when they are not in control, they feel threatened.

3. Pride. Resistance to female equality is also bound up in "the strong sense of entitlement which the hierarchical position grants to males, and which in Highly Resistant Males produces a distorted sense of pride." The perceived "divine right of men" produces a false sense of entitlement that they should be allowed to live an unexamined life free of corrective feedback of any kind. This sense of divinely bestowed entitlement causes them to think that anyone who does anything to embarrass or challenge them has sinned against them and is rebellious against God. Pride expressed as entitlement is, in fact, the likely result of unequal power relationships. According to the Hubbards, the therapist and the client face enormous challenges when the Highly Resistant Male attempts to disassemble his faulty basis of self-worth and to construct a biblically correct basis of self-esteem.

4. Privilege. Resistance to female equality is bound up in the Highly Resistant Male's idea of being privileged. This sense of privilege is derived from, among other things, an incorrect understanding of biblical headship. This doctrine carries with it the idea of "headship" as being a privileged place with the right to privileged treatment by others. Highly Resistant Males tend to believe that men have the right "to be waited upon, to have their needs met first, and to solve problems according to their priorities." An illustration by the Hubbards illuminates the need.

Clinically it is a frustrating task to attempt to assist a High Resistant Male to examine the issue of privilege. "What do you mean?" they ask. "I let her go to see her sister whenever she wants to, and she can write a check without telling me as long as she makes an entry in the checkbook.

She has lots of privileges! More than I do. I don't think I know what you mean by me being privileged."

They miss the point, don't they?

Why Is Gender the Main Issue?

As one surveys the male rulership/female subjugation doctrine, one wonders why gender would be the determining factor in the human struggle for dominance and control. In the first place, none of us is called to dominance and prominence, but to obedience to the Only Pre-eminent One, Jesus Christ. Yet in our humanness, until we come to rest in our relationship with God, we strive for dominance and prominence! This drive expresses itself in hierarchy which we justify with our interpretation of Scripture. This hierarchy normally has produced a chain-of-command dominated by men (patriarchy), but in some cases, it has produced a chain-of-command dominated by women (matriarchy).

But why is this erroneous idea of dominance, so deeply imbedded in our psyche, so gender-based? It seems not far-removed from Freudian psychology in its preoccupation with gender. As Tony Campolo remarks, "Freud argued that all human behavior is sexually motivated. Sex is the driving force behind all we do and say.[4] He goes on to say that Nietzche took it a step deeper, contending that the basic motivation behind human society is "what he called 'the will to power.'" And Campolo summarizes with this poignant statement,

He [Nietzche] would say most of what goes on in the name of sexuality has nothing to do with sex at all. It has to do with *power,* with people trying to gain control over people.[5]

---

[4] Tony Campolo, "Power vs Love," *New Day,* April, 1990: 12.
[5] Campolo, 12.

I would concur. In Christianity, the expression of this drive for power, for control over people, is disguised in the doctrine of authoritarian headship, especially authoritarian male headship. In fact, as Campolo correctly notes, much strife among Christians is not rooted in theology, as it appears, but in the struggle for power with the theological arena serving only as "a cover as people struggle for power."

Is Christianity a Political Power Play?

Yet biblical Christianity is about love. How, then, do the opposing forces of power and love play out in daily life and in theological formulation? Willard Waller, who, noting an inverse relationship between these two elements says, "As love increases, power decreases. And as power increases, love decreases."[6] The one who loves demonstrates sacrifice and vulnerability while the one who "wants to control and dictate the terms of the relationship is the one who loves the least." Campolo notes, "In counseling it's easy to see which one is the guilty party just by watching who exercises the most power."

So the Christian life and its expression as relationship and as ministry is the self-disclosure of God in this world.[7] God is Love. This God Who is Love is also the All-powerful Creator and Sustainer of all things. Yet, in the Incarnation, the All-Powerful One, humbled Himself laying aside His right to Power, and took on the form of a servant. As Campolo says, "Nothing is more power*less* than a man nailed spreadeagled to a Roman gibbet." Yet that is Love.

The lesson is that power and love cannot co-exist. When the Church became a political power after the first 300 years through

---

[6] Cited by Campolo, 12
[7] See Chapter 4.

Emperor Constantine, "something terrible happened." Campolo correctly observes,

> Christians no longer operated from a position of love but from a position of power, and every church historian will tell you that when that happened, New Testament Christianity came to an end.
>
> Nothing is more dangerous than religious people with power. Power solutions are so simple. Love is difficult. But once you have exercised power you have forfeited the privilege of expressing love.[8]

Three Principles of Biblical Relationships

In that I have denounced the traditional rule of male rulership and female subjugation, as being, in fact, not true renditions of biblical Christianity, what do I have to replace these? What I offer, I believe are not laws, but I believe they are attitudes that spring from a regenerate heart and that result in relationships pleasing in the sight of God.

- **Regard.** *To regard* is "to look and to see." It involves paying attention to an individual with the knowledge that that person was created by God, and therefore, is as precious in His sight as anyone else. Hebrews 10:24 expresses this principle well: "Let us observe fully, consider, discover, study one another to incite one another to love and good works." It is an attitude of the heart expressed in active pursuit of the goal. It is the opposite of disregard.

- **Respect.** *To respect* another person is to honor that person. It is an attitude and behavior that occurs both when that person is present and when that person is absent. Again, it is something

---

[8] Campolo, 14.

which requires initiative on our part. Jesus' life exemplifies this principle, and He capsulizes it in what we call the Golden Rule: "So in everything, do to others what you would have them do to you" (Mt. 7:12). It is the opposite of disrespect. The famous prayer of St. Francis of Assisi says it well.

O God, help me to accept the things I cannot change;
Grant me   the courage to change the things that I should
and the wisdom to know the difference.
Help me not so much to be consoled as to console,
To be understood as to understand,
To be loved as to love.
For it is in giving that we receive;
It is in pardoning that we are pardoned;
And it is in dying that we are born to eternal life.

- **Respond.** *To respond* is "to take positive action in relation to another person regardless of their attitude or behavior." It is easy to REACT to undesirable people and circumstances, but as Spirit-filled, Spirit-led people, we are called upon to RESPOND to the Holy Spirit, not to react to another human being. Romans 8:14 tells us that "Those who are led by [i.e. respond to] the Spirit of God are the children of God."

These principles are difficult, perhaps impossible, apart from the enablement of the Holy Spirit. But He does empower us, and that means that men and women can relate to one another according to the will of God. even as the Holy Spirit relates to us—without favoring one gender over the other. This is true in our communities and in our homes. In particular, the following guidelines are helpful regarding the home.

In the Christian home, husband and wife are to defer to each other in seeking to fulfill each other's preferences, desires and aspirations. Neither spouse is to seek to dominate the other, but each is to act as servant to the other, in humility, considering the other as better than oneself. In case of decisional deadlock, they should seek resolution through biblical methods of conflict resolution rather than by one spouse imposing a decision upon the other.

In the Christian home, spouses are to learn to share responsibilities of leadership on the basis of gifts, expertise, and availability, with due regard for the partner most affected by the decision under consideration.

In the Christian home, couples who share a lifestyle characterized by the freedom they find in Christ will do so without experiencing feeling of guilt or resorting to hypocrisy. They are freed to emerge from unbiblical "traditionalism" and can rejoice in their mutual accountability in Christ.[9]

Conclusion

Indeed, biblical equality will be expressed as we repent of prejudice, pride, the drive for power, and the seeking of privilege related to that control. Biblical equality is demonstrated as we rest in Love which is the disclosure of God's very nature to us and through us as we relate to one another. Biblical equality is an aspect of biblical Christianity. It is about us men and women getting to know God intimately and watching Him disclose Himself through us. Keep coming, Holy Spirit!

---

[9] This is an excerpt from "Men, Women, and Biblical Equality." The entire statement, in flyer format, may be obtained from Christians for Biblical Equality, 122 W. Franklin Ave., Suite 218, Minneapolis, MN 55404-2451, or on the website: www.ChrBibEq.org.

Let's Get It Right!

20

What Does Revival Mean
for Women?

The subjugation of women is not biblical, logical or acceptable. The practice is the product of theology influenced by fallen culture. The Lord Jesus Christ, in the New Creation, has re-established the equality found in Creation. And God further confirmed this equality through the activity of the Holy Spirit on the Day of Pentecost. He has continued to confirm this equality through revival history and in the lives of individual believers. The Church, therefore, more than any other group in the world should be promoting gender equality. It is time for Spirit-empowered, Bible-believing Christians to institute that equality.

Indeed, repentance is sorely needed. Recent studies indicate that male domination facilitates—and even promotes—incest, spousal abuse, female slavery, and such practices as female circumcision.[1] This is not acceptable. Nor should the hierarchical and patriarchal theologies of traditional Christianity be acceptable to Christians who claim to be Bible-believing, Spirit-filled, Spirit-led followers of the Lord Jesus Christ. What is needed is an atmosphere that facilitates Holy Spirit-led obedience and good stewardship of the gifts and callings placed on women by the Lord Jesus Christ—not obedience to the dictates of fallen culture masquerading as God's House.

Thus, although patriarchalism has been the accepted norm in

---

[1] "Churches Recruited to Fight Family Violence," *Tulsa World*, 3 October 1993, Religion Section, p. 14; "Anglicans Look at Sexist Problems," *The Telegraph Journal*, Saint John, N.B., Canada, 8 June 1991, 3; "Bride-buying Becoming Epidemic in China," *The Tulsa Tribune*, 8 July 8 1992, sec. Z, p. 1.; "Deadly Inequality: Traditional Bias Toward Males Leaves Millions of Third World Females Lost, Missing, or Dead," *The Providence Sunday Journal*, n.d., 1991-92, sec. D, p. 1.

Christendom for centuries, it is, in fact, an inadequate model for a truly biblical community. The biblical message, in fact, flies in the face of traditional church theology by declaring the biblical fact that women are fully human, made in the image of God, commissioned and empowered by God to be equal partners with men in all realms of life.

The need is obvious and the need is now. God is raising up and commissioning women even as He commissions men. With this commission comes the mighty infilling of the Spirit that empowers us for service, and it behooves us not to grieve the Holy Spirit by rejecting His calling and empowering. Rather, it demands that we—both men and women—bring our theologies, our attitudes, and our actions into agreement with the Author of The Book—the Holy Spirit.

In offering what I have discovered, I challenge the traditional position on biblical womanhood for the same reason that an outspoken host dared to challenge the Church's teaching on slavery. One hundred and fifty years ago, most Christians believed that slavery was a divine institution prescribed by God and confirmed in Scripture. After all, Paul admonishes slaves to obey their masters (Eph. 6:5-8; Col. 3:22-25; 1 Pet. 1;18-25). But a few radicals in the Church believed that black Africans were people made in the image of God just like white Europeans. They believed slavery was a sin. They held the minority view.[2] But they were right.

Historically, the egalitarian view has been the minority view. Even today, in spite of a rich egalitarian birthright, the majority of Pentecostals, Charismatics, and Revival people deny full equality to women by subscribing to a chain-of-command and chain-of-being view of *headship*. Yet, history reveals that the most powerful

---

[2] Ward Gasque, "The Role of Women in the Church, in Society, and in the Home," Crux (September 1983): 9; Tony Campolo, "Power vs Love," *New Day*, April, 1990: 12-14, .

argument for biblical equality is rooted in the ministry of the Spirit.[3]

Why assert this truth? Because we want to keep the River flowing! And to do this, we need to clear up discrepancies between our interpretation of the Bible and our interpretation of the Spirit.

Why assert this truth? Because it is an aspect of Truth, and Truth breaks the shackles of falsehood.

Why assert this truth? Because God is love, and that love cannot flourish in an atmosphere where one assumes superiority over another.[4] An interpretation of *headship* that would grant one lordship/rulership introduces overtones of political control, a model that is in severe tension with the Bible's teaching of the priesthood of all believers, the prophethood of all believers, the servanthood of all believers, and mutual submission. These biblical principals must permeate our perspective and interpretation of individual passages on *headship*.

We need to declare the truth because the Church must be vitally alive with the dynamic power of God. The River must continue to flow and even increase! And this power will be the fruit of integrity. That is to say, only when the Church renounces captivity and discrimination within can it minister true freedom to the captives without. Only when it sets free its own slaves will the world take seriously its preaching on liberty. Only then will it begin to realize the full power inherent in the Gospel. The Spirit of the Lord is upon us and He has anointed us

to preach good news to the poor. He has sent me to proclaim freedom for the prisoners and recovery of sight for the blind, to release the oppressed, to proclaim the year of the Lord's favor(Lk. 4:18)

---

[3] Blumhofer, 11, 14; Dayton, 1.

[4] Gaines S. Dobbins, "Translating New Testament Principles into Present-Day Practices," *A Reader in Christian Education,* ed. Eugene S. Gibbs (Grand Rapids: Baker, 1992), 220.

Who are *the poor, the prisoners, the oppressed?* They are the "circumcised" women of Africa.[5] They are the enslaved women of China. They are the veiled women of Islam. They are the "covered" women of the Church. They are the battered and embittered women of America. They are the prostituted women of the world. Only when the Church truly embraces the egalitarianism inherent in its Spirit-empowered mandate will it minister in the fullness of the Spirit's power and thereby be an adequate voice of Christ's redemption to all people everywhere. Anything less than this eventually stops the flow of The River. Let's not let that happen. Let's get it right this time. Let's be in a flow of The River that is wider and deeper than ever before. People are waiting.

---

[5] Nahid Toubia, *Female Genital Mutilation: A Call for Global Action* (New York: Women, Ink, 1993); Fran Hoskin, *The Hoskin Report: Genital and Sexual Mutilation of Females* (Lexington, MA: Women's International News, 1993).

Selected Bibliography

BOOKS

Aune, David. *Prophecy in Early Christianity and the Ancient Mediterranean World*. Grand Rapids: Eerdmans, 1983.

Bacon, Margaret Hope. *Mothers of Feminism, The Story of Quaker Women in America*. San Francisco: Harper and Row: 1986.

Bainton, Roland. *Women of the Reformation in Germany and Italy*. Minneapolis: Augsburg, 1971.

Beard, Mary R. *Woman as a Force in History*. NYC: MacMillan, 1946.

Bristow, John Temple. *What Paul Really Said About Women*. San Francisco: Harper and Row, 1988.

Brittain, A. and M. Carroll. *Women in All Ages and in All Countries: Women of Early Christianity*. Philadelphia: Rittenhouse Press, 1907.

Bromiley, G. W. *The New Bible Commentary*, 3d ed., D. Guthrie and J. A. Motyer, Eds. Grand Rapids: Eerdmans, 1970.

Bynum, Caroline W. *Jesus as Mother: Studies in the Spirituality of the High Middle Ages*. Berkeley: Univ. of California Press, 1982.

Cairncross, John. *After Polygamy Was Made a Sin: The Social History of Christian Polygamy*. London: Routledge and Kegan, 1974.

Carroll, Bernice A., ed. *Liberating Women's History: Theoretical and Critical Essays*. Urbana: Univ. of Illinois Press, 1976.

Cadbury, Henry J. *Quakerism and Early Christianity*. London: n.p., 1957.

Chilcote, J. *John Wesley and the Women Preachers of Early Methodism*. Metuchen: Scarecrow Press, 1991.

Clark, Elizabeth A. *Women in the Early Church*. Collegeville: Liturgical Press, 1983.

Curnack, Nehemiah, Ed. *The Journal of the Rev. John Wesley A.M.*, 8 Vols. London: Epworth, 1938.

Dunn, James D.G. *Jesus and the Spirit*. Philadelphia: Westminster, 1975.

Fee, Gordon. *Commentary on the First Epistle to the Corinthians*. Grand Rapids: Eerdmans, 1987.

Fox, George. *The Works of George Fox*. 8 Vols. 1706; reprint. New York: AMS Press, 1975.

Gaebelein Hull, Gretchen. *Equal to Serve: Women and Men Working Together Revealing the Gospel*. Tarrytown: Fleming H. Revell, 1991.

Gouge, William. *Of Domesticall Duties*. London: John Haviland, 1662.

Gundry, Patricia. *Woman Be Free!* Grand Rapids, Zondervan, 1977.

Hyatt, Eddie L. *2000 Years of Charismatic Christianity*. 2nd. ed. Dallas: Hyatt Press, 1998.

Jones, R. and M. Maynes, eds. *German Women in the Eighteenth and Nineteenth Centuries*. Bloomington: Indiana Univ. Press, 1986.

Kroeger, Catherine Clark and James R. Beck, eds. *Women, Abuse, and the Bible*. Grand Rapids: Baker Books, 1996.

Kroeger, Richard Clark and Catherine Clark Kroeger. *I Suffer Not a Woman: Rethinking 1 Timothy 2:11-15 in Light of Ancient Evidence*. Grand Rapids: Baker, 1992.

Kung, Hans. *The Church*. Garden City: Image Books, 1976.

Kunze, Bonnelyn Young, *Margaret Fell and the Rise of Quakerism*. Stanford: Stanford University Press, 1994.

Lacy, John. *The General Delusion of Christians Touching the Ways of God's Revealing Himself to and by the Prophets, Envinced from Scriputre and Primitive Antiquity*, Ed. H. Drummond. London: Republished by R. B. Seeley and W. Burnside, MDCCCXXXII.

Ladd, George E. *The New Testament and Criticism*. Grand Rapids: Eerdmans, 1967.

Lerner, Robert E. *The Heresy of the Free Spirit in the Later Middle Ages*. Berkeley: Univ. of California Press, 1972.

Mack, Phyllis. *Visionary Women: Ecstatic Prophecy in Seventeenth-Century England*. Berkeley: University of California Press, 1992.

Mickelsen, Alvera, ed. *Women, Authority & the Bible*, by Alvera Mickelsen. Downers Grove: IVPress. 1986.

Parham, Sarah E. *The Life of Charles Fox*. Joplin: Tri-State Printing. 1930.

Raser, Harold E. *Phoebe Palmer: Her Life and Thought*. Lewiston, NY: Edwin Mellen Press, 1987.

Roberts, Rev. Alexander and James Donaldson. *The Ante-Nicene Christian Library*. 10 Vols. Edinburgh: T & T Clark, 1874.

Schaff, Philip and Henry Wace, Ed. *Nicene and Post-Nicene Fathers of the Christian Church*. 1st Series. 14 Vols. Grand Rapids: Eerdmans, 1978.

___. *Nicene and Post-Nicene Fathers of the Christian Church*. 2nd Series. 14 Vols. Grand Rapids: Eerdmans, 1979.

Schmidt, Alvin John. *Veiled and Silenced: How Culture Shaped Sexist Theology*. Macon, GA: Mercer Univ. Press, 1989.

Sewel, W. *The History of the Rise, Increase, and Progress of the Christian People Called Quakers*. Philadelphia: Friends Book Store, 1774.

Sprenger, Jakob and Heinrich Institoris. *Malleus Maleficarum (The Witches' Hammer)*. Trans. Montague Summers. New York: Benjamin Blom, first printed 1486, reprint 1970.

Storkey, Elaine. *Contributions to Christian Feminism*. London: Christian Impact, 1995.

Tavard, George H
, 1973.

Torjesen, Karen J
 d the Scandal of
   Their Subordinat
3.

Tucker, Ruth A. a
lew Testament
   Times to the Pres

Williams, Selma.
nehart and
   Winston, 1981.

Woodbridge, J. D.
Rapids:
   Zondervan, 199

OTHER

Bilezikian, Gilbert
ette, CBE.
   Wheaton: July

Bratton, Alice. "A
323, Suite 205,
   Tyler, TX 7570

Christians for Bibl
5404. Online
   www.ChrBibEq.

Gasque, Ward. "T
x (September
   1983): 9f.

Hubbard, M. G. a
urnal of Biblical
   Equality 2. (199

Kroeger, Catherin
," *Prism Magazine*
   2, no. 7 (Sept.-

___. "The Challen
g 1994): 7-11.

Mickelsen, Berkel
hristianity Today,
   Oct. 5, 1979: 2

___. "The 'Head' c

Scholer, David M.
8): 21-22.

___. "Patterns of
ity and Governance
   in the Evangelica
Covenant
   Publications, 19

Swidler, Leonard.
97.

Weber, Timothy
l Equality
   (December 198

Willing, J. Fowler.

Wilshire, Leland
l Timothy 2:12."
   New Testament S

DATE DUE

APR 0 7 2009			
APR 0 8 2009			